DOCTOR WHO EXHIBITIONS

THE UNOFFICIAL AND UNAUTHORISED HISTORY

DOCTOR WHO EXHIBITIONS

THE UNOFFICIAL AND UNAUTHORISED HISTORY

Bedwyr Gullidge

First published in 2020 by Telos Publishing Ltd,
139 Whitstable Road, Canterbury, Kent CT2 8EQ, United Kingdom

Telos Publishing values feedback. If you have any comments about this book please e-mail feedback@telos.co.uk

Doctor Who Exhibitions – The Unofficial and Unauthorised History
© 2020 Bedwyr Gullidge

ISBN: 978-1-84583-982-6

Front Cover © 2020 Martin Baines
Photograph of Sentinel Dalek © Roger M Dilley
Image of the *Doctor Who Experience* exterior © Bedwyr Gullidge
Back cover photograph © Richard Leaver
Thanks to Andre Willey for the 'Welcome to Blackpool' postcard scan.

The moral right of the author has been asserted.

British Library Cataloguing in Publication Data. A catalogue record for this book is available from the British Library.

This book is sold subject to the condition that it shall not by way of trade or otherwise, be lent, resold, hired out or otherwise circulated without the publisher's prior written consent in any form of binding or cover other than that in which it is published and without a similar condition including this condition being imposed on the subsequent purchaser.

'It's easy once you know how. You have to make a spectacle of yourself.' – *The Doctor,* 'Silver Nemesis'

'Halt. Approach with Caution. Come forward. Obey the Daleks. We have captured the TARDIS. You may enter but proceed with caution. Move! Move! Move! Move! Halt! Identify! Identify. You may advance. You may advance. The TARDIS is under Dalek control.' Sentinel Dalek

'Halt! Identify. Identify! Obey the Daleks. Obey! Obey! We have captured the TARDIS. The TARDIS is under Dalek control! It is forbidden to smoke. Smokers will be exterminated! Proceed with caution! Move! Move! Move!' Sentinel Dalek

Contents

Author's Note and Acknowledgements	9
Foreword	11
Chapter 1: The Beginning (1963-1973)	12
Chapter 2: Longleat (1973-2003)	21
Chapter 3: Blackpool (1974-1985)	57
Chapter 4: The Turbulent Eighties (1980-1989)	84
Chapter 5: The Wilderness Years (1990-1995)	89
Chapter 6: The *Doctor Who* Experience, Llangollen (1995-2003)	96
Chapter 7: Blackpool II (2004-2009)	107
Chapter 8: *Doctor Who*: Up Close (2004-2009)	119
Chapter 9: The *Doctor Who* Experience, London Olympia (2011-2012)	139
Chapter 10: The *Doctor Who* Experience, Cardiff Bay (2012-2014)	154
Chapter 11: The *Doctor Who* Experience II, Cardiff Bay (2014-2017)	173
Chapter 12: Other Exhibitions	197
Chapter 13: Where Are They Now?	199
Afterword: The Legacy of *Doctor Who* Exhibitions	214
Gallery: Advertising and press pictures from various exhibitions	216
Appendix: Chronology of Referenced *Doctor Who* Stories	238
References	241
About the Author	245

Author's Note and Acknowledgements

A repeat screening of 1972's 'The Sea Devils' on BBC2, twenty years after its original transmission, proved to have a lasting impact on this particular viewer.[1] The iconic imagery of those mysterious creatures rising from the English channel and venturing onto dry land captured the imagination of an impressionable five-year-old. Further episodes of 'Genesis of the Daleks', 'Revelation of the Daleks' and 'Battlefield' screened on the same channel during 1993 cemented an interest in this captivating show.

Growing up with a fascination for *Doctor Who* in the 1990s, or 'the Wilderness Years' as the period has sometimes been called, was tricky. With no new episodes being produced at that time, the BBC's acknowledgment of the show was at an all-time low. Fortunately a steady supply of video releases enabled new enthusiasts to discover its back catalogue and the convention circuit brought fans together with those they admired. However it was the exhibitions in Longleat and Llangollen that really kept the show alive, still exciting and still terrifying.

At a time when the BBC was beginning to think *Doctor Who* was no longer an attraction to the general public, many of its original props and costumes could have disappeared for good. Most already had. By providing storage and revenue, the *Doctor Who* Experience in Llangollen, and the long-running Longleat *Doctor Who* exhibition, were both crucial in keeping the flame alive during the dark times of the 1990s and early 2000s. And now that *Doctor Who* has triumphantly returned to our television screens, a whole new generation has been able to experience the thrill of visiting exhibitions of artefacts from the show.

I have learnt a lot over the course of this project. For example, my research has established that some earlier assumptions about the exhibition Daleks were incorrect. The previously untold story behind the birth of the Llangollen exhibition has also been eye-opening. I would particularly like to place on record my thanks and admiration for David Boyle and all the work he put into launching the *Doctor Who* Experience in Llangollen. It provided me with some precious memories. For instance, on my first visit to Llangollen, Sylvester McCoy, the seventh Doctor himself, just happened to be there. His autograph on the back of my entry ticket remains a prized piece of my collection.

David Boyle passed away in September 2019, before publication of this book. I hope that the story of his achievements and the recollections he shared with me provide a fitting tribute. His partner Julie Whitfield helped facilitate our

---

[1] A checklist of all the *Doctor Who* stories mentioned in this book, and their years of transmission, is given in the Appendix.

conversation, and for that I thank her.

This book has required extensive research, using archive material and contemporary accounts, supplemented by some brand-new interviews. It has taken many months of scouring through articles written at the time – in newspapers, fanzines and magazines – and numerous other sources of information. Wherever possible, accounts have then been checked against photographic or video evidence. This lengthy process has resulted in, I believe, the most detailed history of *Doctor Who* exhibitions ever produced.

So, for those like me who are too young to have visited the original Blackpool *Doctor Who* exhibition in 1974, I hope my words will help you imagine what it was like. Those lucky enough to have been there will hopefully get to relive that amazing experience.

My eternal gratitude is extended to all those who have contributed to this book, and particularly to those who have been willing to share with me their recollections of the various exhibitions. Specific thanks go to Joseph Lidster, Andrew Beech, Mike Tucker, Alexandra and Kevan Looseley-Saul, Christopher Daniels, Bob Richardson and David Prince, who all took the time to talk to me. Thank you too to Mark Barton Hill, Phil Newman, Roger M Dilley, Michael Williams, Ben Croucher and Jenny Martin for sharing additional details that have been of great help. My gratitude is also extended to Richard Bignell, Jon Green and Gavin Rymill for providing further, much-valued sources of information. Throughout the book, Dalek props are referred to by the numbers these latter two historians have assigned them according to the order of their production, as detailed on the Dalek 63·88 website.[2] Individuals who are no longer with us, such as 1980s *Doctor Who* producer John Nathan-Turner, can be represented only by archive material.

For decades *Doctor Who* exhibitions have been the achievement of many talented and dedicated people and I hope this book fully reflects the importance of their contributions. It is a book that seeks to celebrate the work of Lorne Martin, Terry Sampson, Tony Oxley, Charlie Lunn, Bob Richardson, Julie Jones, Martin Wilkie and countless other individuals. It is dedicated to them all.

I would also like to thank the amazing team I was fortunate enough to work with during my own time in the world of *Doctor Who* exhibitions: Bethie, Celeste, Gemima, Harry, Jay and Rhiannon.

Finally, thank you to Susanna, Dixie and all my family for supporting me throughout this process and for driving me to *Doctor Who* exhibitions and events across the whole of the British Isles over the years.

Bedwyr Gullidge, 2020

---

[2] www.dalek6388.co.uk/

Foreword

When *Doctor Who* began in November 1963, television programmes were very different from today's slick, high-definition productions. But the ways in which viewers engage with those programmes have changed perhaps even more radically; and, over the course of its history, *Doctor Who* has played a major part in that revolution.

Prior to the 1980s, a *Doctor Who* episode could generally be enjoyed only once, on its original transmission. Repeats were very uncommon, and this was before the days of affordable home video recording systems, commercial DVD and Blu-ray releases and on-demand services. Some of the show's fans would even go to the lengths of making audio recordings of the episodes to supplement their visual recollections. Thankfully, there was a great deal of tie-in merchandise available to extend the enjoyment, from the Dalekmania of the mid-1960s onwards; but an even bigger thrill could be gained from the opportunity to see original costumes and props in person at an exhibition. Even today, having the chance to look closely at the intricacies of a set or the details of a costume, or even to come face to face with a monster, remains a special thrill.

However, television sets, costumes and props have an intended lifetime based solely on the programme's shooting schedule. They are created specifically to go in front of the cameras, and their design is dictated by budget constraints and the available materials. Consequently, it can prove incredibly difficult to stage an exhibition of them. Even if an item survives the days of use and abuse it receives during the production of the programme, the ravages of time can take a serious toll. For example, rubber and latex masks were commonly used in the making of *Doctor Who* stories, but over time those materials begin to deteriorate and disintegrate. Fortunately, the work of numerous dedicated curators and skilled experts has extended the life of some of these artefacts, preserving them for people to be able to see and enjoy, creating an attraction that would otherwise have been impossible.

Doctor Who has proved to be a trailblazing show around the world in many respects, but no more so than in the field of official exhibitions. These exhibitions, staged over the course of many years, have catered admirably for the viewers' desire to see items from the show's production; and they have recently been emulated by others. For example, in 2015 there began a cross-Europe touring exhibition of costumes and props used during production of the American fantasy series *Game of Thrones*. Similarly, Warner Brother's Harry Potter Studio Tours have created a thriving attraction for fans of the movie franchise and beyond.

Doctor Who was the first show that connected with its audience sufficiently to have the potential for exhibiting items from its history. However, it would take many years to develop fully into the industry we know it to be today.

Chapter 1
The Beginning (1963-1973)

Initially, the only way that viewers could see William Hartnell as the Doctor was via the pictures on their television sets, but this was to change with *Doctor Who*'s rapidly-growing success. Hartnell was in the vanguard of the fledgling practice of personal appearances by television stars. These opportunities for the public to see favourite actors and actresses are relatively commonplace in the 21st Century, with the convention and 'comic con' circuit becoming ever more popular across the world, but during the 1960s they were almost unheard of. Hartnell, though, made a number of such appearances. For instance, in 1964 he opened Pembury Hospital's fête in complete Doctor costume, including wig, cape and stick. This would have been one of the first chances for the public to see a screen-used costume, and it proved very popular, setting the tone for what was to come.

As well as the Doctor, the public clamoured to see his greatest enemies, the Daleks. Original Dalek props were used to promote the show, posing for photographs in the streets of Shepherd's Bush (close to the BBC's studios) and attending other events throughout the 1960s. For instance, Dalek props were loaned out by the BBC or Shawcraft Models, the firm responsible for their construction, to a number of local fêtes around London. In fact, the Daleks quickly became a major draw for events around the UK – not bad for creatures initially written off as a 'bug eyed monsters' by the BBC's then Head of Drama, Sydney Newman. To this day they remain a popular feature at promotional events, with Dalek props being displayed at BBC Studios' showcases and *Doctor Who* series premieres.

The huge popularity of *Doctor Who*, and specifically the Daleks, resulted in the show having a presence at the *Daily Mail*'s annual Boys and Girls Exhibition at Olympia in London during December 1964 and into the following year. Two screen-used Daleks in their 'The Dalek Invasion of Earth' livery were on display, including the Black Dalek commander. Actress Carole Ann Ford, who had played Susan, the Doctor's granddaughter, also made an appearance to generate more press coverage.

The Daleks had proved popular with visitors, so they returned to the Boys and Girls Exhibition three years later, from 27 December 1967 to 9 January 1968; but this time, they did not come alone. A silver and blue Dalek (Dalek 1-7) began a themed Dalek story display that also included a Mire Beast and Fungoids from 'The Chase' and a Varga Plant from 'The Daleks' Master Plan'. In a glass tank, a group of Rills from 'Galaxy 4' were displayed. To bring the exhibits up to date, the organisers also included, from the 1967/1968 series, a

Yeti from 'The Abominable Snowmen'; behind a sheet of frozen 'ice', one of the titular creatures from 'The Ice Warriors'; and, in the design seen in 'The Moonbase' and 'The Tomb of the Cybermen', two Cybermen. The Cybermen costumes were often worn by actors, who posed for pictures. Newsreel footage released by British Pathé in 2014 shows that the Yeti also sometimes menaced visitors: an unforgettable experience for those of an impressionable age.

One of the other features of the exhibition was the display of the winning entries in a competition that the BBC's long-running children's magazine show *Blue Peter* had held to 'Design a Monster' for *Doctor Who* (an exercise that would be repeated years later, resulting in the creation of the Abzorbaloff for 'Love and Monsters'). The three winners had had their designs brought to life by the BBC Visual Effects Department, and the results had appeared on the *Blue Peter* edition announcing the outcome. So, on display at the exhibition were the Aquaman created by Steven Thompson, winner of the 11s-and-over age section; the Hypnotron, which had won the 8-10s category for Paul Worrell; and the Steel Octopus, designed by Karen Dag for the under-8s age group.

By the start of the 1970s, the Doctor had twice regenerated, Jon Pertwee having now taken over the role, bringing an all-action persona and velvet jackets to the character. On 21 December 1971, Pertwee, producer Barry Letts and 1960s companion actor Peter Purves – by that time better known to the public as a *Blue Peter* presenter – appeared on stage at the London Planetarium for the second half of a *Young Observer*-sponsored 'teach-in' event. During this, a number of costumes and props were displayed, including a Silurian (from 'Doctor Who and the Silurians'), a plastic-daffodil-distributing Auton ('Terror of the Autons') and Axon masks ('The Claws of Axos'). The event's conclusion saw two Dalek props from 'Day of the Daleks', the gold-and-black Supreme (Dalek 7-2) and a standard grey-and-black one (Dalek 1-5), emerge on stage to a rapturous ovation.

The following year, a small exhibition was held for two weeks across March and April at the Ceylon Tea Centre on Lower Regent Street in London. The main motivation for this was to showcase the winning entries in a 'Win a Dalek' competition recently run by the BBC's *Radio Times* listings magazine (the prizes for which had been sophisticated remote-control model Daleks rather than full-size props). In the window was the Supreme Dalek 7-2 prop, while on display inside the exhibition were original costumes of Aggedor and Alpha Centauri from 'The Curse of Peladon'.

There was a similar display at the Royal Highland Show in Ingliston, Edinburgh later the same year as attendee Gordon Roxburgh recalls: 'There was a small BBC Marquee that had just the Aggedor, Axon and Mutant costumes on display. Then there were display boards with entries from the *Radio Times* "Win A Dalek" competition. Also in the same tent were Raymond Baxter and James Burke signing copies of the *Tomorrow's World* book. The *Doctor Who* music was playing on a continuous loop as well.'

These displays would prove a precursor to a bigger exhibition later that year.

The potential for successfully displaying items from *Doctor Who* was clearly identified here, from the evident excitement of visitors, particularly youngsters, to see items outside of their television sets. However, it would take a little while for BBC Enterprises (later rebranded as BBC Worldwide and then as BBC Studios) to maximise that potential. Their first step was to set up a new department, headed up by Terry Sampson and called the Exhibitions Unit. Lorne Martin joined the Unit in 1971.[3] It operated from BBC Enterprises' headquarters, Villiers House in Ealing, London, but also had a base at Bilton House in West Ealing. In later years, actress Elisabeth Sladen, who played the Doctor's companion Sarah Jane Smith and who lived in Ealing, would occasionally pop into the latter office for a coffee. Storage units used by the department included Unit 4 on Chase Road in North Acton and one at Alexandra Palace in North London. At the start of the 1990s, seventh Doctor actor Sylvester McCoy recorded segments for the home video release *The Hartnell Years* at 43 Wales Farm Road in London, which he described as 'The BBC Enterprises exhibition store.'

One of the Exhibition Unit's earliest projects was a display of costumes from the BBC's lavish costume drama series *The Six Wives of Henry VIII*. Exhibitions would almost always be a joint venture between BBC Enterprises and a commercial partner. In this case it was the Victoria & Albert Museum in London. The exhibits proved very popular, and a similar success was also achieved with costumes from the *Elizabeth R* production.

BBC Enterprises' next venture was to organise an exhibition at the Science Museum in London, celebrating the special effects used in television production. The BBC TV Special Effects Exhibition ran from 7 December 1972 until 10 June 1973. Parker Hinson Productions Limited, based in Wembley, constructed the attraction in their first contribution to the world of *Doctor Who* exhibitions.[4] However, this was not an exhibition of *Doctor Who* artefacts only, as Kevan Looseley explains: 'It was a special effects exhibition, and the *Doctor Who* exhibition was within that.' Diagrams, photographs and models illustrated various special effects techniques that had been used in the making of other shows such as *Dad's Army*, *Z-Cars* and Open University educational programmes. A press release prepared by BBC Enterprises provided notes on the exhibits, stating that they showed a wide variety of effects 'designed, constructed and operated by BBC Special Effects'.[5] No specific sound or electronic effects were included, as these were the responsibility of other BBC departments. The two centrepieces of the exhibition were specially-constructed: an Old Mill and a TARDIS interior.

The Old Mill was a full-size construction, representing an atmospheric set such as might be used for a drama production at the BBC's Television Centre

---

[3] *Doctor Who Magazine* #175.
[4] *Doctor Who Magazine* #113.
[5] 1972 press release, BBC Enterprises.

studios. Complete with cobwebs and dust, it also featured moving machinery, rats, chains, skulls and life-size figures. Two large mill wheels were created from lightweight timber and driven electronically, the water for them being circulated by an electric pump. The plastic talking skull and rats were similarly motor-driven. Spun plastic latex was used for the cobwebs, while the human figures and owl were made of rubber. To enhance the aged effect, the whole set was dusted with baby powder, giving the impression of a layer of dust. Kevan Looseley recalls how another feature would further unnerve visitors:

'You'd go round the haunted mill and there was a wind machine; something would splat against the window every so often, and you were never sure whether it was a soggy hand or what, but something would blow against the window and make you jump.'

Other displays in the exhibition included a detailed replica of the Lunar Rover used for 1971 Apollo 15 mission; a replica of the Tutankhamen mask; explosion and bullet effects on a number of surfaces such as wood and glass; plus smoke, fog and cobweb machines. For *Doctor Who* fans, however, the highlight was naturally the opportunity to step aboard the TARDIS and see the ship's interior controls for the first time ever.

Entry to this *Doctor Who* section of the exhibition was through a reconstruction of the iconic police box exterior; an idea that would be utilised in other exhibitions for many years to come. Visitors could then move around the TARDIS control room, the centrepiece of which was a replica of the console, referred to in the 1972 press release as the Main Control Panel. Dotted around the roundel-covered walls were some computer banks, and a number of viewing windows with exhibits inside.

This set was specially constructed for the exhibition by Tony Oxley and Charlie Lunn of the BBC Visual Effects Department to replicate the one used by the production team in the television studios. Conveniently, Oxley lived in Ealing, near to the Exhibition Unit's office at Bilton House, and his house had a workshop at the back. He would also contribute to the future exhibition at Longleat.

Of course, the Daleks made an appearance too, in the form of two props also constructed by Oxley and Lunn out of wood and, for the domes, fibreglass. Original Dalek props were unavailable for the exhibition because 'Planet of the Daleks' was shortly to enter production, hence the need for replicas to be used instead. These were not intended to house an operator, as Kevan Looseley explains:

'They were never designed to have anyone inside; they were purely electronic. You could tell because they were quite a lot sharper [than the television versions] at the front. There are various publicity photos of Jon Pertwee crouching between the two of them. Every so often, they would slide forward on rails, threatening death and destruction to smokers, "All smokers will be exterminated".'

The first Dalek was painted gold with black hemispheres, replicating the look of the Supreme Dalek seen in 'Day of the Daleks'. In contrast, the second was given a 1960s livery of silver and blue. Both replicas were in a far more attractive condition than the screen-used props, which had suffered the wear and tear of television production, although slightly smaller in stature and with a more angled front skirt section. Additional motor mechanisms were added by Oxley; these moved the arm and dome, pivoted the eyestalk and flickered the weapon flipper. The Daleks were then placed on an alien planet environment observable through open TARDIS doors; an image that would later be used for a souvenir postcard available from the future Blackpool exhibition.[6]

Behind one viewing window in the recreated TARDIS control room were displayed a Draconian (from 'Frontier in Space'), a Sea Devil ('The Sea Devils') and an Ogron ('Day of the Daleks'). These three monsters made a guest appearance on an episode of *Blue Peter* to promote the exhibition's opening; the segment can now be viewed on the official DVD release of 'The Mutants'. Of particular note is the fact that the Draconian was on display despite having not yet been seen in *Doctor Who* itself: 'Frontier in Space' would not begin its six-week broadcast until 24 February 1973.[7] However, the story's production had concluded in time for the costume to be released for the exhibition.

Other *Doctor Who* monsters thought to have been on display include an Axon ('The Claws of Axos') and a Cyberman ('The Invasion'). An edition of *Doctor Who Magazine* published in February 1994 featured a number of photographs taken by one visitor to the exhibition, Peter Hart.[8] These showed the two Daleks, the Sea Devil, the Ogron and the Draconian. The accompanying feature noted the customary TARDIS police box entrance to the exhibition and also mentioned that the Skybase One model from 'The Mutants' was on display. This latter item was part of a second viewing window display that featured spaceship models on a starry background; also included were Axos ('The Claws of Axos') and, as described in the BBC Enterprises press release, 'Liz, an old tramp rocket', which was the Liz 79 model from 'The Space Pirates'.[9] Amongst the other displays, there was also a model with a miniature UNIT vehicle to show how the heat barrier effect in 'The Daemons' had been achieved.

In attendance at the press launch for the exhibition's 7 December 1972 opening was the current Doctor Jon Pertwee, along with co-stars Katy Manning (Jo Grant), Nicholas Courtney (Brigadier Lethbridge-Stewart) and John Levene (Sergeant Benton). All but Levene were in their respective character costumes from 'The Three Doctors', which would not begin transmission until a few weeks later. Photographs of Pertwee, Manning and Courtney taken on the TARDIS set show Tony Oxley's and Charlie Lunn's specially-recreated control console and familiar roundel-patterned walls. Pertwee, Manning and Levene were also photographed on the Old Mill set.

---

[6] Howe and Blumberg, (2000) *Howe's Transcendental Toybox*, pp327.
[7] www.dalek6388.co.uk/daleks-in-exhibitions/
[8] *Doctor Who Magazine* #209.
[9] 1972 press release, BBC Enterprises.

The New Scientist later described the new exhibition as 'a fairly small show' and bemoaned the entrance cost of 25p per adult and 15p per child.[10] However, despite the entrance fees, the exhibition proved a big hit with attendees. *Doctor Who* was a massive attraction for the general public, and the opportunity to see the TARDIS console, Daleks and other monsters gave visitors a real thrill. Kevan Looseley recalls: 'This thing was so massively popular that the queue to get in had timings on it, as in "One hour from this point," "Half an hour from this point." The queue went around the block. It was absolutely phenomenal.'

The chance to see items from *Doctor Who* up close was clearly a huge attraction to the show's fans. However, the fact that the props and costumes were designed and built to last only for the duration of the television episodes' production posed a significant challenge to the Exhibitions Unit. During *Doctor Who*'s original 26 year run, monsters were created using a number of different materials, but one of the most popular was latex – something still used today. Monster masks and costumes made predominantly of latex suffer from gradual deterioration, as explained by Lorne Martin: 'Many latex suit monsters have simply rotted with age. When all is said and done, they were made to last a few weeks, not a few years.'[11] It was considered imperative that the costumes and props put on public display should showcase *Doctor Who* at its very best, so they required careful storage and presentation. Lorne Martin again: 'You mustn't forget that the creators of the costumes are professionals, and if something is [displayed] looking less than perfect, it is a reflection on those professionals, and quite rightly they will complain.'[12]

As with the original videotape masters of *Doctor Who* episodes, many of which are now missing from the BBC's archives, there was no long-term strategy for preserving the show's props and costumes, or any general recognition within the BBC of their future earnings potential via exhibitions. As a result, only a small selection were retained and stored. Some priceless items were destroyed. For example, the original TARDIS console created in 1963 was broken apart when it was replaced early on in the Jon Pertwee era.

There were examples of individual items being fortuitously preserved, such as Koquillion's mask from 'The Rescue', which was saved by a BBC staff member.[13] But such cases were rarities. Consequently, in the early years of the *Doctor Who* exhibitions, there was a lack of older props or costumes that could be displayed, and the show's most recently-produced series would typically provide the bulk of the exhibits. Popular returning monsters such as the Ice Warriors, the Cybermen and the Yeti were retained for future use, but creations such as the Voord ('The Keys of Marinus') and the Krotons ('The Krotons') never made it into an exhibition.

The items that did however appear in *Doctor Who* exhibitions gave the public an exciting glimpse into the world of *Doctor Who*. For those interested in

---

[10] *The New Scientist*, Volume 56 Number 823.
[11] *Doctor Who Magazine* #175.
[12] *Doctor Who Magazine* #175.
[13] *Nothing at the End of the Lane* fanzine. (2015). Issue 4.

the technical aspects of the show's production, the exhibitions also provided inspiration for future careers. One young visitor was Mike Tucker, who would later go on to work on both the classic and the modern versions of *Doctor Who*. He recalls:

'For me it was just an opportunity to get up close to props that I'd seen on screen; and you got a much better idea of how things were made and how big they were if you could actually get up close to them. In an era before DVDs and behind-the-scenes videos it was only really at the exhibitions and conventions that you got to see these models and props. So it was my opportunity to get to look at them and see how they were built.'

That opportunity still exists today, and hopefully inspires a new generation, but during the 1970s it was a unique chance to enter the world of *Doctor Who*. Although not confined to *Doctor Who*, the BBC TV Special Effects Exhibition at the Science Museum is widely regarded as the starting point for the various dedicated exhibitions that have followed. It can therefore be credited with prompting the creation of the long-running Longleat and Blackpool exhibitions, and all the others that have come since, extending right up to the 21st Century's *Doctor Who* Experience.

The Special Effects Exhibition also featured the first piece of exclusive tie-in merchandise, a pair of 'TARDIS Commander' badges. This is an aspect of the exhibitions that continues and thrives even to this day. It was reported that over 300,000 people had attended, proving that such ventures could prove lucrative.[14] In light of this, the Exhibitions Unit was then tasked with maximising revenues by utilising the significant quantities of costumes and props created for various BBC productions.

Bob Richardson joined the Exhibitions Unit in October 1979 and worked there until March 1982. Lorne Martin was the manager, with Richardson and his colleague Julie Jones both fulfilling the role of Exhibitions Assistant. Richardson recalls: 'Julie was the main organiser and a major influence on the way the exhibitions looked. We shared responsibility for *Doctor Who*.' Over the years, the Unit would develop a close working relationship with the *Doctor Who* production team. The Exhibitions team were ultimately responsible for collecting and storing artefacts directly following the episodes' production.

By the early 1980s, the relationship between the Exhibitions Unit and the production office was particularly close. This extended to it being sent advance copies of scripts at the same time as the actors received them. Bob Richardson remembers: 'Julie and I would read them carefully, using a highlighter to mark up any costumes, monsters, special props and bits of scenery that could be displayed in the exhibitions.' Armed with this information from the scripts, Richardson and Jones would have a 'shopping list' prepared for when studio recording took place. The two Exhibitions Assistants were afforded access to every studio recording session. In an interview that can be found on the DVD

---

[14] *The Stage and Television Today*, published 14 July 1973, from www.dalek6388.co.uk/daleks-in-exhibitions/

release of 'The Underwater Menace', Richardson described the process at Television Centre:

'We had the run of the studio; we were allowed to choose anything we wanted and mark it up with labels. We used to go along with BBC Enterprises labels just saying, "Keep for Enterprises". And at the end of the recording, we put tags on the items that we wanted, and they were ours.'

The Exhibitions team would also liaise with BBC Costume, Visual Effects, Make-Up and Scenic Services Departments prior to recording. The nature of *Doctor Who* meant that a close working relationship was forged with the BBC Visual Effects Department in particular, as Richardson states: 'We worked closely with BBC Visual Effects, who provided models, ray-guns and some parts of the monster costumes. It wasn't always easy. Although we had permission from the various *Doctor Who* producers, VisFx liked to recycle bits of their props and models, so they were sometimes a bit reluctant to part with things.'

Mike Tucker, who worked in the Visual Effects Department during the late '80s, explains: 'When we were working on *Doctor Who* back in the 1980s, at the end of every season, originally BBC Worldwide Exhibitions, and latterly Experience Design & Management, would come along and take away anything that the Effects Department or the Costume Department had made and put them into storage.'

However, Exhibitions didn't always have free access to whichever items they wanted, as Richardson again explains: 'Not everything belonged to the BBC, so we couldn't always get what we wanted. Sometimes a costume would be "make-to-hire" – which means it was created at a reduced cost by an external costumier, but belonged to them after the recording was completed. In the case of make-to-hire costumes, we had to pay a weekly rental charge to have them in the exhibitions, something we were reluctant to do as it was a recurring cost to us. Similarly, computer panels with flashing lights were usually out of bounds as they were frequently hired for the studio and had to go back after the recording.'

The Exhibitions Unit themselves would be responsible for providing all the display items such as mannequins. Over the years, some costumes were unfortunately placed on mannequins of ill-suited size and shape, and consequently were not showcased to their full potential. In any event, the majority of the items on display required constant refurbishment and protection, as Lorne Martin recalled in an interview published in 1991:

'Most of our stock is always on exhibition, and some exhibits may be being refurbished, which is extremely expensive. Also, people should bear in mind that transportation costs are [high] too. In the past when we have lent items of stock, they have been returned damaged and [commonly] missing one or two pieces. Then, to re-exhibit or return them to the studio for a "recall" means spending more money.'[15]

---

[15] *Doctor Who Magazine* #175.

The items for which the Exhibitions Unit were assigned responsibility came not solely from *Doctor Who* but also from other BBC productions. Bob Richardson recalls that they included: 'the puppets from Barry Letts' version of *Pinocchio* [1978]; Dominick Hyde's spaceship [from the 1980 drama *The Flipside of Dominick Hyde*]; a full-size model of Donald Campbell's *Bluebird* car; and the Triffids from *The Day of the Triffids* [1981].' Like the *Doctor Who* items in their care, these things had been expected to be used only for a few studio days, and were not built for longevity. However, the existence of the Exhibitions Unit ensured the long-term survival of many unique items, as Mike Tucker suggests:

'It's a testament, the fact that the BBC back in the '70s did have the foresight to go, "We are going to open these exhibitions." I think a lot of these things survive purely because they were stuck behind a display stand at Blackpool or Longleat for so long.'

After the success of the BBC Special Effects Exhibition at the Science Museum, it was important for the Exhibitions Unit to capitalise on the identified potential. In an interview with John Nathan-Turner published in *Doctor Who Magazine* Issue 175, Lorne Martin recalled a moment when *Doctor Who*'s appeal became glaringly obvious:

'In the middle of the [Science Museum] exhibit was a hint of *Doctor Who*, a little of a TARDIS, a few Daleks and a couple of monsters. Everyone gathered around it, everyone talked about it; Terry [Sampson] and I looked at each other, and I said, "We're on to a winner here."'[16]

Lorne Martin and Terry Sampson were however not the only individuals to identify the potential. During the Special Effects Exhibition's run, the Exhibitions Unit received an enquiry from an individual no stranger to developing visitor attractions. This resulted in the longest-running *Doctor Who* exhibition to date.

---

[16] *Doctor Who Magazine* #175.

Chapter 2
Longleat (1973-2003)

One of the visitors to the Special Effects Exhibition at the Science Museum was Henry Thynne, 6th Marquis of Bath and owner of Longleat House in Wiltshire. The House had been the first stately home opened to the public as a commercial venture, and in 1966 its now-famous safari park first opened its gates. Keen to continue the development of Longleat into one of the country's leading visitor attractions, Lord Bath decided that an exhibition of this nature would be another useful addition. Following conversations with the BBC, a smaller version of the Special Effects Exhibition was set up in an old stable block at the rear of Longleat House. It opened in April 1973. Lorne Martin recalls:

'Our first *Doctor Who* exhibition was very small. It was housed in the same building [as in later years]... but without the extension [that was subsequently added]. There were a few monsters, a TARDIS control console and a Lunar Rover – a visual effects scale model of the vehicle that had been driven on the Moon.' [17]

This initial installation of 1973 featured only the TARDIS control room with a pair of viewing windows, which housed two Daleks, Aggedor from 'The Curse of Peladon', a Sea Devil from 'The Sea Devils' and a Cyberman from 'The Invasion', plus the Lunar Rover model replica in another viewing window on the other side of the room. Originally the Daleks were accompanied by audio taken directly from *Doctor Who*, as Kevan Looseley remembers:

'When it moved into Longleat, the voice track it was using was a line from "Day of the Daleks". There was a sensor that would trip this thing off as soon as you went near it, saying, "Whoever is operating the time machine is an enemy of the Daleks".'

The following year, the Longleat exhibition became one devoted exclusively to *Doctor Who*. It officially opened on 12 April 1974 and ran through to 31 October 1974. Longleat House, the safari park and the other attractions operated seasonal opening times, usually from the Easter weekend through to the autumn. During the 'off season', the *Doctor Who* exhibits were updated, mostly with items from recently-broadcast episodes. Some were also exchanged with the exhibition in Blackpool; as a result, some artefacts would appear at both exhibitions over the years. Once again, Parker Hinson Productions Limited was tasked with the initial construction of the TARDIS control room, complete with fitted flashing lights and sound effects, and with the presentation of the other exhibits.

---

[17] *Doctor Who Magazine* #175.

Maintenance of the costumes and artefacts was however a continuous project, as Lorne Martin recalled in 1991: 'Where possible we try to keep the exhibition up to scratch; sometimes items don't animate, as we're simply waiting for spares and it really does require a constant cleaning operation'.[18]

Exhibitions Assistant Bob Richardson adds: 'A lot of stuff was in very poor condition, and we had a limited budget for conservation work and repair. The result of that was a deliberate decision to keep the lighting levels down on some exhibits to conceal the sad state of them.' The low lighting levels did, however, lead to an atmospheric exhibition that unnerved and thrilled visitors for many years to come.

Longleat would later become notable also for hosting *Doctor Who*'s epic 20th Anniversary Celebration event in 1983, and would become a popular location for further conventions and actor appearances. In 1996 it was said, 'The exhibition attracts around 350,000 visitors a year', demonstrating *Doctor Who*'s continued popularity despite the programme being no longer broadcast on BBC1 at that time.[19] When the attraction eventually closed in 2003, it brought to an end a 30-year *Doctor Who* presence at Longleat, making it the longest-running *Doctor Who* exhibition in the world.

The Exhibition

The exterior entrance to the exhibition took the form of an oversized TARDIS police box. Approximately ten feet tall, its open door gave entry to the attraction. The original exhibition replicated the successful formula of the Special Effects Exhibition, which was still open at the Science Museum at the time. As a result, two further specially-made Daleks were required, and another TARDIS console complete with a central time rotor that would rise and fall. These were again created by Tony Oxley, who in 1975 would receive credits as Visual Effects Designer on 'The Ark in Space' and 'The Sontaran Experiment', and Charlie Lunn, also of the BBC Visual Effects Department.

These two Daleks are now referred to as L1 and L2, the L standing for Longleat. They would undergo a number of changes of appearance later on, but initially their liveries matched those of the ones seen at the Science Museum. Dalek L1 began life in a gold-with-silver paint job complete with black hemispheres, while L2 replicated the silver-and-blue of the 1960s. Both would stay in these colours for the next 15 years.

For the 1974 exhibition, one of the 1973 exhibits, Aggedor, was replaced by an Ice Warrior, as seen in 'The Monster of Peladon' on television earlier that year. A Draconian from 'Frontier in Space' and three 'eight legs' spiders from 'Planet of the Spiders' were also added to the displays.[20]

---

[18] *Doctor Who Magazine* #175.
[19] *Doctor Who Magazine* #245.
[20] *World of Horror* No. 8.

1975

The two-year experiment with a dedicated *Doctor Who* exhibition had proved successful, so for 1975 an extension was added. Visitors now meandered through a dark corridor with display cases on either side, showcasing monsters from a variety of the Doctor's television adventures. The exhibition then concluded in impressive fashion as the corridor led into the replica TARDIS control room. As before, around the sides of the control room were viewing windows where further monster displays were presented, with interactive control panels mounted beneath. The windows were separated by the familiar roundel-patterned TARDIS walls, and a less-than-futuristic fire exit. Over the next 30 years, the display cases would be updated to feature new items as and when they became available.

By 1975, Tom Baker's first season as the Time Lord was drawing to an end. In June that year, issue no. 8 of the monthly *World of Horror* magazine provided one of the first detailed accounts of the exhibition. Simon Short's report – described in the magazine's editorial as 'too informative and entertaining to keep on file'[21] – provides an insight into the exhibition's early days, and suggests that the Exhibitions Unit were quick to include items from the very latest series of *Doctor Who*, broadcast mere months before.

Outside of the exhibition, a loudspeaker played the *Doctor Who* theme tune across the yard, drawing attention to the TARDIS police box entrance and ticket booth. Venturing into the dimly-lit corridor, visitors encountered a model Tyrannosaurus breaking through a brick wall, as seen in 'Invasion of the Dinosaurs'. This began their journey into the world of *Doctor Who*. Another model from the same story, similar to a large doll's house and no doubt used for dinosaur model shots, was also said to be on display.

Behind a long perspex panel stood a cave environment filled with boulders, mirroring the caves at Wookey Hole, location for 'Revenge of the Cybermen'. A trio of Cybermen from the latter adventure formed the centrepiece of this display, and were posed carrying pieces of equipment. The low lighting assisted in making the silver creatures an eerie presence.

The next exhibit was another from Tom Baker's first season in the show's lead role, with a metallic clicking providing a hint. This noise came from the twitching antennae atop the large head of Field Major Styre's robot from 'The Sontaran Experiment'. Styre himself was also present, clutching his helmet under one arm – a pose that would be replicated by later Sontaran displays in various exhibitions. Further along the corridor, past a photograph of Sarah Jane Smith pursued by Linx, the original Sontaran from 'The Time Warrior', was another display case, this time containing a macabre collection of alien head masks. These included an Exxilon ('Death to the Daleks'), an Ice Warrior, a Yeti, a Solonian Mutant ('The Mutants') and a Sea Devil ('The Sea Devils').

At the end of the corridor, a Dalek guard glided forward in a perspex booth,

---

[21] *World of Horror* No. 8.

accompanied by an audio track. Traditional Dalek declarations about ruling the universe were supplemented by a welcome to the exhibition and a warning not to get too close to the dangerous creatures on display. Referred to as the 'Sentinel' Dalek, the replica prop chosen was Dalek L2 in the silver-and-blue livery, complete with flashing dome lights, swivelling eye-stalk and moving plunger and weaponry. The 'Sentinel' Dalek at this time stood guard at the entrance to the TARDIS control room, but in later years it would be moved to the very start of the exhibition.

The TARDIS control room then provided the finale to the attraction, and the surrounding viewing windows showcased a menagerie of monsters. The TARDIS console that Tony Oxley had created for Longleat proved to be a visitor highlight. Fan Peter Trott first saw it several years after it had been installed, but it still made an impressive impact, as he recalls: 'When I first saw the Longleat console *in situ* my eyes lit up; I was just "Wow". It was so beautifully [illuminated].' The console retained the hexagonal shape of the one seen on television, although in a slightly smaller size, but the control panels were different, with more interactive elements, as Trott again remembers: 'It was a cross between different consoles; it had got bits of all sorts on there.' Even at the young age when he first visited the exhibition, Trott felt that he would love to own the console: 'There was that a little bit inside me that went, "Oh, I wish I had that!"' Little did he realise that, many years later, it would indeed come into his possession.

Simon Short's report in *World of Horror* magazine noted that the console was protected by vertical perspex panels placed around its six sides to prevent handling and consequent damage by visitors. These panels, attached directly to the edges of the console, would remain in place for the next twenty years or so. Surrounding the whole of the console was a hexagonal arrangement of metal barriers that would stay in place for the entirety of the exhibition's run.

The display case that had once housed the Lunar Rover was now home to three Exxilons from 'Death to the Daleks'. These creatures were posed worshipping the bright light that illuminated them. Behind stood an Axon creature from 'The Claws of Axos'. To the left was positioned the Wirrn Queen notably seen at the conclusion to the first episode of 'The Ark in Space'. Crawling away to the side and largely hidden from view was a Wirrn larva grub, a crucial part of the creature's life cycle, while above it stood another Wirrn in its final adult form. According to the report in *World of Horror*, some of the cryogenic cells seen on the Nerva Beacon set in 'The Ark in Space' provided a background to this tableau.

On the other side of the room was a second monster collection, featuring a giant clam, Dalek and Davros from 'Genesis of the Daleks'. Dalek L1, in the gold-and-silver paintwork with black hemispheres, featured as part of a monster assortment through one of the other control room windows. Further exhibits in this monster menagerie included a Sea Devil; a Draconian; two Ice Warriors, one with a sonic disruptor attached to its right arm; and a Yeti ('The Web of Fear'). Smaller items on display included a Drashig model ('Carnival of Monsters'); a giant maggot ('The Green Death'); a Cybermat ('The Wheel in Space'); and three giant spiders ('Planet of the Spiders').

Over the next few years, the display cases were regularly updated, with new artefacts added when they became available after use in production of the latest television episodes. The viewing windows in the TARDIS control room were eventually subdivided into four individual cubicles, maximising the space available and allowing for more creative displays than a simple aggregation of monsters. Dalek L1 was placed against the cave backdrop along with several other items, which were frequently rotated. In 1976, for instance, the Axon and one of the Wirrn were positioned there.

1977

The contents of the 1977 exhibition were detailed in the pages of the *Doctor Who* Appreciation Society's *TARDIS* fanzine. The show's fourteenth season had concluded on 2 April 1977 with the final episode of 'The Talons of Weng-Chiang', so new additions from that run of episodes made their debuts in the displays.

After paying the 20p admission charge, the first alien creature that visitors encountered was a Zygon, accompanied by some of the equally alien technology seen during 'Terror of the Zygons'. The display utilised perspex, plastic sheeting and sand to give the appearance that the Zygon was peering out through a window of its spaceship while remaining submerged in Loch Ness. Pulsating lights completed the eerie ambience.[22]

On the right-hand side of the corridor, standing approximately 8 feet tall and made even more impressive by being surrounded by mirrors, was the large Krynoid creature that had lumbered toward the Doctor in the cliffhanger to Part Four of 'The Seeds of Doom'. (This had been an exhibit at the Blackpool exhibition during 1976.)

Adjacent to the Krynoid was Davros from 'Genesis of the Daleks', looking a little worse-for-wear, with 'all but one of his flick-switches ... broken and most of the lights ... not functioning either.'[23] The mask had also lost its shape without actor Michael Wisher's facial features occupying it, and curiously a flashing bulb had been placed inside, lighting up Davros' nose![24]

Back on the left-hand side of the corridor was an exhibit depicting Solon's laboratory on Karn from 'The Brain of Morbius'. The scene included Morbius's brain in its life-support tank; Solon's reflex-testing machine, with a Solonian Mutant head complete with twitching eyes; and other equipment and pieces of Solonian Mutant anatomy scattered on the floor. The Morbius monster itself was also present, and stood nearby to complete the exhibit.

Two models used for different productions were displayed next. The first

---

[22] *TARDIS* fanzine. Volume 2, Number 6.
[23] *TARDIS* fanzine. Volume 2, Number 6.
[24] *TARDIS* fanzine. Volume 2, Number 6.

was the Skarasen puppet from 'Terror of the Zygons', posed as if attacking an oil rig. The second was a model of the Krynoid engulfing Harrison Chase's mansion from the climax of 'The Seeds of Doom'.

A display of artefacts from 'The Robots of Death' was added mere months after the story had been broadcast on television. Replicating scenes set on the Sandminer, D84 was strapped to a table with the glowing Laserson probe suspended overhead. The hooded Taren Capel costume was positioned on the left, with V8 assisting in the operation on the right. At the back of the set stood SV7 on a flight of stairs, observing the scene. The rack of Laserson probes was also positioned at the front of this rather impressive display.

A Kraal from 'The Android Invasion' joined the 'Sentinel' Dalek L2 at the entrance to the TARDIS control room. Unfortunately, the Kraal costume was hung badly on a wire frame, and visitors could see right inside the hollow head mask. Pride of place naturally went to the TARDIS console, 'complete with rising and falling time rotor'.[25] The first of the additional displays surrounding it was the model rock face from 'The Face of Evil', featuring Tom Baker's recognisable features. The next featured a trio of monsters: an Ice Lord; an Ogron, which was missing its hands; and the Sontaran Styre from 'The Sontaran Experiment', with his helmet clutched under his arm.

Residing in the next viewing window was another new addition for that year: a Li H'sen Chang costume and the large golden dragon seen at the conclusion of 'The Talons of Weng-Chiang'. The dragon had formed the centrepiece of the House of the Dragon set and was designed by Roger Murray-Leach. Constructed of polystyrene, it took a freelance sculptor almost 150 hours of non-stop work to complete[26], and would feature prominently on the cover of the story's 1988 VHS release.

The fourth and final main viewing window held the usual menagerie of monsters and other beings. In 1977 this included a golden Time Lord robe and Commander Hilred's costume from 'The Deadly Assassin'; a Cyberman from 'Revenge of the Cybermen'; an Exxilon from 'Death to the Daleks'; two 'eight legs' spiders from 'Planet of the Spiders'; plus Dalek L1 in its gold-and-silver with black hemispheres paintwork.

A final display case held a selection of masks, including a Silurian; a Solonian Mutant; a Draconian, complete with a pair of hands; a Sea Devil; and Sutekh from 'Pyramids of Mars; plus the fabled 'hand' from 'The Hand of Fear'.

1978

Following the transmission of Season 15, the 1978 exhibitions had to include by popular demand the new companion, K-9. The outside of the Longleat exhibition had a new sign added, in the same shape as the show's diamond logo, which proclaimed 'NEW MONSTERS INCLUDING', with a small image of K-9. This year,

---

[25] *TARDIS* Fanzine. Volume 2, Number 6.
[26] *Doctor Who: The Complete History* (2015). Volume 26.

the monster assortment display with Dalek L1 included the K1 Robot ('Robot'); the Morbius monster ('The Brain of Morbius'); a Voc Robot ('The Robots of Death'); a Kraal ('The Android Invasion'); a Fendahl ('Image of the Fendahl'); a Sontaran ('The Invasion of Time'); and a Cyberman ('Revenge of the Cybermen').

1979

In 1979, items in the Longleat exhibition included two astronaut spacesuits and the Nucleus of the Swarm from 'The Invisible Enemy', these having been transferred from Blackpool; the female form of Eldrad ('The Hand of Fear'); two Sontarans, specifically Stor and a helmet-wearing subordinate ('The Invasion of Time'); and a Cyberman ('Revenge of the Cybermen'). Positioned together were a Time Lord robe; the K1 Robot ('Robot'); a Kraal ('The Android Invasion'); and the Morbius monster ('The Brain of Morbius'). The monster assortment featured the giant rat ('The Talons of Weng-Chiang'); a Voc Robot ('The Robots of Death'); plus Dalek L1. A display case covered in fake cobwebs held the demat gun from 'The Invasion of Time'; a single Voc Robot head ('The Robots of Death'); and Morbius's brain held in its jar as seen in 'The Brain of Morbius'.

1980

The Longleat exhibition featured in a *Blue Peter* segment broadcast on 3 April 1980. This included an interview with *Doctor Who* producer John Nathan-Turner and offered a peek at the behind-the-scenes side of the exhibition, which was said to be attracting an estimated 200,000 visitors a year at this time. The four-minute feature – which can be found on the DVD of 'The Leisure Hive' and the Blu-ray box set *The Collection: Season 18* – also showed some of the items on display that year. Naturally given prominence was a Dalek, specifically the silver-and-blue Dalek L2, which was seen moving its manipulator arm from left to right and its eye-stalk up and down. Also on show were the giant rat ('The Talons of Weng-Chiang'), which featured left-to-right head movement; Styggron the Kraal ('The Android Invasion'); the Morbius monster ('The Brain of Morbius'); and a Fendahl ('Image of the Fendahl'), which was now in its own individual display.

Seen being removed from the exhibition was the Nucleus of the Swarm from 'The Invisible Enemy', which had been on display for the 1979 season, having spent 1978 in Blackpool. Added in its place for the 1980 Longleat season was a Mandrel from 'Nightmare of Eden', in an appropriate jungle environment. Other costumes seen being dusted by *Blue Peter* presenter Tina Heath included a Sontaran ('The Invasion of Time'); a Cyberman ('Revenge of the Cybermen'); a Time Lord robe; and the K1 Robot ('Robot').

Transferred from display duties in Blackpool during 1979 to Longleat for 1980 were the Shrivenzale ('The Ribos Operation'); and the costumes for Prince Reynart's duplicate and the Archimandrite from 'The Androids of Tara'.

1981

The following year, a number of new additions could be seen at both Longleat and Blackpool after Season 18 – Tom Baker's last in the lead role – had concluded. The 'Sentinel' Dalek L2 stood guard and welcomed visitors to the exhibition, but the next exhibit was one of the new inclusions: the decayed Master from 'The Keeper of Traken'. Continuing along the corridor, a Mandrel from 'Nightmare of Eden', which had featured in the 1980 *Blue Peter* segment, remained, but now shared the jungle display with a Marshman from the more recent 'Full Circle'. Nearby was another recent acquisition, the model of the radio telescope used for the sequences at the dramatic conclusion of 'Logopolis', when the fourth Doctor fell and triggered his regeneration.

Another new exhibit focused on a story from the 'E-Space' trilogy, 'Warriors' Gate'. This consisted of two Gundan robots and a Tharil. It is thought that it was for this display in 1981 that one of the Gundans had a mechanism installed that caused the robot to swing its axe forward periodically. This movement would be retained for the next 20 years, and was particularly memorable when activated in the much later Llangollen exhibition.

The next display again featured a number of artefacts from a specific story, this time the recent series' first, 'The Leisure Hive'. Included were two Argolin costumes, complete with heads and hairpieces; a Foamasi; and one of the numerous Helmet of Theron props created for the production.

As tradition dictated, the TARDIS control room remained the exhibition's finale. The model of the Jagaroth spacecraft on the surface of primeval Earth, as seen in 'City of Death', had been in Blackpool during 1980 but was installed in Longleat for the 1981 season. A Nimon ('The Horns of Nimon') was accorded its own, separate display within the TARDIS control room, and is thought to have been another new addition this year, having not been seen in the 1980 *Blue Peter* feature. Finally, the monster menagerie remained and featured a Voc Robot; the K1 Robot; the Morbius monster; a Cyberman ('Revenge of the Cybermen'); the Pirate Captain ('The Pirate Planet'); a Fendahleen ('Image of the Fendahl'); Dalek L1; and a Kraal ('The Android Invasion').

The monster display was later adjusted, a Gundan robot ('Warriors' Gate') and the Nimon ('The Horns of Nimon') being brought in to join the Pirate Captain and Dalek L1. The first major change for Dalek L1 was the addition of a short track that allowed for a small amount of forward and backward motion; this was installed at some point prior to 1983 and remained until 1987.

1982

For the 1982 season, masks and weapons from 'Castrovalva' were added to the exhibition, having been seen on television that January. Also present was a scene representing the *K-9 and Company* pilot screened over the previous Christmas period, with K-9 and the Hecate priestess costume on display.

DOCTOR WHO EXHIBITIONS

1983 – Doctor Who Celebration

1983 saw *Doctor Who* celebrate its twentieth anniversary, and one of the highlights was the ambitious Celebration event organised by BBC Enterprises and hosted at Longleat House over the Easter weekend, Sunday 3 April and Monday 4 April. Longleat would host a number of other *Doctor Who* events over the years, but none as high-profile and significant as this. Advanced predictions of 10,000 people attending each day were blown out of the water when approximately 60,000 to 70,000 people made their way to the venue. Although there was some criticism from those who had to queue endlessly or were unable to get in at all, the event is fondly remembered and often referred to as *Doctor Who*'s Woodstock. Like that famous music festival, it proved to be a huge success, demonstrating the popularity of *Doctor Who* to the BBC and setting a template that future events would follow.

Although not the first *Doctor Who* convention, this was the original official convention organised by BBC Enterprises, and it would later be emulated for the fiftieth anniversary at the ExCeL Centre in London. It also marked ten years of a *Doctor Who* presence at Longleat, with the normal exhibition proving a minor part of the event. A number of actors were in attendance, including all four surviving Doctors; various BBC departments had displays; there were screenings of old episodes; and a number of sets used in the production of the yet-to-be-broadcast anniversary special 'The Five Doctors' were exhibited.

Doctor Who Monthly, as the magazine was called at the time, covered the event in its August issue over six pages full of detail and photographs.[27] Later memories of the event were also presented by *Doctor Who Magazine* in 1996 as part of producer John Nathan-Turner's memoirs. He recalled his enthusiasm when approached by Terry Sampson and Lorne Martin of BBC Exhibitions regarding collaboration for this special event. Longleat House was identified as the venue, and planning meetings began in earnest:

'At the very first meeting, it was agreed that the events would all take place in the gorgeous enclosed courtyard to the side of the main house. As the meetings got more frequent, and BBC departments became ever more enthusiastic, the site became larger and larger, eventually totalling six acres. Sometimes one embarks on an idea with scepticism but, in this instance, the various departments of the BBC all decided that they wanted to be part and parcel of this huge celebration. I had agreed with Design that we would allow the sets from "The Five Doctors" to be displayed, even though the post-production on the programme wasn't yet complete and it was months away from transmission. Make-up, Costume, Visual Effects and the Radiophonic Workshop all agreed to display their wares. Suddenly, it was all happening.'[28]

One of those in attendance was Mike Tucker. He recalls, 'My biggest memory is the big exhibition/festival that they did down at Longleat for the twentieth

---

[27] *Doctor Who Monthly* #79.
[28] *Doctor Who Magazine* #237.

anniversary celebration. I am one of many, many people who were there.'
Another individual present was fan and collector Peter Trott, who found the
event the perfect way to celebrate his thirteenth birthday:

'It was my birthday, and I went down with my Mum. My aunt lived down in
Poole in Bournemouth. So they decided to take us to Longleat. We drove in, and
I don't know how we managed to get in and park, but we did. There was this
huge, immense queue. My Mum – she was a law unto herself anyway – just
walked straight in, in front of the queue. She didn't realise what she was doing;
she just walked into the ticket tent and came out with tickets. So we got in.'

Entrance to the *Doctor Who* Celebration was to the right of the main entrance
to Longleat House, at the end of the long driveway with large fountains on either
side. A ticket tent was set up to the side of the right-hand fountain, adult entry
costing £3.50 and a child ticket £1.50; this was where the long queues first began,
and they continued across the site. The event opened at 10am on both mornings
with the Corps of Drums from the Royal Welsh Fusiliers in front of Longleat
House. Displayed by the main entrance to the Celebration, outside of the house,
were 12-foot-high figures of two large Daleks, one yellow and one red; the fifth
Doctor; a Cyberman; a Zygon; and a Sontaran. These were provided by the
Blackpool Corporation, having been previously used as part of the famous
Blackpool illuminations.

On the banks of Half Mile Pond, a series of tents were erected to house some
of the displays, with the first and largest one featuring the aforementioned
studio sets from 'The Five Doctors'. These included the UNIT office and several
areas of Gallifrey, namely the conference room, the Dark Tower corridor and the
Game room.[29] Studio recording on the story had concluded only on the
Thursday of the previous week, so transportation and installation of the sets
occurred on the Friday and Saturday.

Also on display was a TARDIS control room set featuring the Season 20
console; this had been replaced for recording of 'The Five Doctors', but John
Nathan-Turner wanted to keep the new version under wraps until transmission.
Positioned near the console was the robotic companion Kamelion, who had
debuted the previous month in 'The King's Demons'; this is thought to have
been its only public appearance.

The set of the Dark Tower corridor served as a background for the Ergon
('Arc of Infinity') and a Gundan robot ('Warriors' Gate'). Video footage of the
event confirms that the mechanism allowing the Gundan robot to swing its
battle-axe forward was in operation. This supports the conclusion that the
mechanism is likely to have been fitted in 1981. Also present were a Nimon ('The
Horns of Nimon'), a Foamasi ('The Leisure Hive') and Dalek 6-ex, known as the
Tussauds Dalek, still in its original, predominantly light blue colour scheme.

Another item making its debut on public display was the Garm ('Terminus'),
seen onscreen just a couple of months before. The Garm would go on to appear
in many other exhibitions over the years, after spending the remainder of 1983 at

---

[29] *Doctor Who Monthly* #79.

Longleat and in 1984 being transferred to Blackpool.

The BBC Costume and Make-Up Departments shared a tent. Members of the Make-Up team used their skills to perform face-painting for younger visitors, and displayed photographs of their work, such as the aged make-ups created for the Doctor's companions Tegan and Nyssa in 'Mawdryn Undead'. There were also busts displaying make-ups for a Movellan ('Destiny of the Daleks'); Mawdryn ('Mawdryn Undead'); and an Argolin ('The Leisure Hive').

The Costume Department showcased various design sketches, demonstrating the processes involved in creating some of *Doctor Who*'s costumes. Costumes on display at the event included a Cyberman ('Earthshock'); a Harlequin fancy dress outfit ('Black Orchid'); Omega ('Arc of Infinity'); a Vanir ('Terminus'); a helmeted Sontaran ('The Invasion of Time'); Nyssa's outfit from 'Castrovalva'; Black and White Guardian robes; a Time Lord Chancellery Guard; a Chlorian Guard ('The Creature from the Pit'); the Hecate Priestess (*K-9 and Company*); a Kraal ('The Android Invasion'); and the Meglos and Sontaran waxworks created for the then recent Madame Tussauds exhibition. Some of the elaborate costumes seen in other BBC period dramas, plus a Time Lord robe, were also on display in this tent.

The Visual Effects Department had a small tent of their own, where they demonstrated explosive flash effects and other examples of their work. Present here were two Daleks, including one that had been destroyed in 'The Five Doctors'; and the Pharos project model from 'Logopolis'. A K-9 prop, with exposed inner workings, and an assortment of prop weapons, including a Cyberman gun seen in 'Earthshock', were displayed on a table. It wasn't just items from *Doctor Who* that were showcased in this tent, however. Also to be seen here were Marvin the paranoid android and Zaphod Beeblebrox's second head from the BBC production of *The Hitchhikers Guide to the Galaxy*; a gorilla model; a replica of *Star Wars*' R2D2; and a Triffid prop from the BBC's adaptation of *The Day of the Triffids* (1981).

As for many others who visited the event over that weekend, for Mike Tucker it was the prospect of being able to see original props and costumes up close that made it an experience not to be missed. Tucker recalls how attending the Celebration contributed to his career progression: 'If you go back to the props from the '60s and the '70s, because of the crudeness of the materials and because of the rush that these things were done in, for somebody that wants to get into effects work it can actually be quite inspiring.' This inspiration extended to visitors being able to chat to those already in the industry and ask questions about their work and how to break into the industry themselves.

The fourth and final tent on the right-hand side of Longleat House on the bank of Half Mile Pond was dedicated to an auction of original props and costumes, and merchandise stalls. Two auctions took place, at 1pm on each of the days, with items sold including the Cyber Controller helmet from 'The Tomb of the Cybermen' and the demat gun from 'The Invasion of Time'. Guest auctioneers included actors Jon Pertwee, Peter Davison, Nicholas Courtney, Richard Franklin and Carole Ann Ford.

The merchandise that visitors could purchase included baseball caps (priced at £4.50), keyrings, mugs, records and jigsaws. The ever-popular Target novelisations were a hit, with extra stock needing to be brought down from London for the second day. Also printed for the event was a commemorative programme, which was available for only 50p. Inside this programme there was an introduction piece written by the Marquis of Bath, Henry Thynne, who recalled his visit to the BBC Special Effects Exhibition in 1972 that had inspired him to bring the TARDIS to Longleat. Producer John Nathan-Turner also supplied a welcome, and continuity advisor Ian Levine provided an overview of the show's 'twenty year odyssey'. The programme also included some information about the BBC departments on display; a blank area designated for autographs; and the proposed 'Timetable of Events'.

A special *Doctor Who* cinema tent screened selected stories from throughout the show's history, beginning with 'The Dalek Invasion of Earth'. Other stories shown were 'The Dominators', 'Terror of the Autons', 'Terror of the Zygons' and 'The Visitation'. This was a unique opportunity to see these stories at a time before home video releases, and unfortunately the small capacity of approximately 200 people failed to meet the demand.

Like other departments, the BBC Radiophonic Workshop also had a tent to discuss and demonstrate their work with visitors. The Workshop was celebrating its own anniversary of 25 years at the BBC, with staff members Brian Hodgson, Dick Mills, Roger Limb and Malcolm Clarke making presentations.

For some in attendance, however, it was the thrill of seeing *Doctor Who* actors in the flesh, and the chance to get a precious autograph or photo, that drew them to Longleat. A constant stream of autograph sessions took place in the Orangery. John Nathan-Turner had been heavily involved in persuading many of the actors to attend, his aim being to attract all of the surviving Doctors and as many companions as he could convince; Elisabeth Sladen later said that 'Think of the fans' might as well have been his catchphrase during 1983.[30] The late William Hartnell was not forgotten either, as his widow Heather was in attendance.

Hartnell's successor, Patrick Troughton, had proved a particularly tricky sell, as Nathan-Turner recalled in his memoirs for *Doctor Who Magazine* in 1996: 'Reluctantly – and with some helpful prompting from Jon Pertwee – Pat had agreed to attend Longleat. Actually, Pat had done cartwheels to get out of doing Longleat. He would ring me with endless reasons as to why he should not attend, but I was having none of it. "No time to spend with wife Sheelagh? Bring her with you! Don't fancy driving down? I'll lay on a car?" and so on. In the end, Pat decided there was no way I'd let him off the hook. He later admitted that he felt permanently indebted to me, as it had convinced him that he could handle fan events, which, of course, led to him making many such appearances before his untimely death.'[31]

The fourth Doctor, the enigmatic Tom Baker, would also prove tricky to

---

[30] Sladen, E. (2011) *Elisabeth Sladen: The Autobiography*. p.268.
[31] *Doctor Who Magazine* #237.

convince to attend the event, given that he had declined to appear in the anniversary special 'The Five Doctors'. Nathan-Turner explained how his attendance was finally secured: 'I had persuaded all the living Doctors to attend except Tom. Now, as Tom and Terry [Sampson] enjoyed a special friendship, I'd suggested to Terry that, given Tom's non-participation in "The Five Doctors", perhaps it might be more appropriate if he spoke to Tom. Tom always enjoyed the company of Terry and Lorne [Martin], so it was the best possible way of – basically – asking a favour of Tom. (I felt I'd already asked my favour with regard to the use of [footage from the unfinished story] "Shada" [in "The Five Doctors"], and I didn't want to push my luck). Terry duly persuaded Tom to appear at Longleat; it was quite clear that the wider public, at that time, saw Tom as their favourite Doctor.'[32]

For one fan in particular, Tom Baker's attendance was a real thrill and a perfect thirteenth birthday present. As Peter Trott recalls, 'I met Tom Baker there; it was my first time that I'd met him. I was 13, and just like "Wow"!' The effort of Terry Sampson to secure Tom Baker's appearance no doubt brought joy to many others amongst the thousands of fans in attendance. John Nathan-Turner had managed to achieve his goal of attracting all the surviving Doctors, plus Heather Hartnell representing her late husband.

Other *Doctor Who* actors in attendance included Sarah Sutton, Janet Fielding, Mark Strickson, Valentine Dyall, Nicholas Courtney, Richard Franklin, John Levene and Anthony Ainley. From behind the scenes, director Fiona Cumming was also present. Frazer Hines, who had played Jamie opposite Troughton's second Doctor, never reached Longleat, as his car broke down on the M4 motorway.[33]

Two other companion actors who did make it to Longleat were Elisabeth Sladen and Carole Ann Ford. However, when presented with the postcards that they would be signing for the fans, they were horrified at the photographs chosen, which had been taken in haste at the hotel when they were on location for 'The Five Doctors'. John Nathan-Turner recalled this in *Doctor Who Magazine*: 'As we were also promoting "The Five Doctors", masses of pictures of the cast members taken on location were ordered for the artistes to sign. There simply wasn't time to show them the shots for their prior approval, and I had discovered at the end of the event that Lis Sladen and Carole Ann Ford had hated all of their 5,000 pictures!'[34]

The two former companions found a solution, with the help of their husbands, as Elisabeth Sladen wrote in her autobiography: '"I'm not having this", I said. Carole's husband and Brian [Miller, Elisabeth Sladen's husband] were nattering away in the corner – "Over here, boys – we've got a job for you!" Five minutes later every single photo had been submerged in one of the fire buckets of water hidden at the back.'[35]

---

[32] *Doctor Who Magazine* #237.
[33] *Doctor Who Magazine* #237.
[34] *Doctor Who Magazine* #237.
[35] Sladen, E. (2011) *Elisabeth Sladen: The Autobiography*. p.276.

An area was set up in the Longleat House tennis courts to allow visitors to pose for the cameras with certain items and take away a framed photograph. The items in question included a TARDIS exterior, a Marshman ('Full Circle'), a Mandrel ('Nightmare of Eden') and Davros. Dalek 5's skirt section was pressed into use, being hastily converted to create this mock-up of Davros.[36] The Doctor's car Bessie provided visitors with another photo opportunity. These attractions were made possible with the help of photography company Kodak.

The large *Doctor Who* Forum marquee was used for panel discussion interviews with the guests. It was also the location for the official opening ceremony at 10.30 on the Sunday morning and the closing ceremony at 5.30 on the Monday afternoon. Guests emerged from a police box prop and sat at a table discussing their work on the show and answering questions posed by the audience of attendees.

The Longleat exhibition itself was also open and could be found in the far corner, furthest away from the main entrance. With so many other exciting attractions, some visitors to the Celebration missed the permanent exhibition altogether. Peter Trott recalls: 'I knew they had an exhibition [at Longleat], but ... even though I was at that twentieth anniversary thing, I never went into the actual small exhibition there.'

To promote the event, a short announcement had been made on BBC1 at the request of the organising team of John Nathan-Turner, Terry Sampson and Lorne Martin. Details were also included at the end of *Radio Times* programme listings for some episodes of *Doctor Who*, such as Part Four of 'Enlightenment'. This advertising probably accounted for the event attracting such massive crowds, far beyond the expectations of the organisers, including Nathan-Turner:

'Terry, Lorne and I all asked the Presentation Department, who are responsible for all those trails between BBC programmes, to promote our event. (I don't think that we television professionals realised just how effective these plugs were; never mind.) On the eve of the two-day event, we had pre-sold some 13,000 tickets. We all agreed that this meant an eventual attendance of probably double that. How wrong we were! There were, in the end, in excess of 56,000 people. Wiltshire itself ground to a halt. We had a monster on our hands, but this one we couldn't control.'[37]

The excessive crowds on the first day proved hugely problematic, causing traffic chaos across Wiltshire and the surrounding area, with hundreds of disappointed youngsters and exasperated parents being turned away. As John Nathan-Turner explained, the numbers were completely unexpected:

'BBC Enterprises, as it was then called, simply didn't expect anything like such a response from the general audience; and, in all fairness, neither did I. I knew that people were flying in from America, Australia and New Zealand and so on, but it was easy to reckon that they were just a handful of wealthy eccentrics, not an invasion force. Hordes of people were complaining about the

---

[36] www.youtube.com/watch?v=drIjQ88mXPM
[37] *Doctor Who Magazine* #237.

queues, the apparent disorganisation, the lack of intimacy, the overcrowded car parks, the police, the caravan site and so on; we all did our best to ensure that they got something for their money.'[38]

Members of the army were brought in to control the crowds. However, these professional soldiers were not trained in the ways of customer service and so were quite rough with guests. They were also given UNIT badges to fit into the *Doctor Who* universe, which proved profitable for the soldiers as they sold them to visitors, requesting spares from organisers in case they 'lost' them again!

Fortunately, things improved on the second day, with Peter Davison, BBC Enterprises' General Manger Byron Parkin and John Nathan-Turner appearing on Ed Stewart's Radio Two show, broadcasting from the event, to ask people without tickets not to journey to Longleat.

Eight years after the event, Lorne Martin reminisced about the weekend with John Nathan-Turner for *Doctor Who Magazine*. Martin concluded: 'Its main problem, as an event, was that it was too successful. Too many people turned up, and we never, ever thought that people would come from so far away. It's easy with hindsight to identify areas that could have made it better. Being twenty times larger would have helped! It could have covered the entire Longleat Estate, but I still don't think people would have seen everything they wanted. If it had been there for a week, which it couldn't, it would have been better. Nevertheless, I'm glad we did it.'[39]

Nathan-Turner, writing in 1996, reached a similar conclusion: 'I think that Longleat 1983 proved to the powers-that-be, the great and the good, the establishment even, that *Doctor Who* was a force to be reckoned with.'[40] The event's success was without question, and some of the profits allowed for the donation of a minibus to the Sunshine charity, as seen on an episode of *Blue Peter* later in the year and now available as a special feature on the special edition DVD release of 'The Five Doctors'.

The 1983 Celebration at Longleat was indeed a trailblazing event, which has since gone down in fan folklore. In light of its success, and the continued popularity of the Longleat and Blackpool exhibitions, the future looked bright. Subsequently the May 1984 issue of *Doctor Who Magazine* reported that producer John Nathan-Turner had indicated that all the costumes and props on display that year at both exhibitions would be from the latest broadcast season.[41]

1984

Gary Russell composed a *Doctor Who Magazine* feature, published in September 1984, which reviewed that year's versions of the Longleat and Blackpool exhibitions.[42] Photographs taken by Robert Moubert showed some of the items

---

[38] *Doctor Who Magazine* #237.
[39] *Doctor Who Magazine* #175.
[40] *Doctor Who Magazine* #237.
[41] *The Official Doctor Who Magazine* #88.
[42] *The Official Doctor Who Magazine* #92.

on display at Longleat. By this time, the 'Sentinel' Dalek, which had been positioned at the end of the corridor prior to the TARDIS control room, had been relocated to the very start of the exhibition. Unfortunately, its dialogue welcoming visitors was drowned out by the K-9 audio being played deeper inside the exhibition. Another of the early exhibits was the peculiar Ergon from 'Arc of Infinity'. Opposite stood a Terileptil and the beautiful Android from 'The Visitation' plus a Marshman from 'Full Circle'. Next were the two representations of the Malus from 'The Awakening', on display for the first time, mere months after being seen on screen. Gary Russell described them at the time as 'two of the most impressive artefacts I've ever seen.'[43]

K-9 continued to trundle up and down on a single track, informing visitors that he had been built by Professor Marius and that Mark 1 was with Leela. A single Tractator from 'Frontios' benefited from having some luminous paint added to enhance an effect of glowing veins on its body. Omega's and Chancellor Thalia's costumes from 'Arc of Infinity' were also said to be seated together. The TARDIS control room continued to provide the finale. Photos mounted in the wall roundels depicted the Doctor's six television incarnations to date, although Gary Russell lamented that the one of the first Doctor used an image of Richard Hurndall, who had played the role in 'The Five Doctors', instead of William Hartnell.[44]

The control room monster display for 1984 included a Cyberman, apparently with a moving mouthpiece; two Sea Devils and a Silurian ('Warriors of the Deep'); a Fendahl ('Image of the Fendahl'); Dalek L1; a Mandrel ('Nightmare of Eden'); the K1 Robot ('Robot'); and a Dalek Trooper costume ('Resurrection of the Daleks'). Through a glass window, the available merchandise of the time was showcased. Finally, another display case held a smashed Quark head ('The Dominators'); half of the Nucleus's head ('The Invisible Enemy'); a demon mask ('Snakedance'); the Taran crown ('The Androids of Tara'); and a Castrovalvan spear ('Castrovalva').

1985

The following year saw some minor changes at the Longleat exhibition. For instance, the full Sharez Jek costume and Magma creature from 'The Caves of Androzani' were transferred from Blackpool. Additions from Colin Baker's first full season as the Doctor were a Sontaran with weapon from 'The Two Doctors'; and two Varosian guard costumes, complete with the buggy also seen during 'Vengeance on Varos'.

1986

1986 was a time of significant change for *Doctor Who*. The show had escaped a

---

[43] *The Official Doctor Who Magazine* #92.
[44] *The Official Doctor Who Magazine* #92.

threatened cancellation by the BBC and had returned, after a hiatus, with 'The Trial of the Time Lord'. However, this would prove to be Colin Baker's last season in the role.

Times were changing at the Longleat exhibition too. The production hiatus meant that there were no new items that could be added, but during the usual winter closure the exhibition underwent significant redevelopment. Following the closure of the Blackpool exhibition in 1985 and the development of a self-contained USA tour (see later sections of this book), added attention and resources could be dedicated to Longleat. Security was also boosted, in response to some items having been stolen from a Sontaran display.

The environment was improved, with the addition of more atmospheric lighting and set elements that had been utilised in the television show itself. A separate official BBC shop was set up in a nearby stable block, in place of the one that had previously been in the exhibition itself, and this freed up space for the display of extra Daleks – specifically Dalek 1-7 and Dalek N2. These were not behind glass, so the public were able to get up close to them; and the original screen-used ones suffered the brunt of that attention. As Lorne Martin once commented, 'I adore young children, but it's hard to watch *Doctor Who* exhibits being climbed over and bashed in a mock fight. It makes me wince.'[45] One young visitor to the exhibition was Mark Barton Hill. Aged 11 at the time, he was astonished that these screen-used props from 'Revelation of the Daleks' were on display, and remembers them fondly:

'It was amazing! You got to see the actual Daleks, and they weren't the exhibition props but the real thing, up close and touchable. There were two Daleks in grey and black, two of the new cream and gold Daleks and maybe three Cybermen.'

1987

The following year saw a new Doctor debuting on television, and consequently a refresh of the Longleat exhibition was required – and arguably long overdue. The new 'designed' look of the attraction was praised by Stuart Evans in a *Doctor Who Magazine* article.[46] This redesign extended even to the corridors, which were no longer lacklustre but boasted bulkhead features, access panels and ventilation tubes, creating the feel of being on a spaceship. The exhibition ambience was greatly improved, and was now very atmospheric and immersive, with more intricate detailing and lighting throughout.

Replacing the 'Sentinel' Dalek, the first display was a model TARDIS seen materialising and dematerialising onto a generic planetary landscape. To achieve this effect, the so-called Pepper's Ghost illusion was used, with lighting changes onto a screen creating the impression of the model appearing and disappearing. The display lacked the appropriate sound effects. Another model was the next

---

[45] *Doctor Who Magazine* #175.
[46] *Doctor Who Magazine* #127.

and even more impressive exhibit: the 5ft-diameter Time Lord space station used in the spectacular opening sequence of 'The Trial of the Time Lord'. That 35-second sequence was arguably one of the most impressive examples of visual effects viewers had ever witnessed on *Doctor Who*, and the opportunity to see the model up close and examine the intricate detail that had gone into it was a real thrill.

Opposite the space station model was the exhibition's first scene recreation. This was also from 'The Trial of a Time Lord', but in this case the 'Mindwarp' segment. It featured the costumes of the two Mentor characters, Sil and his superior Kiv, separated by that of an alien delegate who had appeared very briefly in the story. The latter costume was actually a modified version of the red Terileptil creature seen in 'The Visitation'. This trio of costumes would remain together until being sold off at auction in 2010.

The large Malus face that had burst through the church wall in 'The Awakening' was the next exhibit, with the added touch of a candle flickering.[47]

A Sea Devil from 'Warriors of the Deep' was displayed in an aquatic environment, although this set was not quite as originally intended. Stuart Evans' *Doctor Who Magazine* article noted that exhibition designer Martin Wilkie had planned to have the Sea Devil visible through bubbling water in a chamber akin to the one seen on television during the story's first episode. A canopy would have poured coloured water between two sheets of plate glass half an inch apart, with an aerator from a fish tank creating the bubbles. Broken glass, a pool of water on the floor and no more money left in the budget meant that the effect was abandoned.[48] However, the Sea Devil still looked impressive in an eerily green-lit case with the walls covered in seaweed.

As the corridor meandered round to the right, the next case featured another costume from 'Warriors of the Deep': a Silurian. This display was a little more random in assembly, however, as the Silurian was paired with Omega from 'Arc of Infinity' and a variety of available helmets and masks. Fortunately, the next display returned to the more considered style of the redesigned exhibition. A strong set-piece was created to replicate the 'Terror of the Vervoids' segment of 'The Trial of the Time Lord'. Control panels and screens represented the deck of the *Hyperion III* spaceship seen during the story. Seated at the controls were two Mogarians. Two Vervoid costumes were also on display, one kneeling and the second lying on the ground covered in leaves. Through a window, a series of asteroids were rotating in space, as if outside the spaceship, adding to the effectiveness of this immersive and well-constructed set.

The final display in the corridor section of the exhibition was dressed to resemble a jungle planet, such as Eden from 'Nightmare of Eden'. Appropriately, a Mandrel from that story was hidden within the shrubs; although curiously it was joined by the Hecate High Priestess costume from the spin-off *K-9 and Company* and the Bandril ambassador puppet from 'Timelash'. The well-

---

[47] *Doctor Who Magazine* #127.
[48] *Doctor Who Magazine* #127.

designed lighting of the redesigned exhibition meant that the Mandrel was one of a number of items that arguably looked more impressive here than they had on screen.

The TARDIS control room once again provided the spectacular highlight and conclusion to the exhibition. The first viewing window to the left of the entrance featured a replica K-9 prop, created from the original mould, in a country house environment representing Aunt Lavinia's home as seen during the *K-9 and Company* pilot. The prop moved forward and back on a small track, and had eyes and buttons that lit up and a nose probe that extended.

The cave setting in the second viewing window was unchanged from the previous year, the miscellany of monsters including the Magma beast from 'The Caves of Androzani'.

The penultimate display had a robot theme and featured the K1 Robot ('Robot'); Drathro and L1 ('The Trial of the Time Lord': 'The Mysterious Planet'); and two Cybermen.

The final hurrah for the 1987 season was the Daleks and Davros, as had been the case for many years in Blackpool. Until this point, the two Longleat Daleks had been separated, L2 acting as the 'Sentinel' and L1 in the monster showcase. Now that they were united, a clever trick was used to make their display seem even bigger. What appeared to be a lengthy, futuristic corridor was actually a pair of mirrors placed at a 90-degree angle to each other. Dalek L1 was placed at the front of the display, with the reflections of Davros and Dalek L2 seen gliding impressively on a short track. The only downside to this was that the telescopic arm and weaponry of the Dalek seen in the reflection appeared to be on the wrong sides of the body.

1988

Doctor Who's twenty-fifth anniversary was marked by the opening of a new Space Adventure exhibition on Tooley Street in London. However, the Longleat exhibition remained open and shared in the celebrations, with new exhibits added. These not only represented the show's most-recently-broadcast season but also featured the addition of two popular monsters from the past; a fitting tribute during the anniversary year. In a significant change, BBC Enterprises had now subcontracted-out the running of the exhibition to M & J Media Ltd, a company headed up by Lorne Martin, with designer Martin Wilkie continuing his contribution to the creation of the displays.

The exhibition entrance remained an oversized TARDIS police box exterior but had the celebratory '*Doctor Who* 25' logo added to the side. Inside, the dematerialising TARDIS model, the Time Lord space station, the Mentors and the Sea Devil displays all remained the same as in the previous year. The first new addition came from the seventh Doctor's debut story, 'Time and the Rani'. Featuring in this exhibit were the Rani's costume, as worn by Kate O'Mara on screen; the giant brain prop; and two of the bat-like Tetraps.

Opposite the Tetraps display was Kane from 'Dragonfire', suffering the gruesome demise caused by his exposure to sunlight. Reminiscent of a 'melting head' effect seen in the Indiana Jones movie *Raiders of the Lost Ark*, this was particularly graphic. The original head and skull used to achieve the effect on television had been constructed by Sue Moore and Stephen Mansfield out of fibreglass and wax. For the exhibition, a new head was needed, with a static melting effect, which was seen largely on the left side of Kane's face. A button outside the case rotated the head to reveal the ghastly visage. This head would later appear for sale on the Prop Gallery website, which at the time of writing features a number of good images that demonstrate how gruesome the exhibit was.[49] Hands also suffering the ravages of the light rays were added to complete the dramatic scene, set in front of ice walls similar to those seen on the planetoid Svartos in the story. The head and hands now belong in the collection of Neil Cole.

The set from the 'Terror of the Vervoids' segment of 'The Trial of the Time Lord', featuring the two Mogarians with two Vervoids, remained in place for a second consecutive year but benefited from the inclusion of the *Hyperion III* spaceship model, now visible through one of the spaceship's portals.

The next exhibit was something a little bit special to mark the show's silver jubilee. Philip Newman described the experience: 'Passing through an archway, you'll find yourselves to all intents and purposes in the London Underground, with white tiled walls, Underground symbol, original poster prints and even a fire extinguisher to complete the illusion.'[50] Lurking in this environment was a Yeti from 'The Web of Fear', a story that had been set predominantly in the London Underground, creating some of the most iconic images of the Patrick Troughton era. This proved to be one of the most creative and impressive exhibits at Longleat, recapturing the essence of a popular story that at that time had been screened some 20 years earlier. Newman reported that, despite its age, the costume remained in surprisingly good condition.

The TARDIS console still provided the conclusion to the tour. K-9 remained in the first viewing window, but adjacent to that was a brand-new exhibit, replacing the monsters' cave setting. This featured another monster that had first appeared in the Troughton era of the show. Beneath the window were a series of interactive controls that controlled the lights within the display. These two touch-sensitive metal plates, when pressed, would reveal an Ice Warrior, bathed in a complementary green or white light. These creatures had first been seen in 'The Ice Warriors', and the scene created for the display replicated the wintery surroundings of that story. A cavern of snow and ice provided a background, while the rest of the chamber was filled with mist to complete the atmospheric spectacle. Pressing the buttons separately would make the lights fade and shimmer, but pressing them together plunged the display into darkness. Activating the lights once again

---

[49] www.thepropgallery.com/kane-edward-peel-bbc-exhibition-melting-head-dragonfire
[50] *Doctor Who Magazine* #140.

would make the Warrior materialise before the visitor's eyes.

The following two displays – the first featuring the K1 Robot ('Robot'), Drathro and L1 robots ('The Trial of the Time Lord: The Mysterious Planet') and an animated Cyberman, and the second Davros and the Daleks – also remained the same as in the previous year.

Despite some of the displays remaining largely unchanged, such great efforts had been made to include the Yeti, the Ice Warrior and the Tetrap to celebrate the twenty-fifth anniversary season that Longleat was more than worth the 50p entrance fee.[51]

The last display case provided a fascinating glimpse into the technical work involved in creating certain monsters and effects. Lined with reflective surfaces, it showcased the animatronic Tetrap head that had memorably featured in the cliff-hanger of Part Two of 'Time and the Rani'. Visitors could manually operate the various moving parts – the three eyes, two ears, mouth and tongue – by using sliding controls mounted outside the case.

The newly-created BBC shop, nicknamed 'The Celestial Storeroom', contained further exhibits: a Cleaner robot and the yellow pool cleaner from 'Paradise Towers', plus an impressive collection of other miscellaneous artefacts. Viewed through a diamond-shaped window, masks and helmets from a wide variety of stories were visible, the central section of this display consisting of multiple variations of Cybermen, from 'The Wheel in Space', 'The Invasion', 'Revenge of the Cybermen' and 'Attack of the Cybermen'. Other items included an Exxilon ('Death to the Daleks'); two Davros masks representing the styles worn on television by Michael Wisher/David Gooderson and Terry Molloy; the Bandril ('Timelash'); Sharez Jek's mask ('The Caves of Androzani'); the Trickster mask ('Kinda'); a Silurian and a Sea Devil ('Warriors of the Deep'); a Sontaran helmet ('The Two Doctors'); a Vervoid ('The Trial of a Time Lord': 'Terror of the Vervoids'); Omega ('Arc of Infinity'); a Voc Robot ('The Robots of Death'); and a Mutt ('The Mutants').

1989

Longleat's exhibition for the 1989 season was again documented by Philip Newman for *Doctor Who Magazine*, in its 150th issue, published in July 1989. The entrance fee had now increased to 70p.[52] Still in position from the previous year were the dematerialising TARDIS model and the Time Lord space station, the latter now on an improved starscape background. In the adjacent case was now a display of various weapons.

One of the major new additions for 1989 was a display featuring the most recent version of the Cybermen, as seen in the anniversary story 'Silver Nemesis'. Two Cybermen with their new shiny chrome finish were joined by the Nemesis statue. Buttons outside the case for visitors to press made the

---

[51] *Doctor Who Magazine* #140.
[52] *Doctor Who Magazine* #150.

statue glow and one of the Cybermen's heads move. An appropriate background was also created, replicating Lady Peinforte's crypt as featured in the story.

Further along the left side of the corridor came the display featuring the Tetraps and the Rani costume from 'Time and the Rani' and, opposite that, Kane from 'Dragonfire': both remained unchanged from the previous year.

Another new addition was not from the latest series but had become available for display at Longleat following the closure of the Blackpool exhibition in 1985. Recreating the scene on the bridge of 'The Pirate Planet', the Pirate Captain was positioned seated at his controls and accompanied by the parrot-like Polyphase Avatron prop, which was still in working order and would rotate its head and spread its wings.

Still *in situ* was the 'Terror of the Vervoids' exhibit featuring the two Mogarians and two Vervoids, on display for the third and final year. The Yeti from 'The Web of Fear' also remained in place.

Tradition continued as the replica TARDIS control room provided the finale to the exhibition. Once again the ever-popular K-9 remained in the first display. The second viewing window again housed the Ice Warrior that had been installed for the 1988 season. In the third display case however was a brand-new installation for 1989. In place of the collection of robots, this now held some of the creepy clowns seen in 'The Greatest Show in the Galaxy'. White canvas sheeting was arranged to resemble the tent of the Psychic Circus. At the back of the display stood the sinister Chief Clown, peering out through the metal bars that had imprisoned the Doctor during the story. Further clown costumes made their public debut here and would reappear at later exhibitions over the next 20 years.

Following the broadcast of 'Remembrance of the Daleks', the two Longleat Daleks underwent a repaint for the first time in 15 years, to match the styles seen in that story. Dalek L2 was painted in the grey-and-black 'Renegade' colour scheme and was fitted with a light in the weapon to simulate a laser. Dalek L1 received a more significant renovation. To match the moulded shoulder section as seen on the 'Imperial' Dalek props on television, the top collar and slats were refitted with additional wooden blocks underneath. The overall look was completed with the appropriate white-and-gold paintwork plus matching lights and arm. It is thought that the 'Imperial'-style sucker and telescopic arm were taken from a screen-used 'Remembrance of the Daleks' prop. The setting was also redressed, with the green gates of 'Radcliffe Builders Merchants' to the right and the destroyed special effects Dalek skirt completing the arrangement.

Further items were displayed inside refurbished stables adjacent to the BBC shop. The extra room allowed for the inclusion of larger items such as Drathro and the L1 tracker robot from 'The Trial of the Time Lord': 'The Mysterious Planet', which had been on display in the exhibition itself during 1988. The robots from 'Paradise Towers' remained in place from the previous year.

DOCTOR WHO EXHIBITIONS

1990

Part 3 of 'Survival', screened on BBC1 on 6 December 1989, was the final new *Doctor Who* episode until 1996. Consequently, the 1990 Longleat exhibition was the last for many years to have the opportunity to feature new artefacts from the production. The entrance price remained at a mere 70p. In May, science fiction magazine *TV Zone* offered a guide to the displays; and in August, a *Doctor Who Magazine* feature provided further details.

Some of the latest artefacts could be viewed immediately on passing into the mirrored corridor. Directly in front, where the 'Sentinel' Dalek had once stood, were two exhibits from 'Ghost Light': Control and a Husk. The Husk, resembling a fly with large eyes, dressed in a tuxedo, is believed to have been a replica created for the exhibition by the BBC Visual Effects Department, with the head and hands cast from the original costume. Later, a background of wooden panels was added to replicate the environment of Gabriel Chase House, the story's setting.

Around the corner and to the immediate right was a suit of armour seen in 'Battlefield'; this is believed to have been the one worn by Mordred but could possibly have been the Knight Commander's. The environment was dressed to resemble the location where the Destroyer was encountered during the story's final episode. An additional feature was the broken wooden planks through which the Brigadier was thrown during that episode, behind which was an exterior image, adding depth to the exhibit. This attention to detail elevated the standards of the exhibition greatly. Curiously, the armour was replaced for some time by the Android from 'The Visitation', but the 'Battlefield'-inspired backdrop remained.

Continuing along the corridor, the display of Cybermen accompanied by the Nemesis statue ('Silver Nemesis') remained from the previous year. Adjacent to this, on the left-hand side of the corridor, were creatures from 'Survival'; this replaced the previous display of Tetraps from Sylvester McCoy's first story. Two Cheetah People were placed in a jungle setting, unlike the quarry location used for the planet seen in the story. However, they appeared more accustomed to that environment, and were seen tending to a fire. Opposite this display, the graphically-disfigured Kane from 'Dragonfire' remained for its final year in this position.

One of the most colourful creations in *Doctor Who*, making it an eye-catching new exhibit here, was the Kandyman costume from 'The Happiness Patrol'. Behind this, hiding away behind bars in the background, was a Pipe person from the same story. These two exhibits had been at the Space Adventure exhibition the year before, and the display was largely unchanged at Longleat.

Another triumph of freelance sculptor and effects designers Sue Moore and Steven Mansfield was their work on the Haemovores and the Ancient One for 'The Curse of Fenric'. The set created for their appearance at Longleat – which replaced the former Vervoid and Mogarian display – replicated the bunker seen during the story, with chemical bombs stacked on the left-hand side. Inside, the Ancient One, the lead Haemovore, was accompanied by three others, two in medieval costume and the third with an Elizabethan ruff. These creatures were carefully posed, reaching out toward the unsuspecting visitors. At the very back stood the gas chamber seen in the story; behind the window was a mannequin in a naval uniform.

The impressive Yeti-on-the-London-Underground set was retained; and at the end of the corridor remained the TARDIS control room. The four viewing windows were separated by the fire exit and surrounded by the familiar TARDIS roundels, inside which were still placed images of the Doctor's television incarnations, now seven in number. For this year, Tony Oxley had rebuilt the control panels beneath the viewing bays. The first window on the left housed Mestor the Gastropod from 'The Twin Dilemma', which had replaced K-9. Next continued to be the Ice Warrior, surrounded by walls of ice and visible through mist and smoke. The clowns from 'The Greatest Show in the Galaxy' were also still on display, for a second consecutive year, as was the permanent Dalek exhibit, which remained as per 1989.

Fifi, the Stigorax pet of Helen A in 'The Happiness Patrol', received a display case of its own; the one that had previously showcased the animatronic Tetrap head, surrounded by mirrors so that the visitor could see the far side of the exhibit. Another creature brought to life by Sue Moore and Stephen Mansfield, Fifi looked very impressive and realistic.

The selection of assorted weapons that had been positioned at the start of the exhibition corridor was now moved to the end, with the final case presenting some of the *Doctor Who* merchandise on sale at the nearby shop, such as the video range, mugs, pencils and T-shirts.

The BBC 'Super Shop' also saw some redevelopment this year, with the addition of display cases featuring a number of interesting artefacts. These included the sixth Doctor's multi-coloured coat; the seventh Doctor's hat and question-mark umbrella; and Ace's bomber jacket. Another case still held the collection of masks and helmets from various stories.

<u>1991</u>

1991 was the first time since the production hiatus five years earlier that no new items were available for the Longleat exhibition – despite which, the entrance fee was raised to a staggering £1. Faced with the prospect of no new artefacts to present, Wilkie instead set about redressing many of the existing displays and resurrecting from storage a number of items not seen at Longleat for a few years.

K-9 returned after a year off, trundling back and forth on a short track and bathed in an alternating red and white light. The next display replaced the armour from 'Battlefield', after it was established that the Destroyer was unavailable to be added. The Android from 'The Visitation' resumed its position here, and was a welcome addition, given its beautiful, colourful jewelled design. Joining it in 1991, however, was the scarred Terileptil from the same story. The background was also redressed slightly to resemble a barn environment.

The display of Cybermen from 'Silver Nemesis' was retained once again, but the Nemesis statue was replaced by the Cyberscope prop seen during the story. New additions came in the form of two 'destroyed' Cybermen, one standing and the other crumpled to its knees and looking a little the worse-for-wear, with parts dating from as far back as 'Earthshock'.

Where the disfigured Kane from 'Dragonfire' had once stood was now an older exhibit in the form of a Sontaran from 'The Two Doctors'. This was the first time a Sontaran had been on display at Longleat since 1986; a period of absence described in *Doctor Who Magazine* as 'hardly surprising, when you bear in mind that when they did, one of them, literally, lost its head!', a reference to the theft that had occurred.[53] A button outside the display case made the creature from Sontar turn its head, and the eyes would glow 'with fierce amber'.[54]

Further down the corridor, the displays from 'Survival', 'The Happiness Patrol' and 'The Curse of Fenric' all remained, with subtle repositioning of the monsters. Replacing the Yeti's London Underground lair were two Tractators from 'Frontios', the Underground station environment substituted by the black-walled tunnels of the planet Frontios.

The TARDIS control room of course remained, but the four displays in the viewing windows all received an update. This first saw the small Malus from 'The Awakening' replacing Mestor the Gastropod. Next to this, where the Ice Warrior had previously stood, was the Svartos environment, now relocated, the extra room allowing for Kane to be joined by the Biomechanoid Dragon, completing the scene from 'Dragonfire'. According to Philip Newman, the delay in getting the latter creature on display had been due to the 'reluctance of the BBC Visual Effects Department' to part with it.[55] The costume was certainly an impressive one, the striking head well worthy of examination by visitors.

The ghoulish clowns from 'The Greatest Show in the Galaxy' had been on display for two years but were now replaced by a new set-up intended to represent a BBC warehouse housing relics from *Doctor Who*'s history. Across the three walls, a series of shelves were crammed full of artefacts, including the Brontosaurus model ('Invasion of the Dinosaurs'); a lion mask ('The Masque of Mandragora'); two Tyrannosaurus embryos in jars ('The Mark of the Rani'); a headpiece on a mannequin head ('Mawdryn Undead'); and the head of the Nucleus of the Swarm ('The Invisible Enemy'). At the front, a number of notable costumes were displayed on mannequins, including Colin Baker's sixth Doctor costume; Sylvester McCoy's seventh Doctor costume, with cream

---

[53] *Doctor Who Magazine* #175.
[54] *Doctor Who Magazine* #175.
[55] *Doctor Who Magazine* #175.

jacket and hat; Sarah Jane Smith's outfit from 'The Five Doctors'; Anthony Ainley's Master costume from 'Survival'; and a Time Lord robe.

Still providing the grand finale were the Daleks, but this display also received an update, with the Special Weapons Dalek being added after its appearance at the Space Adventure exhibition. To accommodate this new arrival, the special effects Dalek skirt was pushed to the front.

Finally, the Husk from 'Ghost Light', which had previously been at the start of the exhibition, was now at the end, but without Control's costume.

1992-1995

As the 1990s continued, so did the Longleat exhibition. With no new *Doctor Who* on television, further changes to the displays became few and far between, but enthusiastic staff and devoted visitors ensured that the attraction remained operational. Items such as a Tetrap and the giant brain ('Time and the Rani'), the Scaroth spaceship model ('City of Death') and a Sontaran ('The Two Doctors') were among those seen during the first half of the decade.

Colin Baker attended the exhibition on Monday 21 September 1992 to record segments for the video release *The Colin Baker Years* in the TARDIS control room area. Exhibits such as Kane from 'Dragonfire' are clearly visible in the background of the shots, as is the TARDIS console. Baker is also seen sat in front of roundels showcasing some of the merchandise available in the exhibition's shop, including videos and books.

Joining the team at Longleat during the mid-1990s was Mark Barton Hill. While training at the Bristol Old Vic, he had been approached by Longleat's Estate Attractions Manager Tim Bentley and asked if he would be interested in some weekend and summer holiday work at the attraction. As Hill remembers, 'When he said that part of this would involve dressing up as *Doctor Who* characters and parading around the exhibition and grounds as a Cyberman or a Time Lord, I instantly agreed.' Less glamorous tasks, such as cleaning, were also part of the job description; but this was by no means unwelcome to Hill, as he relates:

'I particularly enjoyed cleaning and dusting the exhibition first thing every Saturday morning. I couldn't believe that I was in the TARDIS with a dusting cloth and spray, cleaning the console, the Dalek and endless glass screens, but it was a joy.'

1994 saw a now-rare change being made to the exhibition's Dalek display. Dalek L1 had its colour scheme simplified from the 'Imperial' white-with-gold-hemispheres to a more traditional gun-metal-grey-with-black-hemispheres, although the 'Imperial'-style telescopic arm was retained and merely repainted. The street/yard 'Remembrance of the Daleks' background was kept as before, but Davros was now added in place of Dalek L2, which was put into storage. The following year, the set was redressed as a futuristic corridor. The Pepper's Ghost trick, previously utilised in the 1987 refit to show a TARDIS model materialising and dematerialising, was again employed here. A gauze screen was placed in front of a mirror, and when the lighting changed, Davros would appear at the back of the set – an effect that would later be replicated at the *Doctor Who* Experience exhibition.

The Haemovore display was also redressed in 1995 to resemble a graveyard reminiscent of that seen in 'The Curse of Fenric'.

1996 – The Great Fire of Longleat

Doctor Who returned to BBC1 in 1996 for one night only, for a well-received TV movie starring Paul McGann as the eighth Doctor. It would be many years before exhibits from this production would be put on public display. However, the Longleat exhibition had a part to play in the announcement of McGann's casting, a top-secret photo session being held there on Monday 8 January 1996 (during the 'off season' when the exhibition was closed to the general public).[56] Photographs from this shoot, showing McGann stood outside the TARDIS exterior entrance, appeared in many newspapers on 10 January, when the BBC issued a statement revealing the new Doctor's identity. A photograph of McGann inside the Longleat TARDIS control room, clutching a large crystal, later graced the cover of *Doctor Who Magazine*'s Issue 236, dated 13 March 1996.

With interest in the show now renewed, the Longleat exhibition again became a focal point for fans. The scope for changes to the exhibits was still limited, but with the opening that year of the *Doctor Who* Experience in Llangollen, a few adjustments were made. For instance, in place of the Haemovore graveyard, the Cybermen were relocated to a new, futuristic set, with a wounded Cyberman positioned on the ground and another leaning against the glass. The selection of masks continued to be displayed, as did the Android from 'The Visitation' and the Time Lord space station from 'The Trial of the Time Lord'. Also nearby was a K-9 prop that would become particularly noteworthy later in the year. A Mandrel from 'Nightmare of Eden' had replaced a Vervoid within the jungle environment, but Kane and the Biomechanoid Dragon from 'Dragonfire' remained in their Svartos environment.

In the TARDIS control room, two Cheetah people from 'Survival' replaced the now-relocated Cyberman display and were positioned in a jungle scene. A pair of Tractators from 'Frontios', still benefiting from luminous veins painted on their fronts in 1984, replaced the Kandyman and Pipe person from 'The Happiness Patrol', which had been moved to Llangollen. In addition to these, and completing the displays surrounding the TARDIS console, were Dalek L1 and Davros within the futuristic corridor created the previous year.

All of these displays, however, came under threat on Sunday 15 September 1996. This was indeed a dark day for *Doctor Who* exhibitions, as a major fire broke out at Longleat. Newspaper reports later stated that nine

---

[56] *Doctor Who Magazine* #236.

separate fire crews from Wiltshire and Somerset had been sent out to tackle the blaze. *Doctor Who Magazine* also reported on the fire.[57] It stated that the incident had occurred during the afternoon while the exhibition still had public visitors, 'all of whom were swiftly evacuated by staff member Dallas Slade.'[58] After the visitors had been evacuated, firefighters doused the flames and removed monsters and other props to safety outside the building.

It is thought that the blaze began close to where the exhibition's K-9 prop – fortunately not the television original – was displayed. It has subsequently been attributed to faulty wiring within this replica of the Doctor's robot dog. The only part of the prop to survive was its blackened base, which was salvaged and later put on display in the refurbished exhibition as a memorial of the fire.

The heat and smoke caused considerable damage to the building's façade, and the TARDIS control room ceiling suffered particularly badly. Attractions Manager for Longleat Tim Bentley was nevertheless able to confirm that the building's structure remained intact and reusable: 'Fortunately the building that housed the exhibition has escaped the worst of the damage, so we can use it again.'[59] Bentley was also confident that some of the exhibits would go on display once again, stating: 'A lot of the exhibits are badly damaged, but we think that some are repairable, so some of the originals can probably go back on show.'[60] Fortunately the TARDIS console survived largely unscathed, as did Dalek L1 and Davros – complete with the original chair and jacket occupied by Michael Wisher in 'Genesis of the Daleks' – both of which were photographed being carried out to safety after the flames had been quelled. A number of other irreplaceable items were lost completely, and others irreparably damaged.

Some of those items lost in the fire included the Time Lord space station seen in the opening sequence of 'The Trial of the Time Lord', and the Nucleus of the Swarm from 'The Invisible Enemy'. Mike Tucker later noted the regrettable knock-on impact the fire had on future exhibitions: 'An awful lot of items that could otherwise be put on display now got so badly damaged during that fire.'

Nonetheless, out of tragedy emerged opportunity. The damage necessitated a full refit by Experience Design & Management, a company formed in 1993 as a joint venture between Martin Wilkie and Lorne Martin. The pair had long been in charge of all the *Doctor Who* exhibitions and would continue to be so for years to come. Due to a tour with the Bristol Old Vic Theatre, Mark Barton Hill had stopped working at Longleat before the fire. However, he returned in the aftermath and helped out with the big refit, which opened to the public at Easter 1997.

---

[57] *Doctor Who Magazine* #245.
[58] *Doctor Who Magazine* #245.
[59] *Doctor Who Magazine* #245.
[60] *Doctor Who Magazine* #245.

1997

Outside the exhibition, the oversized TARDIS exterior police box entrance was accompanied by a diamond-logo *Doctor Who* Exhibition sign on the ground nearby. The police box itself had been stripped and repainted, but even that hadn't been without problems, as Mark Barton Hill recalls: 'Lorne had paid a chap to strip it down and repaint it. Well, he was fired, simply because he was stripping it down a little *too* much! It was back to its usual form in time for reopening.'[61] Looking fresh and colourful once again, the police box provided a grand welcome to the exhibition.

Hill remembers the frantic preparations on opening day, describing it as 'all hands on deck at 8am to stock the shop, getting ready to open at 10am.'[62] There was clearly a lot to do that morning:

'The Dalek still had its lid off, the Foamasi was still being dressed and lit, Davros's tunic needed a polish, the TARDIS console still had its panels off! And the one thing everybody forgot to check was the soundtrack! Luckily the old system was easy to feed into the new amp, and after a few early arrivals were turned away, [the exhibition] opened as usual for Easter 1997.'[63]

Items at the refitted exhibition included the L1 tracker robot from 'The Trial of a Time Lord': 'The Mysterious Planet' and, against a cave backdrop, two Tractators from 'Frontios'. A video screen showed clips of the various incarnations of the Doctor, and roundels in the TARDIS control room also held images of the actors, cleaned up after the smoke damage. As usual, a number of masks and helmets were also displayed, including a replica Exxilon from 'Death to the Daleks'.

Further full-size costumes on display included, along the main corridor, a Cheetah person ('Survival'); a Mandrel ('Nightmare of Eden'); and, positioned behind a gravestone, the Ancient One Haemovore ('The Curse of Fenric'). Dalek L1, which retained the moulded 'Imperial' plunger seen in 'Remembrance of the Daleks', was paired in a display with a complete Davros, featuring a replica of the mask worn by Michael Wisher in 'Genesis of the Daleks'.

In one of the viewing windows around the TARDIS control room was an environment replicating a scene from 'Robot'; the K1 Robot was stood in an alleyway with stacked wooden boxes blocking its escape. In another of the viewing windows, a number of 1980s-style Cybermen were posed with a classic British red phone box in a redbrick-walled environment; one of the creatures was seen climbing up from beneath the floor, a homage to the famous sequence in 'The Invasion' where they emerge from the London sewers. A destroyed Cyberman was laid on the ground and another was stood leaning against the wall, taking the total number in the display to five. An Ice

---

[61] www.drwholongleat.com/id4.html.
[62] www.drwholongleat.com/id4.html.
[63] www.drwholongleat.com/id4.html.

Warrior was once again placed within an icy vista similar to that seen in the monster's debut story in 1967, but this time it occupied the fourth and final viewing window.

A new K-9 replica, painted pale silver with black lettering, had been created to replace the one destroyed in the fire; the charred remains of the latter were displayed beneath. Further reminders of the disaster visible in the exhibition included the fire-damaged remains of the Android from 'The Visitation' and of the Cleaner robot from 'Paradise Towers'. The Android was in a very bad state; its original vibrant colours were lost forever, left blackened by the heat and smoke. It was practically unrecognisable when, in 2010, it was sold at Bonhams auction house. The severely damaged Cleaner robot, with only half of its upper body remaining, was sold in the same auction for a hammer price of only £100. Back in 1997, some props and costumes were auctioned at Longleat itself, including several salvaged from the fire, such as the head of the Nucleus of the Swarm from 'The Invisible Enemy' and four damaged control panels previously mounted beneath the viewing windows in the TARDIS control room.

1998-2002

In the late 1990s, the BBC filmed a series that went behind the scenes at Longleat. Entitled *Lion Country*, this was a precursor to the current show *Animal Park* presented by Ben Fogle and Kate Humble, but it didn't just focus on the animals that lived on the estate's safari park; it also included features on the *Doctor Who* exhibition. One such feature revealed Attractions Manager Tim Bentley's difficulty in finding someone willing to don a replica Cyberman costume to attract visitors to the exhibition.[64] This was no doubt after the sterling job Mark Barton Hill had done in the role – a tough act to follow.

For a time during 2002, a Dalek replica was placed at the front of the K1 display, probably as a convenient storage solution. This replica prop was Hill's own work. Having spent time walking around the grounds of Longleat House in a Cyberman costume or as a Time Lord, Hill thought it would be great if he could go around in a Dalek instead. The main exhibition Daleks were of course static; and, filled with electronics, they couldn't accommodate an operator. Hence Hill's idea to create a new replica himself. He recalls: 'I thought that the hardest bit to make would be the [upper part], with all the neck rings and stuff, so I took measurements from the exhibition Dalek and got to work.' A number of parts were taken from original, screen-used props – Hill was given an original dome section by producer John Nathan-Turner after some theatre work – and, after completion, this grey and black Dalek could often be seen trundling around the grounds at Longleat, where it remained until the exhibition closed down. Replica bombs matching those seen in 'Destiny of the Daleks' were added to it for a 2002 '*Doctor Who* day' event. Minus these bombs,

---

[64] www.youtube.com/watch?v=ZdZBX7CL0pk

the Dalek later appeared on display at the *Doctor Who* Experience in London and then Cardiff.

John Nathan Turner passed away in May 2002, but he was subsequently remembered in the exhibition's TARDIS control room with a photo in a roundel and a note beneath, acknowledging that he had produced over 150 episodes of the show. Other changes to the exhibition were limited after the refit, but at some point the direction of passage around the corridors was reversed, with the TARDIS control room now providing the opening rather than the finale. However, by the final year, some item exchanges had occurred between the Longleat and Llangollen exhibitions.

2003 – The Final Year

Bringing to an end a 30-year history of *Doctor Who* items being on display in Wiltshire, the 2003 tourist season was the final time that the Longleat Exhibition opened its doors to the public. Throughout the 30-year period, the exhibition's layout had remained largely unchanged. For this final season, the exhibits also remained almost the same as the previous year.

A display case in the shop housed a number of original items, including Sylvester McCoy's costume from 'The Curse of Fenric', complete with duffle coat, and Ace's instantly recognisable bomber jacket. Behind these were the replica Exxilon mask ('Death to the Daleks'); a Voc robot mask ('The Robots of Death'); a Silurian head ('Warriors of the Deep'); plus an arm from a Cleaner robot ('Paradise Towers'). On the other side of the case were displayed Anthony Ainley's Master costume, last seen in 'The Mark of the Rani', and the fire damaged Android from 'The Visitation'. In front of these two costumes was also a Cryon helmet ('Attack of the Cybermen'), and the masks of a Marshman ('Full Circle') and a Mogarian ('The Trial of the Time Lord: Terror of the Vervoids'), plus a Mara banishment mask ('Snakedance') and the Lion headpiece from 'The Masque of Mandragora'.

The Ancient One Haemovore ('The Curse of Fenric'), positioned behind a gravestone, remained the first exhibit visitors encountered on entering the darkened corridor of the exhibition proper. Adjacent to this was a mock-up of a 1960s sitting room, with *Doctor Who*'s first episode, 'An Unearthly Child', playing on the television; an exhibit that had previously featured at the MOMI and Llangollen exhibitions (as described in later sections of this book). A slightly bizarre addition, however, saw a Cyberman emerging from a cupboard to the right-hand side of the scene.

Next came a Vervoid ('The Trial of the Time Lord': 'Terror of the Vervoids'), in a jungle foliage setting, where it looked more at home than it had on the futuristic space liner *Hyperion III* during the story. Further along the corridor, a photograph of a Dalek was illuminated in a roundel. Other images displayed on the corridor walls, and even on the ceiling, included one of the seventh Doctor and his companion Mel in the TARDIS, and one of Davros from 'Revelation of the Daleks'.

Progressing along the corridor, visitors encountered on the right-hand side two Tractators from 'Frontios', and opposite these a Tetrap from 'Time and the Rani'. As the corridor turned to the right, the Daleks were the focus of the next display. This featured Dalek L1, in the gun-metal-grey-and-black livery, Davros, and the Emperor Dalek prop from 'Remembrance of the Daleks'. The Davros exhibit again consisted of the character's original chair and black leather tunic, first seen in 'Genesis of the Daleks' and later modified for use in other stories, and a replica of the original mask worn by actors Michael Wisher and David Gooderson.

Video footage from 3 July 2003 indicates that a second Dalek prop was visible behind Davros, positioned in profile given the cramped space within the display case. This was another replica created by Mark Barton Hill – not the same one as had been paired with the K1 Robot in 2002. It would later be installed at the *Doctor Who* Experience, and would even appear in the television show itself, in 'Asylum of the Daleks'. To the left of the glass front was a speaker grille in which visitors could speak into a voice modulator and impersonate a Dalek.

Further exhibits along the corridor included a Sea Devil from 'Warriors of the Deep' and, within another forest environment, a Mandrel from 'Nightmare of Eden'. Inside the control room, the replica K-9 and the charred remains of the previous version remained on display on the right-hand side. Through a small round window to the left, the materialising/dematerialising TARDIS effect first installed in 1987 had returned. Replacing the K1 Robot was a mockup laboratory showcasing the Morbius monster from 'The Brain of Morbius', which had received a replica head and brain at some point during the 1990s; the replica head included some inaccurate eyestalks with curious pupils stuck onto the end. At the back of the set, facing away from visitors, a white-coated and white-haired figure represented the surgeon Mehendri Solon. Old computer monitors and a peculiar form of chemistry set on a workbench completed the scene.

On the other side of the TARDIS control room were the Cyberman and Ice Warrior displays. The silver creatures' environment was redressed to feature a cave set, while the Martian remained in the fourth and final window.

When the Longleat *Doctor Who* exhibition finally closed, the venue was converted into an artificial Bat Cave, housing numerous Egyptian fruit bats. At the time of writing, this attraction is still going strong.[65] The many *Doctor Who* artefacts were moved to storage and prepared to be combined with items from Llangollen to form a new exhibition in Blackpool.

The Longleat exhibition had entertained hundreds of thousands of visitors over its lifespan, although for many *Doctor Who* fans, it will forever be associated with the incredible Celebration event staged there in 1983, which had been followed up by many other, smaller events in the 20 years before it finally closed.

---

[65] www.longleat.co.uk/main-square/the-bat-cave

DOCTOR WHO EXHIBITIONS

Events at Longleat

Long after the 1983 Celebration, Longleat continued to attract *Doctor Who* actors to make public appearances. In the mid 1990s and into the 21st Century, 'Doctor Who days' were regularly held at Longleat during the August summer holiday. These would involve autograph signings and visitors posing with the actors for photographs, plus auctions of *Doctor Who* memorabilia. Also present, stalking the grounds, would be individuals costumed as monsters, such as Cybermen, Sea Devils and Zygons. Full-size Daleks were also present. One of the Cybermen was often played by Mark Barton Hill:

'I found it particularly hard work being a Cyberman, as the heat in that costume got worse and worse the hotter the summer became; but still I loved it. Predictably, I used to stand stock still, and people would walk past me, and they would say to each other, "Is it a dummy or is there somebody in there …?", and just when they least expected it, usually after someone had stood right in front of me for a photo, I would suddenly jolt into action and scare the hell out of them!'

1996 marked the thirtieth anniversary of the Cybermen's first appearance in *Doctor Who*. To celebrate that landmark, an event was held at Longleat, attended by fourth Doctor Tom Baker and Brigadier actor Nicholas Courtney. The highlight was a battle scene acted out in the grounds of Longleat House. With a number of actors starring as Cybermen, the Brigadier did battle once again with the silver foes. The scene featured explosions and gunfire, all to the delight of those enjoying 'A Quiet Day in the Country'.

18 August 1996 also saw the holding of an auction of *Doctor Who* artefacts, the first at Longleat House since the Celebration event in 1983. [66] The following year, another auction took place. As mentioned previously, this featured some damaged items salvaged from the wreckage of the recent fire.[67] Also that year, Tom Baker, Elisabeth Sladen and K-9 voice actor John Leeson were in attendance to celebrate the twentieth anniversary of robot dog's debut in 'The Invisible Enemy', with special effects expert Mat Irvine bringing along an original K-9 prop.

In 1998, sixth Doctor Colin Baker and Michael Jayston, who had played the Valeyard in 'The Trial of the Time Lord', were guests at Longleat, posing for Polaroid photographs and signing autographs. 1 August 1999 saw another auction of *Doctor Who* items take place, with John Nathan-Turner as auctioneer. This included original June Hudson costume design drawings and a set of four episode scripts for 'The Tenth Planet'.[68]

Nathan-Turner returned to host another auction on 6 August 2000. This included original Dalek components, namely the shoulders of Dalek N5 and the back skirt panel of Dalek 7, which had been removed to create the walk-in

---

[66] www.richardwho.co.uk/auctions/Longleat/19960818/default.asp
[67] www.richardwho.co.uk/auctions/Longleat/1997/default.asp
[68] www.richardwho.co.uk/auctions/Longleat/19990801/default.asp

Dalek exhibit for the MOMI exhibition.

A final auction took place on 5 August 2001, with companion actors Frazer Hines (Jamie) and Anneke Wills (Polly) in attendance and fan Andrew Beech donning a Time Lord guard costume that he owned.[69, 70]

In 2002, the fifteenth anniversary of the seventh Doctor was celebrated, with Sylvester McCoy and Sophie Aldred (Ace) in attendance, accompanied by Nicholas Courtney. The event culminated at 4pm with the actors blowing out candles on a birthday cake.[71] However, as John Nathan-Turner had passed away in May of that year, the *Doctor Who* memorabilia auctions – which he had been responsible for organising – were now discontinued.

Another *'Doctor Who* Day' was held on Sunday 3 August 2003. This celebrated the fortieth anniversary of the first episode's transmission. The recent issue of *Doctor Who Magazine* had included a half-page advert for Longleat that also promoted this event.[72] In attendance were sixth Doctor Colin Baker, Sophie Aldred and John Leeson. Once again, candles were blown out on an appropriately-decorated birthday cake. A number of monsters were also present as usual to menace the visitors, including a variety of Daleks, a few Cybermen, a Sea Devil, a Haemovore, a Sontaran and an Auton. It served as a fitting hurrah, as the Longleat exhibition closed down at the end of that year's holiday season.

Merchandise

The shop at Longleat provided a location for *Doctor Who* fans to purchase books, video releases and audio CDs at a time when internet shopping had not grown to become the colossal force that we know today. It would regularly develop, with new merchandise being added to the items on offer.

During Longleat's opening year, pin badges were manufactured for sale. These featured the diamond *Doctor Who* logo in a choice of either blue or red on a white background. Later, a new version was produced, with the logo in orange on a blue background. The badge was subsequently updated to incorporate the 1980s neon logo. In 1983, the word 'Exhibition' was added, against a royal blue background; the price was a mere 30p. An alternative edition was made especially for the major Celebration event: on a red background was placed the neon logo with 'Celebration Longleat 1983' beneath. Eventually the badge was adapted again to incorporate the Sylvester McCoy-era logo.

In 1976 a set of postcards featuring Tom Baker as the Doctor was produced. One of these was titled 'Welcome to Longleat' and was available at the exhibition.[73] A 'Doctor Who Exhibition' sticker was also produced, and

---

[69] www.richardwho.co.uk/auctions/Longleat/20010805/default.asp
[70] www.richardwho.co.uk/exhibitions/longleat2001/index.asp
[71] www.richardwho.co.uk/exhibitions/longleat20020804/index.asp
[72] *Doctor Who Magazine* #330.
[73] Howe & Blumberg, (2000) *Howe's Transcendental Toybox*. pp.327.

purchasable for 25p. Further postcards, largely featuring publicity stills of cast members, were sold in the shop over the years.

During the 1980s, BBC Enterprises manufactured a number of stationery items for sale in the exhibitions. Pencils, in blue, white or yellow, were priced at 15p each; a retractable pen could be purchased for 60p; and erasers emblazoned with the neon logo were also available. In 1982, a ruler with 'Doctor Who Rules the Universe' printed on it was sold for £1.25. Other stationery items, such as TARDIS and Dalek pencil cases, are also believed to have been sold through the shop.

In 1986, when a stable block close to the main exhibition was pressed into service to house a separate, larger BBC shop, the scope for selling merchandise greatly increased. *Doctor Who* products were also becoming more plentiful at that time, with video releases and the Dapol toys and figures range hitting the shelves. As detailed previously, the additional space also allowed for other, larger items from the show to be displayed.

The shop was later reincorporated with the exhibition but remained one of few places in the UK where fans could pick up the full range of the latest *Doctor Who* merchandise. A product list from 2002 lists some of the less traditional items available shortly before the exhibition closed down: for example, a case for your Nokia 3210, 3310 or 8210 mobile phone would set you back £12.95.

The Longleat Legacy

The Longleat exhibition closed its doors for the final time on 2 November 2003, bringing to an end 30 years of *Doctor Who* costumes and props being displayed at the attraction. *Doctor Who Magazine* reported the sad news, stating: 'The decision to close the exhibition has come internally from Longleat and has nothing to do with any section of the BBC.'[74] Having learned that some fans were organising a petition to protest the closure, the magazine added that readers who wished to voice their concerns were 'advised to send polite messages of protest to' Longleat's General Manager and Land Agent; the appropriate postal address was provided.[75] The magazine also stated that it would be presenting a retrospective feature on the exhibition in a future issue; this never occurred, however, perhaps because editorial priorities understandably changed when production of brand-new *Doctor Who* began the following year.

In a later interview, Martin Wilkie commented on the decision made by Longleat's management: 'That was bad timing. No hard feelings: they knew the new series was coming up, but felt it didn't fit in with animals and stately homes. But it had never fitted in, ever! It was a sad day when we pulled out of

---

[74] *Doctor Who Magazine* #336.
[75] *Doctor Who Magazine* #336.

there.'[76]

Although the exhibition is long-since closed, the shape of its large TARDIS entrance still remains to this day, complete with lamp on top. It is now painted white and hidden by a cave mouth for the Bat Cave attraction that utilises the space inside. The exhibition itself has a lasting legacy, and remains very fondly remembered by those fans lucky enough to have visited it. At the height of its popularity, it was one of only two major exhibitions of *Doctor Who* costumes and props. The other was located in the seaside town of Blackpool.

---

[76] *Doctor Who Magazine* #361.

Chapter 3
Blackpool (1974-1985)

Following the success of the BBC TV Special Effects Exhibition at the Science Museum, BBC Enterprises' Exhibitions Unit looked to maximise the commercial potential of future attractions. Although the Science Museum run ended in May 1973, the same displays were then transplanted to the crypt of Middlesbrough Town Hall. A press preview of this new attraction was held on 4 July 1973. Jon Pertwee was in attendance, having arrived at Teesside airport an hour late, according to a report in the following day's local *Evening Gazette*.[77] Unlike for his appearance at the Science Museum, Pertwee was not in his character's costume, but instead wore a pale suit and tie. He did, though, pose with the TARDIS doors, control console and the Dalek props.

The exhibition remained largely as it had been at the Science Museum, but there were a couple of additions: specifically, some of the giant maggots from 'The Green Death', which proved particularly memorable for visitors, and the screen-used Dalek prop now referred to by aficionados as Goon I, which had been built for 'Planet of the Daleks', broadcast that year. This Middlesbrough exhibition finally closed on 31 December 1973.

Following this successful venture, the BBC Exhibitions team elected to establish a second permanent exhibition in the North of England to complement the Longleat one in the South. Lorne Martin described the situation to John Nathan-Turner for *Doctor Who Magazine*: 'Before we knew what was happening, we had so many exhibits, we started looking for a second exhibition site.'[78]

A number of potential venues were interested in hosting the exhibition, but Lorne Martin and Terry Sampson were determined to locate it in the popular seaside resort of Blackpool. As Martin later explained: 'Blackpool was an ideal choice; especially as the holiday season was always extended because of the famous illuminations. From a commercial point of view, it was very attractive.'[79]

A prominent position on the Golden Mile, the central promenade on Blackpool's seafront, in the shadow of the famous Tower, was considered a prime location, because of the consistent crowd numbers. Martin described the tourist scene of the mid-1970s: 'Remember, in those days, there were no theme parks – no Chessington World of Adventures etc – but the Golden Mile attracted endless crowds. At the time, it was almost certainly the largest area of

---
[77] *Evening Gazette*, 5 July 1973.
[78] *Doctor Who Magazine* #175.
[79] *Doctor Who Magazine* #175.

amusements and attractions in the United Kingdom, and we wanted *Doctor Who* to be right in the middle of it.'[80]

The exhibition was jointly financed by BBC Enterprises and the New Ritz Catering Company, owners of the chosen venue, a café at 111 Central Promenade, opposite Blackpool's Central Pier. Investment costs were very high, thought to be in the region of £40,000, explaining the need for collaboration. With set-up and running costs shared, profits were also split between the two parties. The exhibition was actually housed in an empty basement beneath the café, but this made for a very atmospheric environment. Fan Christopher Daniels remembers a peculiar neighbour to the exhibition: 'I think it ran parallel with the Chamber of Horrors in [the famous waxwork attraction] Tussauds, because that was next door.' Low light levels were again employed in the exhibition to conceal the deteriorating condition of some older items.

The venue was significantly larger than the one at Longleat, as long-time visitor Daniels again recalls: 'That's what I liked about Blackpool. I know Longleat did it, but they didn't do it as well as Blackpool did, because there wasn't enough room. I don't know if this is the memory cheating, but I remember those bays around the TARDIS console, [the ones at Blackpool] were about three times as big.'

The additional space allowed for more substantial displays, with the Daleks proving an obvious choice to be given greater prominence. Two more exhibition Daleks were therefore constructed, again built by Tony Oxley and Charlie Lunn. With subtle differences from the four other exhibition Daleks created previously, Dalek B1 and B2 were given a silver-and-metallic-blue colour scheme, which would be retained for the next ten years. These new Daleks were then mounted onto trolleys, allowing for mechanisms to move them around the display; this is thought to be the first time that Dalek props were seen to move without an internal operator.

The exhibition's interior was again constructed by Parker Hinson Productions Limited. Lorne Martin explains how the exhibits were initially displayed, and how adjustments later had to be made to keep them secure: 'Originally at Blackpool the exhibits were housed behind glass panels rather than being totally [enclosed], but visitors used to throw things at the monsters; sweets, Coke cans etc. One year a "green slime" toy was all the rage; buckets of the stuff found its way all over the monsters, and it was extremely difficult to clean off. Also, at first there was a great deal of damage; masses of bits were ruined or stolen. So, for cleanliness and security, we installed a shop-window-style viewing [arrangement]; though, even then, plastic buttons that animated some of the exhibits were stolen!'[81]

As at Longleat, the exhibition opened during the traditional holiday season, spanning from spring to autumn. As previously noted, the winter months

---

[80] *Doctor Who Magazine* #175.
[81] *Doctor Who Magazine* #175.

offered organisers the opportunity to update displays and exchange artefacts between the two exhibitions, with some therefore appearing at both attractions over the years.

On 9 April 1974, three days before the equivalent event at Longleat, the Blackpool exhibition's ceremonial opening was attended by Jon Pertwee and co-star Elisabeth Sladen, with the attraction officially open to the public the following day. Sladen had joined *Doctor Who* at the start of the season currently being broadcast, and Jon Pertwee's final episode would be seen in early June, making this one of his last appearances as the incumbent Doctor. Writing in her autobiography, Sladen later recalled how the opening of the Blackpool exhibition had actually fallen during production of Pertwee's swansong, 'Planet of the Spiders', the regeneration scene having been recorded only a few days previously. She admitted that she hadn't been 'terribly thrilled at the prospect [of attending the opening], because it promised to be such a whistle-stop visit', but Pertwee had reassured her, saying, 'It will blow your mind, Lissie, trust me.'[82]

Leaving the hotel in which she and Pertwee were staying, Sladen was blown away by the mass of humanity that awaited them: 'I've never seen so many people in my life – and they were all screaming for Jon. I was literally speechless, so stunned I couldn't move. If Jon hadn't put an arm around me to guide me toward the waiting Bessie, I think I'd still be standing there now.'[83]

The massive crowds continued all the way from the hotel to the exhibition, Sladen describing this as one of the most surreal car journeys of her life: 'Somehow Jon negotiated Bessie out of the car park without running anyone over, and we drove at a snail's pace along the promenade. You couldn't see an inch of pavement anywhere. People were lined five deep along the route, all waving and cheering, calling out their appreciation – and, yes, love! – for us. It was like the Queen's Coronation – and we were only off the telly!'[84]

Joining the Doctor and his companion Sarah Jane Smith at the exhibition opening was Dalek Goon I, which since its inclusion in the Middlesbrough exhibition had also been seen in 'Death to the Daleks', broadcast a few weeks beforehand. Some of the other attractions with which Pertwee and Sladen were photographed included a Cyberman, Alpha Centauri ('The Curse of Peladon') and a Draconian ('Frontier in Space'), the latter of which had hung behind it the models used for the Axos spaceship ('The Claws of Axos') and Skybase One ('The Mutants'), as seen at the Science Museum two years previously.

Pertwee commanded the attention of the vast audience, and this meant a lot to Sladen, coming so soon after the emotional blow of recording the regeneration scene. As she recalled in her autobiography, 'I was so glad for Jon; this was how I wanted him to remember *Who*. And this was how I wanted to remember him. Adored by thousands, playing to the gallery, living and

---

[82] Sladen, E (2011) *Elisabeth Sladen: The Autobiography.* p.147.
[83] Sladen, E (2011) *Elisabeth Sladen: The Autobiography.* p.148.
[84] Sladen, E (2011) *Elisabeth Sladen: The Autobiography.* p.148.

breathing *Doctor Who*.'[85]

With the Blackpool exhibition now up and running, the first season saw it open daily through to 1 November 1974. One regular visitor was Roger M Dilley, whose family would spend their summer holidays in Blackpool specifically because of the exhibition's location there: 'It started as a weekend trip with my Mum when I was in my teens and progressed to a full week's family holiday over the years. Each day I would have breakfast, hop on a tram to Central Pier, and my family wouldn't see me again until dinner. Such was my enthusiasm for the place; I would spend hours photographing the exhibits and just drinking in the atmosphere. By the end of the first day I knew the soundtrack off by heart! Obviously, spending so much time there, I got to know the staff pretty well, and I was allowed to wear original costumes for promotional purposes outside the exhibition.'

Pertwee's successor Tom Baker later recorded some in-character promotional video messages that played repeatedly on television monitors inside the exhibition. Two of these can be found as Easter Eggs on the special edition DVD release of 'The Ark in Space'; one has Baker stating that he is 'going to Blackpool' and suggesting that viewers brush their teeth; the other, which came at the end of the exhibition, has him saying, as he departs, 'Shh! Whatever you do, tell everybody about it. And mind the steps!', followed by an off-camera noise implying that he has tripped over.

These videos were never broadcast, but episodes of *Doctor Who* would often be followed by a voice-over announcement promoting the two permanent exhibitions. Fan Peter Trott recalls: 'I always remember, at the end of every episode back in the '70s, they used to mention there were exhibitions at Longleat and Blackpool.' This type of announcement would not be repeated for later exhibitions such as the *Doctor Who* Experience, due to the tightening of rules on advertising on the BBC, but as Trott confirms: 'That's what they used to do back then in the '70s, and possibly even in the '80s.'

The Exhibition

As at Longleat, an oversized replica TARDIS exterior provided the entrance to the exhibition, leading to the ticket desk, with the familiar *Doctor Who* theme tune playing through a speaker to publicise the attraction. A young Christopher Daniels recalls this clearly: 'I can remember from childhood it was just fantastic to see the TARDIS on that corner opposite the Central Pier, just standing there, and the theme sort of wafting along the seafront. It was just great.' The wall outside the venue was painted with a prominent advertisement pointing the way to the entrance. Over the years this would be regularly updated, notably in 1985 when portraits of the six Doctors were added. The Doctor's car Bessie and a Dalek would often be displayed in front of the sign, and staff members and helpers in monster costumes would

---

[85] Sladen, E (2011) *Elisabeth Sladen: The Autobiography.* p.148.

encourage passers-by into the exhibition. Roger M Dilley reminisces: 'One year I was allowed to wear an "Earthshock" Cyberman costume outside. At only 5' 3¾" tall, I was nicknamed the Cyberdwarf!'

In a piece contributed to the charity anthology *Behind the Sofa*, League of Gentlemen comedy team member Jeremy Dyson recalled visiting the exhibition during its opening year of 1974, noting that the entrance, 'took the form of a TARDIS parked at the side of a building adjacent to Louis Tussauds waxworks.'[86] He added: 'Still young enough for the border between what's imagined and what's perceived to be very leaky, [I] felt like I was actually going to enter a space that was bigger on the inside than it was on the outside.'[87] On entering the darkness, Dyson came to the head of a staircase, where the sound effects from inside the exhibition floated through the air: 'Fear, thrill, joy – all intermingled in a moment of pure intensity as I gripped my mother's hand. And then I heard it, calling from the bottom of the staircase. That familiar electronic vibrating tonality. Speech rendered empty of humanity. The sound of pure terror.'[88] Gripped by the fear of an impending Dalek encounter, the seven-year-old Dyson was left at the top of the staircase while his family explored 'the glories of the universe displayed beneath the Blackpool pavement.'[89]

Those visitors who did dare to venture down the staircase entered a dark and winding corridor that largely replicated the layout of the Longleat exhibition. Either side of this winding path were display cases with various props and costumes, which over the years would be updated and feature new items as and when they became available.

As at Longleat, the corridor eventually led into a replica TARDIS control room with viewing windows around its walls, providing the exhibition's grand finale. The control console in Blackpool was the same one that had been created originally for the BBC TV Special Effects Exhibition at the Science Museum and had last been seen in Middlesbrough. Fan and collector Peter Trott remembers: 'The console was always the highlight of both the Blackpool and the Longleat exhibitions. It was the centre of those exhibitions.'

When the Blackpool exhibition first opened, the majority of the items on display were simply transferred from Middlesbrough. The two Daleks from the original Science Museum exhibition were however joined now by the two additional replicas created specifically for this new venture.

As at Longleat, the first Dalek to be seen by visitors was a 'Sentinel', positioned at the start of the corridor. In this case, though, the prop used was the gold-and-silver-with-black-hemispheres Dalek SM1, instead of the silver-and-blue design as used at Longleat. In addition to the motorised appendage movements installed for its previous exhibition appearances, it was now given a voice track provided by actor Michael Wisher. Hidden speakers played

---

[86] Berry, S (ed) (2013) *Behind the Sofa*. p.147.
[87] Berry, S (ed) (2013) *Behind the Sofa*. p.147.
[88] Berry, S (ed) (2013) *Behind the Sofa*. p.148.
[89] Berry, S (ed). (2013). *Behind the Sofa*. p.148.

messages commanding visitors not to smoke in the exhibition and triumphantly proclaiming that the Daleks had captured the TARDIS.

A Dalek scene also provided the memorable climax to the displays, being placed in the final viewing window in the TARDIS control room. A cavern environment was created for this, replicated in areas of the control room itself, around which visitors progressed in a clockwise direction. Three Daleks were to be seen here. Dalek SM2 remained static, but the two new, trolley-mounted Daleks specially built for the exhibition moved about on railway-like tracks. Dalek B1 simply circled around Dalek SM2, but Dalek B2 had a longer route, disappearing through a gap in the set and reappearing from behind some rocks. Also on display were a few of the 'eight legs' from 'Planet of the Spiders'.

Other items installed for 1974 included the helmeted Sontaran costume from 'The Time Warrior' and, poking its head through a brick wall, the Tyrannosaurus model from 'Invasion of the Dinosaurs'. Both of these would be transferred to Longleat the following year, the former after being removed for use in production of the new story 'The Sontaran Experiment'.

Fan Christopher Daniels remembers visiting the exhibition in its debut year: 'The first time I ever went in the Blackpool exhibition, it was the last season of Jon Pertwee, when it first opened. I was only about four or five at the time, my brother was a little bit younger, my sister was older. We went in, and I always remember seeing the big dinosaur at the bottom of the stairs, with its head poking through, from "Invasion of the Dinosaurs".'

Despite his young age at the time, Christopher has clear memories of the exhibits: 'I remember being immersed into this world ... I remember seeing the Draconian, the Ogron [and so on] the first time.' Daniels also recalls the giant spiders making an appearance.

The Blackpool exhibition proved a big hit with fans in general. Roger M Dilley enthuses: 'I *loved* that place. I spent a week of my annual holidays down there every year for several years ... My family never saw me!'

The Dalek display underwent only a few changes over the years. For example, occasionally Dalek B1 and Dalek B2 would swap tracks; and in 1976, the large Krynoid from 'The Seeds of Doom' was added. However, all of the other displays, both behind the TARDIS control room viewing windows and along the preceding corridor, would be regularly updated.

1975

One of those who visited the *Doctor Who* exhibition in Blackpool during 1975 was a young Andrew Smith, later to write for *Doctor Who* on both television and audio: 'For me, the greatest of all exhibitions was the first one I visited, based on the Golden Mile in Blackpool from 1974. I visited ... during a family weekend break in October 1975. I can pinpoint the date because "Planet of Evil" was broadcasting at the time. I was 13.'

For those who walked along the Golden Mile in Blackpool, the oversized

TARDIS exterior stood out. The recognisable shape of the time and space machine provided a gateway into the world of *Doctor Who*. As Smith again recalls: 'The entrance was through a TARDIS attached to the building. I remember descending steps into the basement where the exhibits were on display, past a video welcome message from Tom Baker pointing the way for us.'

An early issue of the long-running *TARDIS* fanzine provided the first written account of the Blackpool exhibition, in the form of an article by Stuart Glazebrook and a second, shorter piece by Geraint Jones. Although published in April 1976, this described the exhibition as it had appeared the previous year; the issue stated that both of the permanent exhibitions were closed at the time, but would reopen over the Easter weekend, with reported changes to include new monsters from the show's recently-broadcast Season 13.

For a small ticket price of 30p for adults, 15p for children, visitors were able to enter a world of *Doctor Who* beneath the street level of Blackpool, where a familiar grating metallic voice declared that the TARDIS was under Dalek control. Inside, the iconic *Doctor Who* theme tune rang out, and visitors were menaced by a pterodactyl from 'Invasion of the Dinosaurs' overhead. On reaching the bottom of the steep flight of stairs, the first exhibit to be seen was a new addition: a Wirrn from 'The Ark in Space' emerging from a cocoon. The head of the insectoid alien moved from side to side, causing its antennae to sway, and the exhibit was lit with a pulsing green light. Adjacent to this was a piece of artwork (originally produced for a *Radio Times* special marking *Doctor Who*'s tenth anniversary) representing the regeneration transitions from William Hartnell to Patrick Troughton and finally to Jon Pertwee.[90] Beneath this was a sign stating that, with the exception of the Daleks, all exhibits were originals used in the recording of *Doctor Who*.

Another new addition to the exhibition was the K1 Robot from Tom Baker's debut story 'Robot'. Making its public debut here, this impressive costume would also be displayed from time to time at Longleat (as detailed in the previous chapter), and would later appear at both the MOMI and Llangollen exhibitions before returning to Blackpool and finally being seen at the *Doctor Who* Experience. Given its height and size, it naturally dominated any display in which it was placed. Designed by James Acheson, the main body was constructed out of aluminium sheeting, while the arms were made of a combination of balsawood and more aluminium. Pincer-like hands and a head containing flashing lights rounded things off. The costume had been very heavy and uncomfortable for actor Michael Kilgarriff to wear in the television production, but the sturdy materials used meant that it survived the test of time much better than others made of latex and rubber. The spectacle of the large K1 Robot on display in Blackpool in 1975 certainly made a lasting impression on a young Andrew Smith:

'One of the first exhibits I saw was the Giant Robot from Tom's opening

---

[90] *TARDIS* fanzine. Volume 1, Number 5.

story, "Robot". And it left me gobsmacked. Tall, impressive, a lovely piece of design, and *"an actual thing that had actually been in the TV series"*, my brain was shouting at me. My fan gene was well and truly engaged at that point.'

For the 1975 exhibition, the robot had a glowing red light place inside its head and its disintegrator weapon positioned under its left arm. An audio soundtrack was also played, with lines taken from the television story, such as 'I can bring about the destruction of humanity' and 'Go! Go now or I shall destroy you all.'[91] The exhibit was said to be able to 'radiate an aura of menace that is quite unnerving, yet strangely fascinating', and to be worth the entrance fee alone.[92]

Further along the dark corridor, the next display featured Brontosaurus and Stegosaurus models from 'Invasion of the Dinosaurs', posed on a drab cityscape. The next exhibit was a more substantial one, featuring the Royal Beast of Peladon, Aggedor, last seen in 'The Monster of Peladon', stood on its hind legs with claws outstretched. The report of this in *TARDIS* was unfavourable: 'The majestic figure of Aggedor resembles a stuffed bear in a museum.'[93] Also in the display were some static 'eight legs' spiders from 'Planet of the Spiders' and, according to Geraint Jones, some giant maggots from 'The Green Death'.

Continuing along the corridor and past a wall-mounted photograph of Sarah Jane Smith with Aggedor, visitors encountered another model exhibit from 'Invasion of the Dinosaurs', in the form of a Triceratops in a London underground station. The dinosaur moved its head from side to side, with accompanying growling and grunting sounds.

Further models, made by a teenage *Doctor Who* fan, provided a representation of sets such as the Doctor's UNIT workshop, a Dalek interrogation room, the Master's TARDIS control room and the giant spiders' throne room. There were nine of these highly detailed model recreations in total, and they also included miniature representations of a Sea Devil, Alpha Centauri and a Quark.

The final display in this corridor again featured a Wirrn from 'The Ark in Space', but this time it was the impressive swarm leader.

Now moved to just outside the TARDIS control room, the 'Sentinel' Dalek SM1 in its gold livery stood guard, barking out orders in the familiar staccato style: 'Halt! Identify. Identify! Obey the Daleks. Obey! Obey! We have captured the TARDIS. The TARDIS is under Dalek control! It is forbidden to smoke. Smokers will be exterminated! Proceed with caution! Move! Move! Move!'[94]

The TARDIS console itself, as in Longleat, was surrounded by a barrier and protected by a transparent case to ensure its longevity. Dotted around the walls of the room however were interactive panels that visitors could operate.

---

[91] *TARDIS* fanzine. Volume 1, Number 5.
[92] *TARDIS* fanzine. Volume 1, Number 5.
[93] *TARDIS* fanzine. Volume 1, Number 5.
[94] *TARDIS* fanzine. Volume 1, Number 5.

Along the right-hand side of the room, mounted against a barren and alien backdrop, remained a number of alien creatures that had been installed for the exhibition's opening in 1974. These included a Cyberman from 'The Moonbase', Alpha Centauri as first seen in 'The Curse of Peladon' and a Draconian from 'Frontier in Space'. A new addition was an Axon from 'The Claws of Axos', which was unfortunately described by Glazebrook as having 'dull red external organs, which look pathetic; it must be the worst exhibit on show, bearing a strong resemblance to a poorly stuffed ragged sack.'[95] Glazebrook was equally scathing of another new exhibit, a Yeti, which seemed to have a face 'made from *papier-mâché* then tacked onto the head. To make things worse, this mask has two eyes and a silly looking mouth cut into it.'[96] Further exhibits included a Sea Devil ('The Sea Devils'); two Ice Warriors last seen during 'The Monster of Peladon' ; and 'a cluster of Exxilons' ('Death to the Daleks') covered with sackcloth, making them appear 'quite drab and meaningless.'[97, 98]

The Dalek cavern once again provided the exhibition's grand finale, housing the three Daleks SM2, B1 and B2. This display was largely the same as in the previous year, but now featured a Silurian from their first appearance in 'Doctor Who and the Silurians'. Hidden away at the back of the set, the Silurian was partly covered with a fabric sheet draped over the right arm and part of the torso, camouflaging it against the rocks, no doubt to conceal some damage or missing section of the costume.

Finally, a single Ogron ('Day of the Daleks'), clutching a weapon in its right hand, stood guard as visitors exited toward the souvenir booth. In an amusing anecdote, Stuart Glazebrook noted the presence of 'a Cyberman head on the counter which is used to inflate *Doctor Who* balloons!'[99]

Andrew Smith recalls the remainder of the exhibition: 'I followed a route through the displays that included Cybermen and a Wirrn, and a functioning TARDIS console behind barriers. I shouldn't think I blinked once – I was in awe.'

In wrapping up his review, Glazebrook described the Blackpool exhibition of 1975 as a 'superb show', but added there were 'things which could be improved, sure – but then I must say that the good things far outweigh the bad'. He concluded by writing, 'I heartily urge anyone who is in the area to "Defy the Daleks"' – a reference to a slogan that formed part of the artwork on the exhibition's exterior wall on the Golden Mile.[100]

Similarly, Geraint Jones praised the exhibition, describing it as 'really great' and adding, 'With a bit of imagination it can be a *Doctor Who* adventure just for you! I know you will enjoy it; it will be the best day of your life – it was

---

[95] *TARDIS* fanzine. Volume 1, Number 5.
[96] *TARDIS* fanzine. Volume 1, Number 5.
[97] *TARDIS* fanzine. Volume 1, Number 5.
[98] *TARDIS* fanzine. Volume 1, Number 5.
[99] *TARDIS* fanzine. Volume 1, Number 5.
[100] *TARDIS* fanzine. Volume 1, Number 5.

mine!'[101]

With Tom Baker now established in the lead role, *Doctor Who* entered a new period of popularity at this time. The exhibition in Blackpool would play its part as the ratings reached stellar levels in the second half of the 1970s.

1976

1976 saw Styre the Sontaran and his robot from 'The Sontaran Experiment' transferred to Blackpool following a season at Longleat. This year also saw the launch of a 'Design a Monster' competition: visitors to the exhibition were invited to draw a monster design on an A4 piece of paper and submit it, along with their entrance ticket, to 'Exhibitions Organiser, BBC Enterprises, Villiers House, Ealing Broadway, London W5 2PA'. The winner was promised a day for two in London, including a 'spectacular visit to the BBC Television Centre'. Hopefully this included an opportunity to watch a recording session of *Doctor Who* itself.

1977

The *Doctor Who* exhibitions of 1977 were again reviewed in the pages of *TARDIS* fanzine, with Stuart Glazebrook and Richard Leaver composing the Blackpool feature. As at Longleat, new additions had been made, featuring items from the most-recently-transmitted Season 14.

On descending the staircase into the darkness, the first exhibits to be seen were masks of a Sea Devil ('The Sea Devils'), an Exxilon ('Death to the Daleks') and a Solonian Mutant ('The Mutants'). At the base of the stairs, two Voc Robots, V5 and D33, 'reached out menacingly', their elegant costumes and masks being a thrill to examine up close. [102]

'The Android Invasion' was showcased next, with two Kraal costumes, accompanied by two white-helmeted androids working on the Sarah Jane Smith android duplicate. The scene was completed with some power cables and flashing electrical devices.

Another story to receive a significant display of artefacts was the 'Pyramids of Mars'. A scene was created to replicate the Tomb of Sutekh. Sutekh himself was seated with his jackal-like head revealed, his mask being positioned on his lap. Next to him, an open sarcophagus contained a Guardian Mummy robot, complete with golden bandages. At the front, the Marconiscope prop that had also featured in the story completed the impressive exhibit.

Further along the corridor, on the left-hand side, two Sea Devils were housed, emerging from the murky depths of what appeared to be an underwater set. This illusion was created by projecting lights through a shallow trough containing bubbling water onto a fine mesh behind the

---

[101] TARDIS fanzine. Volume 1, Number 5.
[102] *TARDIS* fanzine. Volume 2, Number 6.

window of glass.

Next along the corridor, surrounded by a series of mirrors, stood the always-impressive K1 Robot ('Robot'), which still had red lights flashing within its metallic cranium.

The impressive Sandminer miniature from 'The Robots of Death' was another item displayed at Blackpool in 1977. One person who remembers this exhibit in particular is Mike Tucker: 'I've got photos of it from display the year that the story went out on television. I've spoken to [fellow effects designer] Mat Irvine, and he remembers going to the exhibition and setting that up and running the motors to a transformer to get the Archimedes screws to spin round.' Those screws at the front of the Sandminer appeared to cut through a rocky terrain of *papier-mâché*, while a glow illuminated the model from underneath. The model was a relatively large one, measuring between 4 and 5 feet in length, and was constructed of fibreglass, metal and timber. Although one of the most impressive miniatures created for *Doctor Who*, it was displayed for only the one year at Blackpool. Its whereabouts are now unknown, and the likelihood is that it was simply disposed of when taken out of the exhibition.

Opposite the Sandminer was a classic piece from the second Doctor's tenure: one of the robot Quarks that had first appeared in 'The Dominators' and had been last seen during the Doctor's trial at the conclusion of 'The War Games'. The Quark had its arms unfolded, ready to blast the visitors, and suffered only from a misaligned spike on the top of its spherical head.

As usual, the 'Sentinel' Dalek SM1, in the gold colour scheme, stood at the entrance to the TARDIS control room. The first exhibit within the control room itself was a new addition: the giant rat created for 'The Talons of Weng-Chiang', mounted in a replica sewer. The rat's eyes glowed red and the head turned from side to side, as seen during the 1980 *Blue Peter* feature about the Longleat exhibition. A soundtrack of dripping water completed the atmospheric scene. Positioned adjacent to this, and also from 'The Talons of Weng-Chiang', were Mr Sin and the distillation chamber used by Magnus Greel.

The next display presented both forms of Eldrad the Kastrian from 'The Hand of Fear': the feminine shape as played on screen by Judith Paris and the more masculine form as portrayed by Stephen Thorne. Signage on the wall read 'CONTROLLED AREA – RADIATION SOURCE EXPOSED. DO NOT ENTER' – advice not heeded by a lone Zygon, which had crept into the scene.

Another mixture of alien creature exhibits included an Exxilon ('Death to the Daleks'), described as 'slumped against a wall'[103]; Alpha Centauri, from the two Peladon stories, which had suffered damage to its large eye[104]; two Cybermen; and Styre's robot from 'The Sontaran Experiment'. Also displayed with this menagerie were a pair of Time Lords robes from 'The Deadly Assassin', one in the light purple or heliotrope of the Patrexes and the other in

---

[103] *TARDIS* fanzine. Volume 2, Number 6.
[104] *TARDIS* fanzine. Volume 2, Number 6.

the orange of the Prydonians. Finally, the decayed form of the Master, as he had appeared during that same story, was positioned toward the front of the display.

The two Cybermen seen here were a peculiar mix of a 'The Wheel in Space' helmet attached to a 'Revenge of the Cybermen' body and vice versa. Exhibitions assistant Bob Richardson explains how older Cybermen existed in pieces rather than as complete costumes: 'There were several vintage Cybermen, and tea chests full of spare bits – plastic tubing, silver wellies and those plastic balls with holes in them, used to join up the silver tubing on their arms.' In light of this, it is no surprise that occasionally pieces would become mismatched.

Prior to 1977, the Silurian in the Dalek cavern had been replaced by an Ice Warrior, specifically the original Warrior with the oversized helmet that had been used for the advance filming at Ealing studios for 'The Ice Warriors'. A humanoid Krynoid from 'The Seeds of Doom' was also added to the cavern, possibly in time for the 1976 season but definitely by 1977, and had Dalek B1 circling around it. This repainted Axon costume that had been used during production for the humanoid Krynoid would most likely have come from the exhibition in the first place. It didn't always remain in the cavern but was also used to promote the attraction, being photographed outside of the Golden Mile entrance in 1977. In place of the Krynoid when Glazebrook and Leaver attended for their *TARDIS* fanzine article were the lion headpiece and plain outfit from 'The Masque of Mandragora'.

The last exhibit prior to the small retail booth – which continued to sell a range of mementos – was Magnus Greel's warped face mask, seen only briefly in 'The Talons of Weng-Chiang'. Finally venturing up the stairs, back to the real world, visitors passed a case in which were displayed a Drashig, a Krynoid seed pod, and a Cybermat as seen in 'Revenge of the Cybermen', along with some spaceship models.

<u>1978</u>

The following year, fan Tim Dollin visited the Blackpool exhibition in early April 1978, and described the experience for the fourth edition of *Gallifrey* fanzine. On descending the staircase into the gloom of the exhibition, the first thing the visitor saw was a large screen playing video clips from the show; Dollin commented that these would get 'stuck' on the image of a Voc robot from 'The Robots of Death'. A case on the wall held the hand of Eldrad from 'The Hand of Fear', but the first major display was the impressively-arranged scene from 'The Robots of Death' that had been at Longleat the previous year. It therefore comprised D84 strapped to a table and the hooded Taren Capel costume, with V8 and SV7 stood nearby.

The next exhibit, however, was a new addition, from the recently transmitted Season 15. Two astronaut spacesuits from 'The Invisible Enemy' were displayed on mannequins, and to their right was the Nucleus of the

Swarm from the same story, against a glistening silver background. This set-up would be moved to Longleat the following year.

Another new display came from 'Underworld', broadcast a few months before the exhibition's latest reopening. To the left stood a Minyan costume, complete with large domed helmet and shield weapon. Another mannequin was dressed to resemble the character Tala, complete with blonde wig; this was posed facing away from visitors, so as to conceal the face, and grappling with a Seer; another costume complete with oversized helmet.

Dollin's account also mentioned here dolls of the Doctor and Leela, suspended on fine wires, and an inaccurately labelled model, probably of the lighthouse from 'Horror of Fang Rock'.

Further along the corridor was housed the most recent addition to the TARDIS crew: K-9. A replica of the robot dog was installed, as the screen-used prop was needed by the production team for the following season's recording, which began in April 1978. Dollin noted that a number of screws were visible on the replica, unlike on the K-9 seen on screen.

In another change, the 'Sentinel' Dalek SM1 had been swapped for a grey Dalek, guarding the entrance to the TARDIS control room.[105] Inside, the first viewing window held another new display, featuring items from 'Image of the Fendahl'. Dominating the scene was the large Fendahleen, complete with horrific tentacles protruding from its circular mouth. Also on display were the long, flowing golden robes worn by actress Wanda Ventham as Thea transformed into the Fendahl core, and the skull that triggered the events of the story. The atmospheric scene was assisted by some sparing lighting and by 'the use of green luminous paint on the floor of "the cellar" and around Thea's eyes.'[106] Adjacent to this display were the Mr Sin puppet, holding out his knife, and the large golden dragon statue; two items from 'The Talons of Weng-Chiang' that had been at Longleat the previous year.

The 'cavalcade of monsters' display for 1978 featured a Sontaran, Alpha Centauri, a Kraal, an 'eight legs' giant spider, a Zygon, a Cyberman and a Time Lord. Curiously, Dollin commented that the Kraal, the Zygon and the Cyberman were 'encased in a plastic cubicle'.[107] At some point the display was developed so that the monsters were mounted in individual cubicles against a tinfoil backing.

The exhibition's grand finale was, as usual, the Dalek cavern, in which remained the Ice Warrior, along with the large Krynoid that had been at Longleat the previous year. Also added to the display was one of the Cybermen seen the previous year, specifically the combination of 'The Wheel in Space' helmet and 'Revenge of the Cybermen' body, along with a Cybermat from the latter story.

In the final display case, another Kraal from 'The Android Invasion' was

---

[105] *Gallifrey* fanzine, No. 4.
[106] *Gallifrey* fanzine, No. 4.
[107] *Gallifrey* fanzine. No. 4.

paired with one of that story's titular androids, specifically a 'service mechanic'-costumed figure with white overalls and helmet with a tinted visor.

A Silurian mask was also mounted in a display case surrounded by copies of the *Doctor Who Sound Effects* LP record, which had been released that year. The latter could of course be purchased in the little shop at the exhibition. Beyond the shop, a small television screen showed Tom Baker, in character as the Doctor, bidding visitors farewell with the words, 'Goodbye. It's good, isn't it?' (a clip later included in the *More Than Thirty Years in the TARDIS* video documentary).

1979

The following year, John Bok wrote about the exhibition for the *Doctor Who* Appreciation Society's *TARDIS* fanzine. Curiously, he began with a suggestion to phone the Ritz Café next door to check that the attraction was open before attempting a visit.

Once again, a number of new additions had been made to the exhibition, utilising items from the recently-broadcast Season 16, revolving around the Doctor's search for the six segments of the Key to Time. However, the first display case remained the same as in 1977, and presumably 1978, presenting a collection of masks including an Exxilon ('Death to the Daleks'), a Sea Devil ('The Sea Devils') and a Solonian Mutant ('The Mutants'). At the foot of the entrance staircase came a set featuring items from 'Pyramids of Mars'. A cobweb-covered Sutekh, complete with jackal head, was accompanied by one of the golden-bandaged 'Guardian' Mummies and an Egyptian sarcophagus. Nearby, the purple-velvet-lined case that had held the hand from 'The Hand of Fear' now housed a lump of Jethryk rock from 'The Ribos Operation' – the first of the fresh inclusions in the exhibition.

Next, the coronation scene from 'The Androids of Tara' was recreated in Blackpool. Prince Reynart's duplicate was positioned on the throne with the face removed to expose the android's inner workings. Also present were the costumes for the Archimandrite and swordsman Farrah plus a number of others worn by supporting artistes during the coronation scene. Opposite this display was another new addition, namely the Shrivenzale monster and a guard costume from 'The Ribos Operation'.

The Nucleus of the Swarm from 'The Invisible Enemy' had been removed from the next display case and transferred to Longleat for 1979. Replacing it was Voc Robot V5 from 'The Robots of Death'. The next exhibit was another of the items on display for the first time, namely the model of the huge swamp-creature Kroll created for effects scenes in 'The Power of Kroll'. Measuring 66 inches long, it also had mechanisms fitted to make it twitch and move. Bok noted: 'One of its tentacles had a fine wire attached to it, which made the tentacle rise up and down periodically. Also, its head bobbed up and down and inside its mouth was an orange light, which gave off a very eerie glow.

Altogether a most impressive exhibit.'[108] The model would later appear at other exhibitions before being sold off in 2010.

Adjacent to Kroll was a model of the Krynoid engulfing Harrison Chase's mansion from the climax of 'The Seeds of Doom'; this had been seen at Longleat in 1977. Opposite was another model, this time of the city of Zanak from 'The Pirate Planet'.

'Sentinel' Dalek SM1 had now been restored to its position guarding the entrance to the TARDIS control room. The background had also been changed to match the cavern set elsewhere in the exhibition. However, John Bok noted that the Dalek prop was 'suffering from dislodged solar panels and a cracked iris'. [109] Bok also mentioned that areas of the control room interior had been improved, with a third of the cavernous environment now covered with computer equipment, and a swirling pattern on the floors and ceiling creating a more futuristic backdrop.

The first viewing window in the control room housed the Pirate Captain costume from 'The Pirate Planet'. Seated on a black leather chair, he was accompanied by the Polyphase Avatron parrot robot plus two of the guard costumes also seen during the story. The Pirate Captain would reappear at several other *Doctor Who* exhibitions in the future. Next to this exhibit was the K-9 replica with the same audio playing as in the previous year. The replica was mounted on a short track that should have enabled it to move forward and back, but this was not working when John Bok visited.

The second viewing window housed a display focusing on the most recent season finale, 'The Armageddon Factor'. On a pedestal stood the incomplete Key to Time prop, the missing final segment being held by the Shadow, positioned nearby. Also on display were the costume of Princess Astra, played on screen by Lalla Ward, and the uniform of either Merak or Shapp from the same story.

The cavern scenario featuring the menagerie of monsters was still in place, but by this point the Kraal from 'The Android Invasion' had been poorly repaired, with a cartoonish pair of eyes and mouth painted onto the original mask, creating a comical expression of surprise. Remaining on display in their separate plastic pods were a Cyberman, 'with a drunken look, as he was slumped knock-kneed against the back of the cubicle'[110], along with a Zygon and a Sea Devil. The Ice Warrior was positioned nearby and had also been touched up with some luminous paint to the tips of its scales. Moved into this area, too, was the Herrick costume from 'Underworld', complete with shield blaster, that had been on display elsewhere in the exhibition the previous year; however, this was poorly lit and could easily have been missed by visitors. The Krynoid creature had been brought closer to the viewing window as well, and again touched up with some luminous paint.

---

[108] *TARDIS* fanzine. Volume 4, Number 5.
[109] *TARDIS* fanzine. Volume 4, Number 5.
[110] *TARDIS* fanzine. Volume 4, Number 5.

Still *in situ* from the 1978 season were the trio of Daleks, Cyberman and Cybermat, but the correct helmet had now been added to the 'Revenge of the Cybermen' suit. At the front of this display was also an 'eight legs' spider from 'Planet of the Spiders'.

The final new addition to the exhibition from the Key to Time season was the Taran Wood Beast from 'The Androids of Tara'. The dim lighting in the corridor actually aided this costume; the broad daylight in which it had been filmed on location having revealed its less-than-terrifying facial features.

In another display case was a selection of weapons created for the show, a Silurian mask and the hand from 'The Hand of Fear', now moved close to the end of the exhibition. The final case before the exit displayed a Sea Devil mask in two separate halves. Lastly, adorning the walls of the staircase back to the real world were a number of still photographs of the first four Doctors.

1980

As a new decade began, the team of BBC Enterprises' Exhibitions Unit again managed to secure for display a new batch of artefacts straight from the latest *Doctor Who* season. 1979's Season 17 had included a Dalek story, 'Destiny of the Daleks', and the acclaimed, Paris-set 'City of Death', both of which were represented at the Blackpool exhibition, entrance to which still cost a mere 30p.

Details of the 1980 displays can be gleaned from a number of separate accounts: in its Issue 26, *Doctor Who Weekly* (still some time off from being renamed *Doctor Who Monthly* and eventually *Doctor Who Magazine*) presented its first feature on the exhibitions, focusing on a visit to Blackpool; one of the readers of that issue was fan Christopher Daniels, who was prompted to make a return visit; and an issue of the fanzine *Kronos* featured a David Duffin-written review of the attraction.

Through the darkness, the introductory Dalek audio track was heard, matching the one that accompanied the 'Sentinel' Dalek at Longleat. Unchanged once again was the display case showcasing masks of an Exxilon, a Sea Devil and a Mutant. The lump of Jethryk from 'The Ribos Operation' also remained, but a new item added to the exhibition was the spaceship model from 'The Horns of Nimon', suspended against a space background.

The Erato monster from 'The Creature from the Pit' next made its exhibition debut. It was lit with an appropriate green light and rigged up to pulse. Although commentators often deride Erato as an unsuccessful monster on screen, Christopher Daniels remembers being impressed by its display here: '[It also included] some of the soldiers around it, the Chlorian guards, posed as if they were recoiling from it. There was a dummy dressed as Lady Adrasta as well. And there were the Wolfweeds.'

This was a great demonstration of the thought and attention put into the Blackpool exhibition by the BBC Exhibitions team, utilising more than just the basic costume pieces. Similarly impressive was a jungle setting provided for a trio of debuting Mandrels from 'Nightmare of Eden', effectively matching the environment of the planet Eden as seen during that story.

Nearby, Scaroth the Jagaroth from 'City of Death' sat in his spaceship, complete with illuminating lights on the controls and the backdrop of a prehistoric planet Earth. Christopher Daniels remembers this display particularly: 'It frightened the bejesus out of me. I don't know why. I remember [Scaroth] was just sitting there, and I just felt my legs go to jelly.' Also seen here was a model of the Jagaroth ship, used during production for the film sequence of the craft exploding; this had been 'touched up with sickly purple and green luminous paint'. [111]

Another model spaceship on display in the corridor was the *Empress* intergalactic cruise liner from 'Nightmare of Eden', hung against a black backdrop with painted stars.

The 'Sentinel' Dalek still guarded the entrance to the TARDIS control room, but by this time Dalek SM1 was beginning to look the worse for wear and had lost the sucker from the end of its telescopic arm; this had been replaced by a poor plastic replica. Inside the control room, another new exhibit featured Soldeed and Sorak guard costumes from 'The Horns of Nimon'. K-9 was still present here, too, on his short track. This display really encapsulated what Christopher Daniels grew to love about the exhibition: 'The thing I liked about the original Blackpool one was it wasn't just the stuff that was on display, it was the bespoke [representations] of the episodes; you had bits of the scenery. When you went into the main area where the TARDIS console was, the first one was a big scene of Skonnos from "The Horns of the Nimon". I can quite vividly remember that.'

The display of miscellaneous monsters for 1980 included a Voc Robot from 'The Robots of Death', a Cyberman, a Sea Devil, a Zygon, and a Movellan from 'Destiny of the Daleks'.

Following the broadcast of the latter story, the Dalek set had received a complete overhaul for 1980. The scenery now matched that of Skaro as seen during the story, with the addition of computers, monitors and cables, all given the weathered look of the abandoned Dalek city, plus the suspended animation chamber in which Davros was imprisoned. The Davros seen here, which replaced Dalek SM2, was the complete 'hero' costume and mask as used during production. Daleks B1 and B2 continued on their tracks around the set, B1 now circling around Davros, and curiously both were kept in the silver-and-blue livery from the 1960s rather than given an updated colour scheme. The only change was that Dalek B2 now had a black lower collar section.

The fish-like costume for one of the alternative Romana regenerations was added, along with two more Movellans, completing the 'Destiny of the Daleks' scene. It was *Doctor Who Weekly*'s description of this that drew fan Christopher Daniels back to the exhibition for the first time in a couple of years, as he now recalls: 'The bit I really wanted to see was the Dalek scene. *Doctor Who Weekly*, as it was then, had an article about the exhibition as a whole, and there was a

---

[111] Duffin, D. *Crystal of Kronos* fanzine.

very blurred photograph of that scene across the centrefold. "Destiny of the Daleks" is a story I've always liked, and that photograph really seized my imagination. I remember, when I went to see it, Davros sitting there and the Daleks on the tracks and the ruined bunker. Even now I want to build a version for my Sevans Dalek model kits to stand in. I'm going to do it eventually!'

A moving transparent brain of a Dalek was mounted on the wall to the left of the final viewing window that housed the Dalek display. A miscellany of weapons then provided the attraction's final exhibit for that year.

1981

A poster advertising the exhibition proclaimed that Meglos, Foamasi, Marshmen, Gundans and Melkur were 'NEW FOR 1981'. Following the broadcast of Season 18, Tom Baker's last as the Doctor, a number of significant updates had been made to the displays, with all the stories of that latest season represented. Admission now cost 50p.

'The Leisure Hive', the opening story, was the subject of a display featuring two Foamasi and three Argolins mounted in a recreation of the Tachyon Recreation Generator hall with its central cabinet. Christopher Daniels remembers this in particular, saying: 'That was the beauty of the original Blackpool, it had those bespoke sets. They had "The Leisure Hive"; they had the Tachyon Recreation Generator room.'

The next story, 'Meglos', benefited from two displays; the first featured the spacecraft used by the Gaztak plunderers and the second placed the Zolfa-Thuran cactus amongst the bell plants from Tigella.

Another spaceship model exhibit was the *Starliner* from 'Full Circle'. In addition, a cave had been constructed to match that seen in the story, with Marshmen and Marsh Spiders inhabiting it.

Once again a story was represented by a model used during production, and for 'State of Decay' the obvious candidate was the vampires' tower, otherwise known as the spaceship *Hydrax*.

The final story of the so-called 'E-Space trilogy', 'Warriors' Gate', supplied a significant number of exhibits. These included a Gundan robot costume, which would become a regular display item in the years that followed. It was joined here by Lazlo the wounded Tharil and the privateer's M-Z weapon, the latter of which had an interactive element whereby visitors could press a button to make the large dish rotate and fire a strobe light simulating a laser. This feature is again fondly remembered by Christopher Daniels:

'They had the MZ, the big weapon from "Warriors' Gate", and you could steer it. It was in the Gateway set. They had the Gundan in there too. There was a joystick on the fascia in front of you, so you could actually steer the dish, press a button and the weapon fired; it made a noise and lit up. It was great fun, having the chance to play about with something that was in the series. I was only about 10 or 11 at the time. It just turned on its axis.'

Interactive elements are more familiar to visitors of modern exhibitions – allowing them to 'fly' the TARDIS, for example – but even back in 1981 the BBC Exhibitions Unit was able to include some of these in the Blackpool displays. The statuesque Melkur from 'The Keeper of Traken' would become a popular item at a number of exhibitions over the years but made its debut at Blackpool in 1981. At this point, red eyes had been added to the screen-used costume.

The final exhibit from Season 18 was the Monitor's costume from 'Logopolis', on a mannequin with features resembling those of actor John Fraser, who had played the character in the story; he was described in a *Doctor Who Monthly* feature as presiding 'over his mathematically precise workers'.[112]

The monster collection of this year featured a Cyberman, a Zygon and a Sontaran, all from stories broadcast during the previous decade. Certainly the exhibition had not been dedicated solely to Tom Baker's final season; notably, the Dalek control room set remained as before, featuring Daleks, Movellans and Davros from 'Destiny of the Daleks'.

1982

With the arrival of a new incarnation of the Doctor, played by Peter Davison, the Blackpool exhibition also received a refresh, benefiting from an influx of new items from Season 19.

First came the beautiful android costume from 'The Visitation', which would go on to appear at a number of other exhibitions over the next 15 years. It was accompanied by the Soliton Gas Machine prop from the same story; an item that would later be acquired by the Prop Gallery website.[113]

Progressing along the corridor, on the right-hand side could be found two of the monstrous Terileptils, also from 'The Visitation'. Curiously, the blue-hued mask was paired with the red-hued body on the creature closest to the visitor, at odds with how it had appeared on screen. Directly opposite was the TSS machine from 'Kinda', and further along, the instantly recognisable Trickster mask from the same story.

Around the corner, a series of displays ran along the left-hand side of the corridor. The first of these showcased Monarch the Urbankan from 'Four to Doomsday'. Next came the Pharos Project model that had featured prominently in the demise of the fourth Doctor in 'Logopolis'. Spinning around, the visitor would then encounter K-9, housed in a display case with a number of model spaceships and other craft.

The gold-and-silver 'Sentinel' Dalek once more guarded the entrance to the TARDIS control room. Moving around to the right of the control console, the first display featured two of the new Cybermen and the Cyberscope prop from 'Earthshock'. The monster assortment this year held, from left to right, Stor the

---

[112] *Doctor Who Monthly* #53.
[113] www.thepropgallery.com/soliton-gas-machine-the-visitation

Sontaran from 'The Invasion of Time', a Mandrel ('Nightmare of Eden') and a Foamasi ('The Leisure Hive'). At the front of the display was the decayed Master costume, complete with mask worn by actor Geoffrey Beevers in 'The Keeper of Traken'. Next to this monster assembly was the Tharil and Gundan display from 'Warriors' Gate', which remained in its former position. Similarly, the Davros and Daleks exhibit remained the same as in the previous year.

Before the visitor ventured back upstairs to the real world, one of the last exhibits featured a Plasmaton from 'Time-Flight'. Next to this were two halves of Sea Devil mask stuck to the wall and draped in one of the creatures' blue 'string vest' costumes, as it had been seen in 1979, on top of which was added an 'eight legs' giant spider from 'Planet of the Spiders'.

1983

One visitor to Blackpool in 1983 was writer Paul Magrs, who shared his memories in the Steve Berry-edited book *Behind the Sofa*. His description was as follows:

'Jazzy and tacky, sepulchral, dark – jam-packed with rubber monsters and polystyrene rocks. There was stuffing hanging out of Cybermen, and holes in the Yeti's fur, and poor automated K-9 looked as if he hadn't enough room to run around in his paddock, bizarrely filled as it was with the decapitated heads of monsters. But every bit of it was magical. These were pieces of the true cross, treasures from ancient civilisations, and nuggets of gold from the Moon. This floppy dinosaur, this Fairy Liquid spaceship, this TARDIS console looking like a bingo machine. This was the day that *Doctor Who* seemed more real than anything else in the world.'[114]

In *Doctor Who*'s twentieth anniversary year, however, much of the attention was directed toward Longleat, as it hosted the epic Celebration event.

1984

Writing in *Doctor Who Magazine*, Gary Russell reviewed the Blackpool and Longleat exhibitions of 1984. Blackpool's 'Sentinel' Dalek SM1, like Longleat's, was relocated for this year, becoming the first exhibit encountered by visitors. Dalek B1 was also moved to accompany it. On the right-hand side of the corridor was a display from 'Warriors of the Deep', featuring three Sea Devils and a Silurian. Further along, another Silurian and a Sea Devil were accompanied by the Myrka.[115]

The next display presented a variety of creatures from different stories, including a Terileptil ('The Visitation'); a Gundan ('Warriors' Gate'); a blobby Axon ('The Claws of Axos'); and the 'Logar' silver spacesuit from 'Planet of

---

[114] Berry, S (2013) *Behind the Sofa*, p182-183.
[115] *The Official Doctor Who Magazine* #92.

Fire'. Also included were a Plasmaton and Kalid's globe from 'Time-Flight'. An adjacent display case held a number of smaller miscellaneous items. These included the coronet of Rassilon from 'The Five Doctors'; the Mara snake from 'Snakedance'; Sutekh's mask and jackal head from 'Pyramids of Mars'; plus a Jacondan headpiece from 'The Twin Dilemma'.

Opposite these displays, and taking up that whole side of the corridor, were a further three cases. The first housed Mestor the Gastropod from 'The Twin Dilemma', making its exhibition debut here. In the second was the titular flower from 'Black Orchid'. The final one showcased the full Sharez Jek costume and the Queen bat from 'The Caves of Androzani'.

This year, as at Longleat, the photographs of the Doctor displayed at the entrance to the TARDIS control room included one of Richard Hurndall as the first Doctor, rather than of one of William Hartnell.[116]

Also making their exhibition debuts at Blackpool during the 1984 run were the Tractators from 'Frontios', accompanied by the imprisoned Plantagenet in his spherical ball from the same story, and the large Magma creature from 'The Caves of Androzani'.

Christopher Daniels recalls visiting the exhibition again during 1984: 'I remember the one year they had the Garm [from 'Terminus'], and it was moving backwards and forwards with its eyes lit up.' Accompanying the Garm was a Vanir costume from the same story.

The Dalek display was once again refreshed this year, following the February 1984 broadcast of 'Resurrection of the Daleks'. The background had been adjusted in 1982, with the addition of columns and archways, but these were now replaced by brick walls that vaguely matched the warehouse environment seen during the story. A more major change, though, was that the display had been halved in size, with only one track and a single Dalek, Dalek B2, circling Davros. All of the Daleks had however received a fresh coat of paint, for the first time in over 10 years. To match the look of those recently seen on screen, they were given a gun-metal-grey-and-black livery – although some of the paint had noticeably splashed into the wrong places.

The Davros chair as seen in 'Resurrection of the Daleks' was installed, but curiously it was accompanied by the previous mask, as worn most recently by David Gooderson in 'Destiny of the Daleks'. Completing the display were two of the Dalek Trooper costumes and the destroyed Dalek prop also seen during 'Resurrection of the Daleks', and probably also the destroyed Dalek that featured in 'The Five Doctors'.

The monster section this year saw appearances from a string-vest-wearing Sea Devil from 'The Sea Devils' and a Zygon from 'Terror of the Zygons', accompanied by the decayed Master from 'The Keeper of Traken', the Pirate Captain with Polyphase Avatron from 'The Pirate Planet', and K-9.

In the final section of corridor, the Yeti from 'The Five Doctors' was on display, seemingly installed the previous year. Pinned to the wall of a display

---

[116] *The Official Doctor Who Magazine* #92.

case was also Peter Davison's cricketing-inspired second costume.

The screen that had once played Tom Baker's video clip now showed the regeneration scene from 'The Caves of Androzani'. Finally, the last display case featured an assortment of artefacts, including another Sharez Jek mask, the bird caps worn by the Black and White Guardians from 'Enlightenment' and some stills from 'The Five Doctors'.

1985

Colin Baker's debut full season, Season 22, broadcast during 1985, was very well represented at the Blackpool exhibition. The stories had featured three classic monster races, the Cybermen, the Sontarans and the Daleks, and examples of all were on display. This would be the final year that the exhibition was open.

Throughout 1985, screen-used prop Dalek 6-ex was positioned outside the exhibition, exposed to the wind and rain of the North West coast plus the attentions of the exuberant British public. The prop was in the gun-metal-grey-and-black colours, with the exception of the solar panel section, which for some reason was gold.

Many exhibits remained in place from the previous year. The first of these were 'Sentinel' Dalek SM1 and Dalek B1, and the three Sea Devils and Silurian from 'Warriors of the Deep'. Opposite this display remained the mixture of costumes from the previous year. Further along the left-hand side of the corridor was, once again, Mestor the Gastropod from 'The Twin Dilemma'.

Around a corner, the right-hand wall featured another display case, containing a variety of items. These included Sutekh's mask and jackal head ('Pyramids of Mars'); a Cyberman helmet; the lion mask from 'The Masque of Mandragora'; the Mara snake from 'Snakedance'; a Voc robot ('The Robots of Death'); and a Kraal mask from 'The Android Invasion'. This display was also bulked out with weaponry such as Dalek Trooper guns from 'Resurrection of the Daleks'.

Next came a Sontaran and the Kartz-Reimer module from 'The Two Doctors' and a Varosian guard costume from 'Vengeance on Varos'. The Black Orchid plant remained in position from the previous year.

Within the TARDIS control room and around to the right, the first exhibit was the Tractators and their excavating machine, as had also been in place during 1984. The next however was a new addition, namely a Cryon and the Cyber Controller from 'Attack of the Cybermen'. Through the middle viewing window could be seen the transparent incubating Dalek and the gravestone statue of the Doctor from 'Revelation of the Daleks'. Curiously, the gravestone featured a trail of blood across the Doctor's features, which had not been particularly apparent on screen but was in keeping with the original script, which described 'blood gushing out from underneath'.

This year's version of the monster menagerie display included a Marshman ('Full Circle'); a Zygon ('Terror of the Zygons'); a Mandrel ('Nightmare of

Eden'); the Garm ('Terminus'); K-9; the Cyberscope that the Cybermen had used in 'Earthshock'; and an 'eight legs' giant spider ('Planet of the Spiders'). Adjacent to this and visible through the final viewing window was of course the Dalek exhibit. Despite the recent broadcast of 'Revelation of the Daleks', the 'Resurrection of the Daleks' display remained *in situ*, the only change being that Davros now had the correct style mask, as worn by Terry Molloy in the story.

As before, adjacent to the Dalek display was the animated Dalek brain mounted on the wall. The final exhibit was then the Pirate Captain from 'The Pirate Planet'.

Footage of the Blackpool exhibition during its last year can be found on the DVD and Blu Ray releases of 'The Trial of a Time Lord', specifically on the disc containing Parts Five to Eight of the story. The segment begins with two Cybermen and a Dalek menacing, or rather being menaced by, children outside of the exhibition. A subsequent clip clearly shows the Dalek area, with Dalek B2 circling a rather hunkered-down Davros, a destroyed Dalek and a barely-visible Dalek Trooper costume from 'Resurrection of the Daleks' plus, for some reason, a spacesuit from 'Enlightenment'. There is also a shot of two of the Sea Devils from 'Warriors of the Deep', and one of the monster assortment display. In addition, we are treated to close-ups of a Tractator ('Frontios'), which wiggles its antennae, and of two static Cybermen. Shots inside the TARDIS control room reveal the images of the Doctor's various incarnations still present, mounted within wall roundels.

The exhibition finally closed its doors in October 1985, after eleven years in operation.

Merchandise

The Blackpool exhibition was serviced by a small souvenir sales counter that stocked postcards, stationery, badges, games and jigsaws. Over the years, tens of thousands of items would have been sold over this counter. Many of the stationery items were the same as the ones available at Longleat. A postcard featuring a colour photograph of Daleks SM1 and SM2, taken at the original Science Museum exhibition, first became available in 1974 when the Blackpool exhibition opened. It was manufactured by Larkfield Printing Co Ltd[117] and was given away as a complimentary gift during that debut year. In 1976, a series of postcards featuring Tom Baker as the Doctor were produced. Equivalent to those produced for Longleat, one of them was titled 'Welcome to Blackpool'. Further postcards, largely featuring publicity stills of cast members, would be sold in the shop over the years.

For visitor Andrew Smith, however, it was the opportunity to purchase Target novelisations of the television stories that had the biggest impact: 'Probably the most significant thing that happened to me that day was when I

---

[117] Howe & Blumberg (2000). *Howe's Transcendental Toybox*, pp.327.

passed the last of the exhibits and found myself in a shop. My eye was caught by a display of novels on the shelves. It turned out they were Target novelisations of TV stories. The novels were few in number at the time, but the titles excited me and I bought three – *Doctor Who and the Abominable Snowmen* (my first memories of *Doctor Who* include vivid recollections of the Yeti), *Doctor Who and the Cybermen* (the novelisation of the TV story "The Moonbase") and *Doctor Who In An Exciting Adventure With the Daleks*. I took these books home and devoured them within days. I placed mail orders for more, and I started something that would hone my own writing skills. From then on, starting with "Pyramids of Mars" and for the next four years, I started audio recording the episodes as they were broadcast. Then I would write them up as my own "novelisations". I still have several of them, complete with my artwork front covers. In between writing my own (original, non-*Who*) stories, I learned what dialogue looked like on the page, and some of the rules of story structure. Within a year or so I was writing original scripts and storylines and submitting them to the *Doctor Who* production office. In 1980 I was asked to develop one storyline into a script that became the TV story "Full Circle". A success that had its beginnings when I took those steps into the Blackpool exhibition in 1975.'

In his *Kronos* fanzine article, David Duffin listed a few of the other items on sale at the exhibition in 1980. The customary badges and posters were amongst the cheaper items. More expensive ones included a 9ft-long scarf, priced at £8.21, and *Doctor Who Sound Effects* and *Doctor Who and the Pescatons* LP records for £2.99 each.

In 1981, a T-shirt with the neon-tube-style logo was on sale. In 1984, there was a car sticker stating 'We've seen the BBC Enterprises *Doctor Who* Exhibition Blackpool'; this featured the earlier, curved logo and was priced at 25p.[118] During Blackpool's final season, a baseball cap was available, with the neon-tube-style logo against a white background on an otherwise black cap.

Events

The highlight of the year in Blackpool is always the switching on of the world-famous illuminations. On 5 September 1975 the new Doctor, Tom Baker, did the honours, accompanied by Elisabeth Sladen, Ian Marter, who played Harry Sullivan, and even director David Maloney. In her autobiography, Sladen later recalled that she had been determined to take a much-needed holiday, but had felt obliged to attend the event after receiving a phone call from her excited mother, who had been invited by Terry Sampson of BBC Enterprises to watch the switching-on of the lights. However, she considered it a great experience.[119] A reported 20,000 people watched the event; as Sladen recalled, 'The crowds

---

[118] Howe & Blumberg (2000). *Howe's Transcendental Toybox*, pp.347.
[119] Sladen, E (2011). *Elisabeth Sladen: The Autobiography*, p.199.

were ten deep, all yelling and waving their *Doctor Who* scarves and toys.'[120]

The following year, the Blackpool exhibition provided several costumes for another event attended by Tom Baker.[121] A special report of this occasion on 12 July 1976 was composed by Stuart Glazebrook for *TARDIS* fanzine.[122] Baker was accompanied by a variety of *Doctor Who* monsters as, in the Doctor's yellow roadster Bessie, he led a procession of 'over 200 floats along the seemingly endless miles of the Blackpool Prom'.[123] The actor so synonymous with *Doctor Who* also appeared on the Radio One Roadshow that day to promote the event. After materialising in a limousine, he posed for pictures with Wilnelia Merced, who had been crowned Miss World 1975 (and who some seven years later would become the wife of entertainer Sir Bruce Forsyth). Brigadier for the day was Terry Sampson, BBC Exhibitions Manager, complete with UNIT uniform, overseeing proceedings and monitoring the alien hordes. The Lord Mayor and Lady Mayoress joined Sampson and Baker in Bessie for the eight-mile parade route. The monsters following the car were a Cyberman, an Exxilon, a Zygon, Styre the Sontaran, Styggron the Kraal and a Sea Devil. As Glazebrook wrote:

'The whole length of the Prom was packed with cheering people on both sides of the road as Tom flashed smiles and waved to young and old alike, all jostling for a good look at these strange celebrities. The monsters played their part well, giving their armed guard a rough time as they ran around, menacing the crowds, unfortunately upsetting a few children, and I think, a few adults too!'[124]

The poor individuals stuck inside those monster costumes of rubber and latex, walking the eight-mile length of the promenade, in the heat of a July afternoon, must have suffered terribly. Glazebrook described the aftermath: 'I joined the aliens as they collapsed by the beach exhausted! Costumes were unzipped, unplugged and untied and masks were temporarily thrown aside. Never have I seen six wearier men!'[125]

The *Doctor Who* exhibition maintained a regular presence at events of this kind during the yearly Blackpool festivities, and this helps to explain why so few of the props and costumes still survive to this day. Roger M Dilley recalls being asked to don a Voc robot costume one year as a part of the carnival procession along the Golden Mile:

'I actually walked most of it, menacing the people either side of the Promenade. Believe me, it *isn't* just one mile! One thing I remember most vividly of that day is that the inside of the Voc mask was very rough and prickly. I swear to this day I am *still* carrying a tiny bit of it embedded in my nose!'

---

[120] Sladen, E (2011). *Elisabeth Sladen: The Autobiography*, p.202.
[121] *Doctor Who Monthly* #53.
[122] *TARDIS* fanzine. Blackpool Extra.
[123] *TARDIS* fanzine. Blackpool Extra.
[124] *TARDIS* fanzine. Blackpool Extra.
[125] *TARDIS* fanzine. Blackpool Extra.

Many years later, with *Doctor Who* back on the television screens and an exhibition sited in Blackpool once again, tenth Doctor David Tennant performed the official switch-on of the illuminations. This event in 2007 saw Tennant following in the footsteps of Jon Pertwee, Tom Baker and sixth Doctor Colin Baker, who all made *Doctor Who*-related appearances in Blackpool. Footage on the DVD of 'The Trial of the Time Lord' reveals that at the end of August 1985 Colin Baker was accompanied on a visit to the exhibition by companion actress Nicola Bryant (Peri) and producer John Nathan-Turner. Appropriately, all three arrived in Bessie. Baker and Bryant, both in character costumes, signed autographs for a crowd of young fans by the exhibition's TARDIS console and commented on how hot the place was with so many people crammed inside.

End of an Era

Blackpool was the planned filming location for 'The Nightmare Fair', the story originally intended to open *Doctor Who*'s twenty-third season in 1986. The final line of 'Revelation of the Daleks' was to have set this up but was trimmed to remove the word 'Blackpool' after the season was postponed by the BBC and subsequently reformatted. Any *Doctor Who* promotion of Blackpool became unnecessary after that, as the exhibition closed its doors for the final time in October 1985, the lease on the building having expired.

Roger M Dilley's parents had recently retired to St Anne's on Sea, just along the coast from Blackpool, and he had assumed that this would enable him to make regular visits to the exhibition. He recalls the shock he felt on learning this was not to be: '[My parents] moved into the bungalow in the autumn and I visited them for the Christmas break. As we drove past the exhibition to go shopping, I noticed that the TARDIS door was open. "How exciting," I thought. "They must be setting it up for the new season." My folks dropped me off and we arranged to meet up later. I descended into the unusually silent gloom of the exhibition. No flashing lights. No Dalek voices warning me, "Smokers will be exterminated!" No cases of monsters ready to lurch toward me. I felt my way through the gloom to the only source of light emanating from the TARDIS control room. It had been completely gutted. No console, and all that remained of the outer viewing gallery walls was being ripped apart by workmen. "Hello," I said. "Are you getting the Exhibition ready for next year?" "No. They've closed it down. We're just clearing it out." And at that point my world came crashing down! My Mum said when she saw me later that she knew something awful had happened. She'd never seen me so upset.'

All the contents in the exhibition were stripped out. It is probably at this point, therefore, that certain pieces from *Doctor Who*'s history were simply discarded into skips and lost forever. However, some of the artefacts were retained and made available for display at the still-ongoing Longleat exhibition. Others would also feature in a new venture, the *Doctor Who*

Celebration USA Tour. The Daleks that had been displayed at Blackpool fell into the care of Martin Wilkie, Lorne Martin and BBC Enterprises. Dalek SM2 was given an overhaul and a fresh paint job of silver with black hemispheres and was then pressed into service as a promotional tool for BBC Enterprises in Australia. It was kept in excellent condition, and in 1995 was loaned to the Powerhouse Museum in Sydney for their SPFX: Secrets Behind the Screen exhibition. More recently, in 2013, it was used as one of a number of *Doctor Who* exhibits displayed at the ABC Centre in Sydney, celebrating the show's fiftieth anniversary. The other exhibition Daleks proved useful as sources for Dalek spare parts. Dalek B1 was partly cannibalised for the repair of Dalek 6-ex prior to a charity auction. Similarly, Dalek SM1 and Dalek B2 donated various parts to repair existing props for production of the television story 'Remembrance of the Daleks', allowing for *Doctor Who* to present one of the largest Dalek armies ever assembled.

Chapter 4
The Turbulent Eighties (1980-1989)

Doctor Who endured a turbulent time during the 1980s, but producer John Nathan-Turner was adept at keeping the show in the public eye, and exhibitions played a significant role. There were lows, such as the Blackpool closure in 1985, but there were also a number of highs, including original costumes being taken to America for the first time. By 1989, the show was no longer in production at the BBC, but exhibitions of items created during this decade helped to cement it in the public consciousness.

Madame Tussauds, London

The decade began with a *Doctor Who* display, referred to as the '*Doctor Who* Experience', designed by the team at the famous waxwork attraction Madame Tussauds. This was the first time since the BBC Special Effects Exhibition closed in June 1973 that *Doctor Who* items had been on display in London, the city where at that time the show's studios were actually based.

Tom Baker achieved the notable feat of being the first person to have two waxworks on display at the venue at the same time. In addition to a waxwork of the fourth Doctor, there was also one of his cactus-featured doppelganger Meglos from the 1980 story of the same name. Both sculpts of Baker were created by Judith Craig, and the waxwork Doctor would later be used in publicity photographs for the twentieth anniversary special 'The Five Doctors', in which Baker himself declined to appear. Baker was an enthusiastic model for the waxworks, attending the studios at Madame Tussauds for a number of sittings. The costume chosen for the mannequin was a replica of that seen throughout his last season in the role; it now resides in the private collection of Alexandra and Kevan of the Who Shop in London. *Doctor Who Magazine* covered the exhibition in Issue 48, published in January 1981, and featured a number of photographs of Baker posing with some of the exhibits.

The exhibition was designed by a team headed by Michael Wright, who described it as 'a total experience'.[126] Sound and lighting effects added to the atmosphere, and exhibits were set against elaborate backgrounds that had taken over four months of work to create.

The exhibition opened to the public at the Madame Tussauds site on Marylebone Road, London on 29 August 1980. In addition to waxworks of the fourth Doctor, Meglos and Lalla Ward's incarnation of companion Romana,

---

[126] *Doctor Who Monthly* #48.

exhibits included K-9, Davros, a Sontaran seated at a control console, a Nimon ('The Horns of Nimon'), a Foamasi ('The Leisure Hive'), a Marshman ('Full Circle') and a Dalek.

The Dalek displayed here boasted the shoulder section from Dalek 6 paired with a skirt section now referred to by aficionados as 'the exhibition skirt'. The latter had been constructed some time previously to replace the damaged skirt section of a 'goon' Dalek from 'Planet of the Daleks' used for public appearances at various locations across the UK. It is easily identifiable because it is wider than usual – having been made in two halves for ease of transportation – and because the rear panel is at a steeper angle. It was regularly paired with the upper body of Dalek Goon IV – one exception being that in a *Pebble Mill at One* appearance in 1978 it was paired with that of Dalek 7 – and as such was used in the production of 'Destiny of the Daleks', becoming a then-unique example of an exhibition prop gaining screen-used prop status afterwards.

From this point, Dalek 6-ex was also referred to as the 'Tussauds Dalek', because in addition to its unique skirt dimensions it had an equally unique paint job. Despite no Dalek having ever appeared on television in this livery, it was given a light blue body, supposedly Porsche Riviera Blue[127], with black collar and solar panels and silver hemispheres. After the Madam Tussauds display concluded, it was moved into storage before appearing at the Longleat Celebration of 1983. It would later have more appearances on television before moving into a private collection.

In a bonus interview on the Big Finish audio release 'Gallery of Ghouls', a story featuring sinister waxworks, Lalla Ward recalled that, due to delays, the Tussauds waxwork of Romana had not been ready for display at the time of the exhibition's opening; a fact that explains why relatively few photographs of it exist. Ward also revealed that the body was reused from an old Audrey Hepburn waxwork, as a new one was being created for the British actress.

The exhibition was due to close on 31 March 1981 but proved so popular that it remained open until the following year.

Garden Festival, Liverpool

In 1984 the International Garden Festival took place in Liverpool, running from 2 May to 14 October. The venue was an area of redeveloped land, which had been derelict and needed to be cleared of industrial waste as a part of a regeneration project. In addition to a number of sponsored gardens and a replica of the Beatles' Yellow Submarine, there was a large BBC tent. Inside were displayed a number of items and props from various programmes. However, stationed outside, on a sandy and rocky area designed to mirror an alien planet, was a TARDIS exterior police box, two full-size Daleks and a K-9. These are all thought to have been replicas constructed by Martin Wilkie. The

---

[127] www.sixthdoctorcostume.blogspot.co.uk/2010/11/bonhams-costume-sales-previous-auctions.html

two Daleks were given a grey paint job a little lighter than that of the gun-metal grey ones seen on screen in 'Resurrection of the Daleks'. In another variation from the screen-used props, the hemispheres and solar panel collar were painted silver. One of the Daleks also had some damage to its left side. The TARDIS however was more accurate, with a stacked roof and a shade of blue paint that was a reasonable match to that seen on the screen-used police box during Season 20.

Doctor Who USA Tour and Celebration

Following the closure of the Blackpool exhibition in 1985, many of the artefacts became available to be displayed elsewhere. Producer John Nathan-Turner's desire to bolster *Doctor Who*'s popularity in the USA resulted in a touring exhibition being mounted inside a 48ft-long trailer. This was titled simply the *Doctor Who* USA Tour. It involved co-operation and significant investment from Monarch International, a US company specialising in imports and exports, and the BBC's US distributor, Lionheart Television International. Costs were recovered from visitor entrance fees and from the sale of exclusive merchandise, including mugs, badges, T-shirts and keyrings bearing a memorable USA Tour logo, which was also emblazoned on the shop's plastic bags.

The trailer was specially constructed in Warrington by a company called Vanplan, and was unsuitable to be driven on British roads. Its exterior was adorned with artwork by Andrew Skilleter, well known to *Doctor Who* fans for his numerous covers for the Target *Doctor Who* novelisation range. The bright and colourful design featured the Dark Tower as seen in 'The Five Doctors' in an alien landscape that also provided the backdrop to the shop counter. TARDIS exterior doors at both ends of the trailer provided the entrance and exit from the exhibition. The Wembley-based Parker Hinson Productions Limited, who had worked with BBC Enterprises since 1971, was once again called upon to construct the exhibition interior.

A press launch was organised in the UK, featuring Colin Baker, Nicola Bryant (Peri) and Janet Fielding (Tegan), accompanied by a Cyberman and a Cryon from 'Attack of the Cybermen', along with the Doctor's roadster Bessie. Baker and Fielding donned screen-worn costumes for this event. August 1986's edition of *Doctor Who Magazine* featured Baker, Bryant and Fielding on the cover, and inside published numerous other images from the launch.[128]

After the trailer had been shipped to America, another publicity event was held on 8 May 1986, this time with Peter Davison and, amazingly, the notoriously anti-*Doctor Who* BBC One Controller Michael Grade in attendance.

The Tour began in Washington DC, and some of its subsequent stops were in cities selected to coincide with conventions being held there. The six surviving Doctors, including newcomer Sylvester McCoy, all made

---

[128] *Doctor Who Magazine* #115.

appearances during the Tour's duration.

Tony Burrough, a BBC set designer who had worked on five *Doctor Who* stories including 'The Keeper of Traken', had been appointed exhibition designer. Inside the trailer, the first display was of a replica TARDIS control room; the control console was mounted in one corner, and the room also featured a rather elaborate ceiling plus the obligatory roundelled walls. The console is believed to have been a new construction, with panels and time rotor differing from those of the one last seen in Blackpool.

The next artefact was Dalek N1, which had been seen on screen in 'Revelation of the Daleks'. Having been refurbished for the tour by Mike Tucker of the BBC Visual Effects Department, it boasted a new, glossy coat of paint, although still in the 'Imperial' white-and-gold livery. Mechanisms had now been fitted that rotated the dome and moved the weapon and the eye stalk, which had a unique pupil design. Being on the other side of the Atlantic precluded this Dalek's availability for use in the production of 'Remembrance of the Daleks' in 1988, the year that the Tour made its final stop.

The Tour exhibits were placed behind two-way reinforced mirrors, with spotlights and sound effects enhancing the atmosphere. They consisted of a mixture of full costumes and original masks. The full costumes, some of which were rigged to move and light up intermittently, included a Sea Devil and a Silurian ('Warriors of the Deep'), a Sontaran ('The Two Doctors'), a Tractator ('Frontios'), and the Cyber Controller ('Attack of the Cybermen'). These items had been pressed into service following the closure of the Blackpool exhibition, along with the Ergon ('Arc of Infinity'), which had been on display at Longleat.

Masks were particularly suited for inclusion in a touring exhibition, their smaller size making them easier to transport. Those featured in the USA Tour included Davros (Terry Molloy style); Sutekh (both full mask and jackal head, 'Pyramids of Mars'); a Cryon ('Attack of the Cybermen'); a Voc robot ('The Robots of Death'); and a Mutt ('The Mutants'). Masks of Styggron the Kraal ('The Android Invasion') and a Marshman ('Full Circle') shared a display with the Hecate priestess headdress from *K-9 and Company*.

Other exhibits included K-9; the smaller Malus handheld puppet ('The Awakening'); a 'The Moonbase'/'The Tomb of the Cybermen' Cyberman helmet; and Mestor the Gastropod ('The Twin Dilemma'), which was inaccurately called 'Nestor' in the accompanying flyer.

Outside the trailer, fans could pose with the Doctor's roadster Bessie, just as Colin Baker and others had done during the UK press launch.

After a change of name to the *Doctor Who* Celebration & Tour '87-'88, and two years spent visiting over 180 locations the length and breadth of America, the exhibition finally came to an end. The trailer was later left to rot in a scrapyard in Derbyshire, with Andrew Skilleter's wonderful artwork gradually weathering and fading away.

The World of _Doctor Who_ Exhibition at Space Adventure, Tooley Street, London

On 15 November 1988, Sylvester McCoy and Sophie Aldred (Ace) opened a new World of _Doctor Who_ Exhibition located on London's Tooley Street within the established Space Adventure attraction, which at that time housed the largest commercial flight simulator in Europe, allowing visitors to take a virtual journey through the universe. The event was used to celebrate the show's twenty-fifth anniversary, and was attended by actors, press and members of the production team. It included a preview screening of Episode 1 of 'Silver Nemesis' accompanied by a highlights trailer for the remainder of the story, presented in a similar style to a classic 'B' movie, with a voice-over by Cyber Leader actor David Banks.

Items on display from the show's latest season, which had begun transmission the previous month, included the Special Weapons Dalek from 'Remembrance of the Daleks', the Kandyman from 'The Happiness Patrol' and Cybermen from 'Silver Nemesis'.[129] The Special Weapons Dalek had a motor fitted that moved its weaponry up and down. Similarly, another Dalek, Dalek 14, with its 'Imperial' colour scheme, was fitted with motors that moved all three of its protuberances. During the exhibition's run, eager collectors would remove some of the gold pieces that had been attached to this Dalek's solar panel slats, leaving them bare white.[130] In August 1989, the Emperor Dalek prop from 'Remembrance of the Daleks' was also added to the displays.

Mike Tucker recalls contributing to the exhibition: 'Robert Allsopp, Derek Handley and I did a "Cyberman heads through the ages" display, we did a couple of Davros heads, and we did an Exxilon.' Other exhibits included a Sea Devil with head rotation from left to right ('Warriors of the Deep'); a Sontaran with glowing red eyes ('The Two Doctors'); a Plasmaton ('Time-Flight'); and a Pipe Person ('The Happiness Patrol').

In December 1988, BBC Two's _Behind the Screen_ programme broadcast an interview with producer John Nathan-Turner, revealing two other monster costumes that were on display, namely a Tractator ('Frontios') and a Silurian ('Warriors of the Deep'). The interview was conducted beside a TARDIS control console that was also amongst the exhibition's highlights.

While the exhibition was running, the Space Adventure shop sold a number of _Doctor Who_-related items, including a ruler printed with the wording 'I've Journeyed through the World of _Doctor Who_ Exhibition', a pencil and an eraser.[131]

Although writers David J Howe and Mark Stammers were in discussion with the managers of the exhibition about a special magazine publication to accompany it, nothing happened with this and the exhibition closed in November 1989, after a year _in situ_ at Tooley Street.

---

[129] www.youtube.com/watch?v=XD7hTYaTOp4
[130] www.dalek6388.co.uk/where-are-they-now/
[131] Howe & Blumberg (2000). _Howe's Transcendental Toybox_, pp.345-346.

Chapter 5
The Wilderness Years (1990-1995)

Despite *Doctor Who* being no longer in production at the BBC during the 1990s, the show remained popular with the public and continued to generate income for BBC Enterprises. Two exhibitions were organised in the early years of the decade: the first was the high-profile Behind the Sofa exhibition at the since-closed Museum of the Moving Image (MOMI) in London's Southbank Centre; the second, a much smaller affair, brought *Doctor Who* artefacts to the Isle of Wight for the first time.

Behind the Sofa Exhibition at the Museum of the Moving Image (MOMI), London

A press launch for the Behind the Sofa exhibition was held on 4 July 1991 with lots of former companion actors in attendance, including Carole Ann Ford, Nicholas Courtney, Deborah Watling, Bonnie Langford and Sophie Aldred. Initially set to run until 30 November that year, the exhibition was so well-attended that it remained open for longer than anticipated and was then moved to other locations. This popularity was due in part to extensive promotion via leaflets, newspaper and magazine advertisements and other publicity, including one particularly memorable poster featuring the image of a sink plunger with the tagline 'Find out how it conquered the galaxy'. Entrance tickets cost a reasonable £4.95 for adults, £3.50 for children, £4.20 for students and £15.00 for families of up to two adults and four children. [132] Opening hours were from 10am and 6pm, seven days a week.[133]

The exhibition received almost unanimous praise from fans, partly because of the extensive collection of original costumes on display, which was thought to be the biggest ever assembled at that time. It also became a favoured location for recording of *Doctor Who*-related video clips, and these offer a good opportunity to see what it was like.

Tom Baker recorded his introduction for the VHS video release of the unfinished and untransmitted story 'Shada' on 4 February 1992, the two-tape set being released that July. Baker is seen moving through the Behind the Sofa exhibition, having supposedly sneaked in through an emergency exit. Items visible in this material include the Magma Creature ('The Caves of Androzani'); Zog (from the stage play *The Ultimate Adventure*); a Tetrap ('Time

---

[132] *DWB* #92 and *Doctor Who Magazine* #175.
[133] *Doctor Who Magazine* #175.

and the Rani'); the K1 Robot ('Robot'), which prompts Baker to declare, 'Beat you, cock'; Cybermen; a 'walk-in' Dalek (described in more detail below); and Davros. As Baker moves across the room, there are also shots of Kiv the Mentor and the Alien Delegate ('The Trial of the Lord': 'Mindwarp'); a Yeti ('The Web of Fear'); a Gundan robot ('Warriors' Gate'); a Vervoid ('The Trial of the Time Lord': 'Terror of the Vervoids'); a Sea Devil ('Warriors of the Deep'); an Ice Warrior; and finally a Krarg from 'Shada' itself.

Baker's additional 'Shada' links, bridging the gaps in the story left by scenes uncompleted due to industrial action at the BBC, were also recorded at the exhibition. They were performed in character as the Doctor at the suggestion of Baker himself, according to John Nathan-Turner, who had persuaded him to be involved.[134] They reveal a number of other items on display, including the Android from 'The Visitation'; a Mandrel ('Nightmare of Eden'); the Melkur ('The Keeper of Traken'); a sarcophagus prop from 'Pyramids of Mars'; and K-9. These sequences can all now be found on the subsequent 'Shada' DVD and Blu-ray releases.

The video's credits reveal that the Krarg costume was provided by Lorne Martin, indicating that it might have been part of the established exhibitions collection. However, it was displayed for the first time at MOMI, to tie in with the VHS release. According to WhoSFX on Twitter, it had actually been withdrawn from a Bonhams auction catalogue a few months before the links were recorded.

The Behind the Sofa exhibition also featured in material recorded for other VHS video projects, including Peter Davison's links for *Daleks: The Early Years* and Colin Baker's for *Cybermen: The Early Years*, both released in 1992, and interviews with Dalek operator John Scott Martin, voice artist Roy Skelton and designer Raymond P Cusick for the *More Than 30 Years in the TARDIS* documentary, released in 1994.

In his sequences, Davison can be seen leaning against Dalek N1, which had appeared in 'Revelation of the Daleks'; it remained in its ivory-and-gold 'Imperial' livery and retained the movement mechanism fitted for the USA tour in the late 1980s. This display had a white plastic background featuring spherical hemispheres and geometric shapes mirroring the concentric circles of the Dalek eyestalk; parts of these vacuum-formed panels were created using a screen-used eyestalk sawn in half to create the shape.

Dalek N1 was accompanied by the Davros-concealing Emperor Dalek casing constructed for 'Remembrance of the Daleks'. The domed top section of the Emperor had been sourced from a large prop eyelid used in a BBC medical show called *Bodymatters*.[135] The lower skirt section originated from Dalek N5, which had been constructed from the original moulds used to create the Necros Daleks for 'Revelation of the Daleks' but had not appeared in that story. Additional parts came from props predating 'Revelation of the Daleks',

---

[134] *The Essential Doctor Who: The Time Lords* (2016), p52.
[135] www.dalek6388.co.uk/remembrance-of-the-daleks/

along with the neck section from a Blackpool exhibition prop, which had a differently-patterned mesh from usual screen-used ones. The skirt section had actually made a second appearance in 'Remembrance of the Daleks', as part of a grey-and-black 'Renegade' Dalek. Two small holes had been made in it, to allow for that Dalek to be pulled into position on location for its destruction scene, and then for the Emperor Dalek to be pulled onto the set of the Dalek spaceship's bridge, and those holes were still visible during its exhibition life. In between the location filming and the studio scenes, the prop had of course been stripped of its 'Renegade' livery and repainted in the 'Imperial' one. The domed top section had then been added, completing the dramatic look of a new and unique Dalek. Although used only once in a televised story, this Emperor prop proved to be a popular addition to Behind the Sofa's inventory. It would be prominent in many subsequent exhibitions over the following years.

Colin Baker's links for *Cybermen: The Early Years* were recorded with him sat in front of a display of Cyberman helmets and then stood beside a full Cyberman costume. Further interviews recorded at the exhibition for the same video release featured voice artist Roy Skelton, director Morris Barry and actress Wendy Padbury. Morris Barry was also seated in front of the display of Cyberman helmets to record his introduction for the 1992 VHS video release of 'The Tomb of the Cybermen'; this clip, which shows a closer view of the display, can now be found on the story's Special Edition DVD released as part of the *Revisitations 3* box set. Helmets featured in the display, some of which were noticeably damaged, included examples from 'The Wheel in Space' and 'The Invasion', and the Cyber Leader's black-handled variant from 'Revenge of the Cybermen'. Two other helmets were mounted onto the black wall behind; one from 'The Moonbase'/'The Tomb of the Cybermen' and the other of the most recent redesign from 'Earthshock' onwards.

Either side of this display of helmets stood two full Cyberman costumes from the 1980s. The whole display utilised the entrance/exit doors of the Cyberman ship seen in 'Silver Nemesis', with a metallic-silver-lined backdrop and a black doorway, the latter being where the helmets were mounted.

The aforementioned 'walk-in' Dalek, which featured prominently in the opening Peter Davison segment of the *Daleks: The Early Years* VHS release (material not currently available on DVD), was an exhibit specially created for Behind the Sofa. It took the form of a Dalek that had some of its back panels removed, allowing visitors to venture inside, move the plunger and weapon and see what it was like to inhabit a Dalek prop. The prop in question, referred to as Dalek 1-7, had the shoulder section of an original Dalek from 'The Daleks' and the skirt section of one created for 'The Chase'. It was positioned in front of mirrors, allowing those inside to see their Dalek reflection.

Another Dalek included in the Behind the Sofa exhibition but not seen in any of the video footage now available on DVD is referred to as Dalek 2-8. This was made up of an upper half dating from the very first Dalek story and a narrower-than-usual skirt section constructed for 'The Evil of the Daleks'. This prop had been rescued by visual effects pioneer Bernard Wilkie but was showing the wear and tear of years of rough handling. The top half was hanging over to one side and the paintwork was in far from pristine condition. However, it offered a rare opportunity for visitors to see a genuine 1960s Dalek.

Adjacent to the 'walk-in' Dalek was their creator Davros, retaining the look from his appearance in 'Revelation of the Daleks', including black torso and Terry Molloy-era mask. The mannequin used for this was not ideal, however; resulting in Davros leaning forward, amusingly giving the impression that he had fallen asleep. In another, intentionally witty touch, the K-9 prop was displayed with a dog bowl and a bag of Winalot dog food! Aside from these diversions, the displays were consistent with those featured in previous exhibitions, although effort had been made to add complementary neutral backgrounds.

The exhibition was detailed in a two-page, Philip Newman-written feature in Issue 178 of *Doctor Who Magazine*. Once again, visitors entered via a TARDIS police box exterior. Inside, in keeping with the exhibition's theme, a mannequin of a young viewer was crouched behind the sofa of a 1960s-style living-room, watching as the show's first ever episode, 'An Unearthly Child', was shown on a television set of the era. Nearby, another police box, this time a model approximately 5ft tall, was mounted against a starry background to show the famous time/spaceship travelling through the universe.

A few familiar outfits were on display in glass cabinets, including those of the sixth and seventh Doctors, and those of companions Ace and Adric. However, for many fans, the main attraction was the numerous monster costumes on show. These included the Garm ('Terminus'); a Silurian ('Warriors of the Deep'); Mestor the Gastropod ('The Twin Dilemma'); a Plasmaton ('Time-Flight'); Omega ('Arc of Infinity'); and Sil ('Vengeance on Varos' and 'The Trial of the Time Lord': 'Mindwarp'). The Sylvester McCoy era of the programme, being the most recent, was well represented, with a seated God of Ragnarok from 'The Greatest Show in the Galaxy'; the Giant Brain prop created for 'Time and the Rani'; and the Dalek transmat device from 'Remembrance of the Daleks'.

The fanzine *Doctor Who Bulletin* (*DWB*) reported in 1991 that also on display at the MOMI exhibition were three creatures from the proposed big-screen *Doctor Who* movie *Last of the Time Lords* that, ultimately, never came to fruition. These included a rather demonic head mask, complete with horns.

Another interesting display showcased some of the *Doctor Who* merchandise that had been released over the years. This included badges, toys, money boxes and all variety of Dalek models. Behind the Sofa made its own contribution to this aspect of *Doctor Who* history, as a range of exclusive items could be bought from the exhibition shop. A pencil, a badge, a mug and four specially-designed T-shirts were just some of the mementos that fans could take home from their visit. The T-shirts proved particularly popular and were even advertised in the leaflet promoting the exhibition. They were priced at

£9.99 each but were available only in Large or Extra Large sizes. One of them featured words representing the *Doctor Who* theme tune ('Diddly dum'), a design that was also reproduced on the mug.[136] A monochrome poster featuring a photograph of the Doctor and a Dalek from 'Planet of the Daleks' and a colour facsimile of the *Dr Who and the Daleks* movie poster had both been sold by MOMI in the late 1980s and may have remained available during the exhibition's run. Four further posters, originally intended only for use in advertising the exhibition on the London Underground, were also made available to purchase after it was realised that fans were making off with them to keep as souvenirs.[137]

To coincide with the MOMI exhibition, a *Doctor Who* weekend was staged at the adjacent National Film Theatre (since renamed the BFI Southbank). Such was the popularity of this event that some fans who wanted to attend were left disappointed, as the majority of the 200 tickets were snapped up in advance sales to members of the British Film Institute (BFI). Prominent fan Jeremy Bentham opened proceedings with a history of *Doctor Who* from its beginnings in 1963. The event then continued with presentations by a number of individuals who had worked on the show, starting with Bernard Wilkie and Jack Kine, formerly of the BBC Visual Effects Department. Headline act on the Saturday was Colin Baker, who discussed his time as the sixth Doctor. Costume designer June Hudson told fans about her work, as did theatre director Carole Todd, who had brought *The Ultimate Adventure* to the stage. Brigadier actor Nicholas Courtney then closed the first day. The Sunday saw contributions from visual effects designer Mat Irvine; director Fiona Cumming; Sophie Aldred (Ace); *Doctor Who Magazine* editor John Freeman; Dick Mills of the BBC Radiophonic Workshop; writer and script editor Terrance Dicks; and finally 1980s producer John Nathan-Turner and seventh Doctor actor Sylvester McCoy.

Even after the exhibition's departure from MOMI on the South Bank, *Doctor Who* continued to be represented there into the late 1990s. Dalek L2, which had been in storage after updates to the Longleat exhibition, spent a period on display in the foyer area, and amongst the Museum's other treasures, visitors could see a TARDIS police box, an 'Earthshock'-style Cyberman and the K1 Robot. Director David Maloney was interviewed standing outside the venue for the BBV-produced independent documentary *30 Years of Time Travel and Beyond*, with the Dalek and police box clearly visible inside.

Behind the Sofa Exhibition at the Paisley Museum, Paisley

Following the end of its run at MOMI, the Behind the Sofa exhibition reopened in the Paisley Museum in Scotland, as reported by Liam Rudden in Issue 189 of *Doctor Who Magazine*. Described as 'a good deal smaller than its MOMI

---

[136] Howe & Blumberg (2000). *Howe's Transcendental Toybox*, pp.259.
[137] Howe & Blumberg (2000). *Howe's Transcendental Toybox*, pp.338.

counterpart', this remount with publicised by way of a special press launch held on 20 March 1992, with Jon Pertwee in attendance. It then opened to the public from 28 March 1992 until 30 June 1992. [138]

Highlighting the draw of *Doctor Who*, Paul Wetherall from Paisley Museum was quoted as saying, 'Since Behind the Sofa opened, the number of visitors to the Museum has increased by between two and three-fold!'[139]

To coincide with the exhibition, an event was held on 31 May 1992 at the Paisley Arts Centre, with Tom Baker, Nicholas Courtney, John Nathan-Turner and Carole Ann Ford taking part in talks and question-and-answer sessions hosted by one-time *Doctor Who* production manager Ian Fraser.

Behind the Sofa Exhibition at the Exploratory, Bristol

The Behind the Sofa exhibition was next relocated once again to the Exploratory venue at Temple Meads in Bristol. This version was reported as being largely unchanged from how it had appeared in London, and presumably therefore in Paisley. It ran from 18 July 1993 to 1 November 1993.

The Needles, Alum Bay, Isle of Wight

A small *Doctor Who* exhibition was then mounted in a large tent at popular tourist spot the Needles on the Isle of Wight. This is thought to be have been during 1994, following the closure of the Behind the Sofa exhibition in Bristol.

One of the displays featured the Mentors Sil and Lord Kiv with the alien delegate that had appeared in 'The Trial of a Time Lord': 'Mindwarp' and had been displayed together in Longleat as far back as 1987 before appearing at MOMI. Other exhibits included the large Malus ('The Awakening'); Drathro and the L1 robot ('The Trial of the Time Lord': 'The Mysterious Planet'); a Vervoid ('The Trial of a Time Lord': 'Terror of the Vervoids'); Haemovores ('The Curse of Fenric'); a Mandrel ('Nightmare of Eden'); a Cyberman and the Nemesis statue ('Silver Nemesis'); the Pirate Captain and Polyphase Avatron ('The Pirate Planet'); Cheetah People ('Survival'); and a God of Ragnarok with the Chief Clown and another clown from 'The Greatest Show in the Galaxy'.

Care was taken to place the items in appropriate environments making for as effective a display as possible. For example, the Haemovores were positioned in a graveyard; the Malus was mounted against a stone wall; and the Mandrel was at home in a jungle. In addition to the larger displays, a selection of monster masks were also exhibited, including those of an Exxilon ('Death to the Daleks'); a Gundan robot ('Warriors' Gate'); and a Silurian and a Sea Devil (both from 'Warriors of the Deep').

No *Doctor Who* exhibition would be complete without the Daleks, and in this case 'Imperial' Daleks I2 and I4, created for Season 25's 'Remembrance of

---

[138] *Doctor Who Magazine* #189.
[139] *Doctor Who Magazine* #189.

the Daleks', were used. Both required new lamps to be fitted onto their domes. They were positioned in a mock-up of the cellar beneath Coal Hill School, complete with transmat prop, as seen during the story. After the exhibition closed, the two halves of these Daleks were mistakenly mixed up; Dalek I2-I4 moved on to the Llangollen exhibition, but Dalek I4-I2's whereabouts are currently unknown.

An Uncertain Future

Although *Doctor Who* exhibitions had proved popular across the UK and USA, the 1990s were continuing with the prospect of no further episodes of the show being made for television, and an inevitable decline in public interest. Consequently, the surviving costumes and props now had an uncertain future. The BBC had already sold off a number of items from their substantial stores, the first of a series of *Doctor Who* auctions at Bonhams in London having taken place on 11 May 1991. The possibility of further unique and precious artefacts disappearing forever into private collections was becoming increasingly likely. However, an unlikely saviour was to be found in the form of a model railway manufacturer.

Chapter 6
The *Doctor Who* Experience, Llangollen (1995–2003)

North Wales is perhaps not the most obvious location for a *Doctor Who* exhibition, but in 1995 the town of Llangollen in Denbighshire became home to the *Doctor Who* Experience. This was just one part of an attraction that included a model railway world and also provided an opportunity to observe the manufacturing process of a notable range of *Doctor Who* merchandise. Located at the Lower Dee Exhibition Centre on the bank of the River Dee, it was open all year round, giving it an advantage over the seasonal Longleat exhibition. Becoming a popular location for fans to visit and meet *Doctor Who* personalities, it helped to keep the show in the public eye at a time when, save for one evening in 1996, there were no new episodes broadcast.

The exhibition was the idea of husband-and-wife team David and Pauline Boyle, who under their Dapol brand name were best known for marketing model railway components. In 1987 Dapol had been granted a licence to produce *Doctor Who* action figures and other merchandise – a venture that had led to them being contacted by many fans who wanted to see first-hand how the range was manufactured. At that time, the company's activities were split over a number of different locations, as David Boyle explained: 'We were already operating from a very large, 33,000-square-foot factory in Winsford. We also had subsidiary units in two other places ... and a small warehouse in Northwich. So we were quite well spread out, and were looking to see if we could combine the production into one area.' This desire to streamline Dapol's operations, coupled with *Doctor Who* fans' enthusiasm to observe the manufacturing process, was what ultimately sparked the idea of an exhibition – something that would have the added benefit of generating extra income for Dapol at a time when it was facing stiff competition from Chinese companies. 'There was such a demand from people to visit us that we opened up the factory,' Boyle recalled. 'We made it into a tour and charged people to go around. That then subsidised the operation.'

Taking advantage of his existing relationship with BBC Enterprises, Boyle began exploring the possibility of adding a formal *Doctor Who* exhibition to the factory tour, as he explains: 'Through the offices of Experience Design we met two of the top people, Martin Wilkie and Lorne Martin. Lorne Martin was a wonderful guy. We discussed potentially having a *Doctor Who* exhibition as part of the tour.'

A suitable factory for Dapol's needs was identified in the town of Llangollen. 'It was a big building,' Boyle recalled, 'which had been totally refurbished by the Welsh Development Authority. We had an agreement with them, and we decided we would buy the building, which was a phenomenal amount of money that we had to invest. When we discussed this with the BBC, they said that they would be prepared to work with us and establish a *Doctor Who* exhibition for a period of time. So, thinking about this, we started to move our production from Winsford and Northwich to Llangollen.'

With the new premises purchased and the BBC interested in providing artefacts for an exhibition to complement the factory tour, the transition began. At that point, however, a disastrous fire threatened Dapol's very existence, throwing everything into doubt. David Boyle reflected on the tragedy: 'It was during this transition period that we had our major destruction. A fire was started deliberately in the Winsford factory by a gang of kids. We couldn't believe it. I'd gone from a multi-millionaire to owing the bank more money, all because of a box of matches.' With no insurance money forthcoming, the investment in the new Llangollen factory having already been made, and practically everything in the Winsford factory having been destroyed, it seemed all was lost.

Fortunately, some items had already been moved, including lots of stock products, and were now safe. However, seventeen expensive moulding machines had been destroyed, and the moulds and tools had all been exposed to intense heat and then doused in water when the fire was extinguished. Crucial to the business's continuation were the injection moulds, stored on racks and numbering about 2,500 in total. David Boyle recounted how he saved Dapol by retrieving these moulds:

'The moment the fire was put out and cleared, we could just about climb into the area. The pallet racks had kept the roof above from falling completely through. However, it had come down on top of the racks, and once it had burnt away, it had then been doused with water. So all of these moulds were covered in filth. Black, burnt filth everywhere. So I went in and opened every single mould with a crowbar and hammers and chisels. I then sprayed the faces back to back with a compound called Turbo, which was provided by one of our suppliers – an absolutely wonderful product. It took me a whole day, a whole night and half the next day to complete that. When I'd finished it, I was slimy and covered in muck. I walked out into the road, took all my clothes off, got into my car, drove home, had a shower and then came back with new clothes on to start to work again. I know that that saved all but two of the moulds. We then moved the moulds from Winsford to Llangollen by lorry, and there they were stored until we could wash them clean and prepare them.'

Boyle's determination in salvaging the moulds meant that Dapol could continue to manufacture its model railway products and remain in business. But there was still the daunting prospect of filling the newly-acquired exhibition centre. 'The BBC came to see us,' said Boyle. 'Lorne Martin particularly. We spent a long time discussing, and in the end they said to me that if I could set up Llangollen properly, they would be prepared to put together a *Doctor Who* exhibition to put on display the costumes that had come back from America, and additional new ones.'

Following the USA tour and the Behind the Sofa and Isle of Wight exhibitions, the remaining artefacts not installed at Longleat had been put into storage. The BBC's willingness to supply them for display in Llangollen was due in large part to their wish to avoid the ongoing cost of maintaining this extensive collection. Had it not been for Dapol's initiative, these costumes and props would probably have been sold off; but now they would actually earn the BBC a regular income, as Boyle explained: 'The BBC no longer had to pay for the costumes to be in storage, because we protected them and looked after them, and [under our licence for the exhibition] we then paid them a percentage of the money that came from the people that visited us, which was quite wonderful when you think about it. So it was a win-win situation for everybody.'

Mounting a *Doctor Who* exhibition was still a bit of a gamble, given that the show was no longer in regular production and arguably at its lowest ebb of popularity, but David Boyle had faith in it: 'There was no *Doctor Who* available, it was not showing; as far as a lot of people were concerned at the time, *Doctor Who* was finished. Being a lifetime *Doctor Who* fan, I had trust that things would change, that it would come back again, but there was no-one in the BBC with this optimism, and the general belief was that it was over.'

Boyle's confidence has since been borne out, with *Doctor Who* regaining its rightful place atop the BBC's global brands. In the 1990s, however, few people saw that coming. Experience Design & Management, formed in 1993, came on board with the project, assisting in the design of the exhibition. The company had grown out of the partnership between Lorne Martin and Martin Wilkie, who had contributed to several *Doctor Who* exhibitions over the years. Llangollen was to be one of their first new projects. However, to deliver the exhibition required more investment from Dapol. 'This was not a free gift from the BBC, make no mistake about that,' noted Boyle. 'We had to pay for the building, the cabinets, the TVs, the display stands and everything. This cost me an absolute fortune. I was already horrendously in debt. I had to go around and scavenge every penny I could find to be able to get the money to properly house the exhibition.'

After several years of hard work, the Boyles finally managed to open their new attraction. The whole exhibition centre totalled 18,000 square feet and incorporated a model railway world and a Llangollen town museum in addition to the toy and model railway factory and the *Doctor Who* exhibition. Three floors of the building were utilised, with the factory and *Doctor Who* exhibition covering the ground and first floor. Despite the cost involved, detailed attention was given to ensuring that the *Doctor Who* artefacts on display were properly preserved and cared for. The exhibition had very low lighting levels, and the objects were positioned behind reinforced glass so that they could be kept at a consistent temperature.

Overcoming the setback of the earlier fire, David and Pauline Boyle had succeeded in delivering a fantastic attraction appealing to a wide variety of people, be they *Doctor Who* fans, model railway enthusiasts or those simply intrigued by the factory's manufacturing processes. At the time, the *Doctor Who* exhibition was the largest ongoing display of original items from the show and was advertised as the biggest science fiction exhibition in the world.

David Boyle was in periodic contact with John Nathan-Turner at the BBC to discuss issues relating to the action figure range, and it was the producer who made a suggestion for adding to the exhibition. 'I'd paid all the expenses of setting up the exhibition,' Boyle recalled, 'built it up and put it in. And then [Nathan-Turner] said to us, "Well, we've got some more stuff and equipment, can we extend the exhibition?" I said, "Of course you can." So we paid them another big sum, I think somewhere in the region of £50,000 to £100,000, for them to build the glass cabinets with all the displays in the corridors. So there was a second-stage expansion in Llangollen.'

Colin Baker was in attendance for the exhibition's opening on 17 June 1995, becoming the first of many *Doctor Who* luminaries to visit the venue. Admission prices in 1999 for the *Doctor Who* Experience section were £5.50 for an adult and £3.25 for a child, which seems very reasonable by comparison with more recent exhibitions. A souvenir brochure from the time claimed that visitor numbers exceeded 50,000 people a year; particularly impressive given that the show was no longer regularly broadcast on television.

Like Longleat, the Llangollen exhibition became a favourite location for *Doctor Who* fans. One of these visitors was Joe Lidster, who would go onto write for Big Finish's *Doctor Who* audio range, episodes of *Torchwood* and *The Sarah Jane Adventures*, plus the walk-through adventure starring Peter Capaldi for the later *Doctor Who* Experience in Cardiff. 'I went to the Llangollen exhibition years ago when I was at university,' he says. 'I can't remember a huge amount about it, to be honest, but it was fun.' Another visitor was Chris Parrot, who would later work as a designer on the *Doctor Who* Experience in London Olympia. He remembers the exhibition fondly, saying, 'When I was little we had great times at Dapol. All the staff made an amazing effort with us as a family, and one time I even sat in the Whomobile!' The latter vehicle, specially made for Jon Pertwee to use in his final season as the Doctor in 1974, was sometimes parked outside the exhibition for visitors to see. Another of the Doctor's vehicles, Bessie, which had debuted in 'Doctor Who and the Silurians', was also at the exhibition, sometimes outside the building but at other times in a corridor close to the factory entrance. This was in fact a replica owned by David Boyle rather than the original car, but another example of the notable items that drew fans to Llangollen.

The Exhibition

After climbing up a few steps, visitors encountered a replica Dalek guarding the entrance to the Dapol building and providing an early photo opportunity. If weather conditions were unfavourable, the Dalek would be moved inside the building, where a reception desk stood in the centre for tickets to be purchased. In one corner of this area was a glass case displaying a Cyberman of the style featured in 'Silver Nemesis', but with a matt silver helmet as opposed to the shiny ones seen on screen. Visitors could then enter the exhibition straight ahead or visit the Dapol shop up some stairs to the right. Occasionally, volunteers wearing monster costumes or in a replica Dalek would patrol the exhibition and creep up on unsuspecting fans.

The exhibition was spread over three galleries and featured many of the items that had been previously on display elsewhere. On entering, the first sight was often a replica TARDIS police box, but occasionally a Dalek would take its place in front of a brick wall. Around the corner was one of the oldest surviving Daleks – Dalek 2-8 or the 'Wilkie Dalek', so named after Bernard Wilkie, who had rescued it from being junked – as previously seen at the MOMI exhibition.

Opposite the 'Wilkie Dalek' was a 1963-style front room set-up, with *Doctor Who*'s first ever episode, 'An Unearthly Child', playing on a vintage television set. This was again as previously seen at MOMI, although an adult viewer mannequin had now been added, seated on the sofa behind which the young boy mannequin still crouched. Another item transferred from MOMI was the miniature TARDIS model on a starry background to show it in flight across space. A Dalek with the colour scheme of those in 'The Evil of the Daleks' was also in this area, placed in front of a series of mirrors; a photograph of this featured on a postcard available in the shop.

Gallery 1

Following entry through a set of oversized TARDIS doors, visitors reached a recreated TARDIS control room. This included a replica of the console used on television from 'The Five Doctors' through to the end of the show's original run in 1989. In fact, only half of the console was built; it was placed flush up against a mirrored wall to create the illusion of the full six-sided item. 'I seem to remember them not having a complete TARDIS console,' Joe Lidster confirms, 'but rather half of one and a mirror to make it seem complete. I hope it was the case, as that's a very *Doctor Who* way to deal with budget limitations!' A Time Lord costume was at times stood next to the console, and some roundelled walls were placed opposite the mirrored one. Between these roundelled walls was a doorway through which began the displays representing the Doctors.

Some of the rarest articles to have survived were found in the display cases here, including walking canes used by William Hartnell. Hartnell's immediate successors were represented by a pair of trousers and braces worn by Patrick Troughton in 'The Two Doctors' and Jon Pertwee's cape from 'The Five Doctors'. Between the cases, a small television screen played clips of the Doctor's regenerations. Also on display was one of Tom Baker's iconic scarves, of the Season 18 style seen from 'The Leisure Hive' to 'Logopolis'. On a hanger nearby was a waistcoat worn by Baker in 'The Power of Kroll' and 'The Armageddon Factor'.

The Peter Davison, Colin Baker and Sylvester McCoy Doctors were represented by complete costumes. Baker's ensemble was accompanied by the colourful waistcoat from 'The Two Doctors', and both cream and brown versions of McCoy's jacket were displayed along with his screen-used question-mark umbrella.

A selection of surviving companion costumes were also to be found in one corner. These included Turlough's school uniform ('Mawdryn Undead'); Nyssa's costume from 'Terminus' and butterfly mask from 'Black Orchid'; Adric's regular outfit ('Full Circle'); Peri's clothes from 'The Mysterious Planet' segment of 'The Trial of the Time Lord'; and Sarah Jane Smith's pink costume from 'The Five Doctors'. As the latest on-screen companion, Ace was represented via her iconic baseball jacket along with the grey dress seen in 'The Curse of Fenric'.

Adjacent to these companion costumes was a display of six Cyberman helmets, charting the development of the silver creatures over more than 20 years of on-screen adventures. This was very similar to the one previously seen at MOMI, but also included the Cyber Controller's helmet from 'Attack of the Cybermen'.

In the next display case were two costumes typifying the 'monster era' of Patrick Troughton's second Doctor; a Yeti from 'The Web of Fear' and an Ice Warrior that had debuted in 'The Ice Warriors'. Behind these were various Cyberman costume pieces from the 1980s, including the undersuit, gloves and chest unit. Also displayed was a Time Lord costume; this was in a style similar to those seen in 'The War Games', but according to collector Andrew Beech dated from 'The Five Doctors'. A further miscellany of costumes was stored in what was described as the 'TARDIS wardrobe'.

In the intersecting corridor between the galleries were cases showing examples of Dapol's merchandise and a reproduction of the *Doctor Who and the Daleks* movie poster with a plaque acknowledging the two big-screen adventures that had starred Peter Cushing. Other *Doctor Who* artwork and *Radio Times* covers lined the corridor, alongside another display case commemorating the Dapol factory fire that had nearly prevented the exhibition from opening.

Gallery 2 – The 'Hall of Monsters'

The second gallery was titled the 'Hall of Monsters' and featured a wide variety of monster costumes from the show. Perhaps allowing for the fact that some younger visitors might have been frightened by the prospect of coming face to face with hideous creatures from across the universe, it was possible to skip this part of the exhibition and move straight on to the third gallery if desired. However, those children – and adults – who bravely ventured forth found themselves in a dimly-lit area complete with atmospheric sounds, making for an eerily memorable experience.

The monster costumes, which continued into the third gallery, were displayed in loosely chronological order according to their first on-screen appearances. First up was a Silurian, although this was not a costume from the creatures' 1970 debut story but one from their return in 'Warriors of the Deep'. Activating a button on the side of the display case caused the creature to flap its arms; just one of the subtle movement mechanisms fitted to certain exhibits, adding to the unnerving atmosphere for younger visitors. The next monster was from Jon Pertwee's second season as the Doctor, one of the blobby Axon creatures from 'The Claws of Axos'; this had also been seen at the Blackpool exhibition on opening in 1974. Omega's costume from 'Arc of Infinity' was curiously paired with the jacket worn by Pertwee's Doctor in 'The Time Monster' and 'The Three Doctors' and briefly tried on by Sylvester McCoy's in 'Time and the Rani'. A button on the side of this display case illuminated the lights on the Omega headpiece. Another creature represented by its second on-screen appearance in 'Warriors of the Deep' was a Sea Devil. A strobing light effect neatly illuminated this monster, which would turn its head and open and close its mouth.

Next came the Morbius monster from 'The Brain of Morbius', looking robustly healthy despite its tumble down a cliff on the planet Karn. In the final year, this costume was moved to the Longleat exhibition, where a laboratory scene was created to mirror the story's *Frankenstein* inspiration.

The next display case boasted a collection of artefacts from a number of different stories: an 'eight legs' giant spider from 'Planet of the Spiders'; a Brontosaurus model used in the production of 'Invasion of the Dinosaurs'; and a large Egyptian sarcophagus from 'Pyramids of Mars'.

Not to be confused with the hideous monstrosities in the gallery was the ever-faithful K-9, accompanied by the Hecate priestess costume from the spin-off *K-9 and Company*, an arrangement similar to that seen at Longleat in 1982. K-9 could have its visual receptor grille illuminated by the press of an exterior button.

The Pirate Captain from 'The Pirate Planet', as first exhibited at Blackpool in 1979, was again accompanied by his robot parrot, the Polyphase Avatron, perched on his right shoulder. Another exhibit from the Key to Time season, again first seen at Blackpool in 1979, was the large Kroll miniature created for 'The Power of Kroll'. In the same cabinet was a Mandrel from 'Nightmare of Eden', a regular exhibition feature, particularly at Longleat, along with a *Mona Lisa* painting used in the production of the ever-popular story 'City of Death'.

As previously mentioned, the exhibits were all placed behind reinforced glass to help ensure their longevity. This had an added benefit in the case of the Gundan robot from 'Warriors' Gate', as when it swung its battle-axe in the familiar movement first seen at Longleat during 1981, the blade of the axe now hit the glass, making it appear that the robot was trying to break out. Deliberate or not, this certainly made for a frightening encounter for those younger visitors who had bravely ventured into the 'Hall of Monsters'.

Sharing the next display case were a Marshman from 'Full Circle' and a Krarg from 'Shada'. The latter costume was the same one memorably installed at MOMI to coincide with the infamously incomplete story's video release. Another element borrowed from the MOMI exhibition was the prop doorway from 'Silver Nemesis', which was reused as a backdrop for another Cyberman display. At some point prior to the Llangollen exhibition's closing, Adric's costume was repositioned from the companions' area in the first gallery to this Cybermen display in the 'Hall of Monsters', evoking memories of the young Alzarian's demise in the classic story 'Earthshock'. The prop Cyberscope from 'Silver Nemesis', previously on display at Longleat, was also added to complete the scene.

The following case featured an Argolin costume, loaned by Andrew Beech, and a Foamasi from 'The Leisure Hive'; the Melkur statue from 'The Keeper of Traken'; masks and spears from the fifth Doctor's debut story 'Castrovalva'; the Trickster mask from 'Kinda'; and Plasmatons from 'Time-Flight'. Also on display was the animatronic scarred Terileptil head from 'The Visitation', accompanied by a complete Terileptil costume consisting of the red-hued body coupled with the blue-hued mask, as first seen at Blackpool back in 1982. At some point during the exhibition's run, the blue-hued mask was either removed or lost and the animatronic head relocated to replace it.

Nearby, the end of Peter Davison's time as the Doctor was commemorated with the Magma beast creature, the head of the Queen Bat and Sharaz Jek's mask, all seen during 'The Caves of Androzani'. Other items on display from the fifth Doctor's era included the Garm from 'Terminus'; a full-length pink-and-yellow snake puppet and a black-and-yellow snake head used as representations of the Mara during 'Snakedance'; a Mawdryn headpiece from 'Mawdryn Undead'; and, mounted on a wall, the Ergon head from 'Arc of Infinity'. In the next display case, the large Malus face from 'The Awakening' was accompanied by a Jacondan headpiece and Mestor the Gastropod from 'The Twin Dilemma'. Opposite were a Tractator from 'Frontios' and a Sea Devil mask from 'Warriors of the Deep'. The smaller Malus hand puppet from 'The Awakening' was housed in a small display case of its own, with glowing red eyes and its head rotating from side to side.

A selection of weapons from a variety of stories was exhibited nearby, including a Sontaran rifle from 'The Two Doctors' and a Kontron crystal deflector gun and Karfelon laser rifle from 'Timelash'. The next few exhibits came from Colin Baker's last story, 'The Trial of the Time Lord'. These included the L1 Robot and Drathro ('The Mysterious Planet'); Sil, Kiv and the Alien Delegate ('Mindwarp'); and two Vervoids, the latter being displayed with an additional Vervoid mask plus hand pieces ('Terror of the Vervoids'). A Mogarian costume and an additional Mogarian mask ('Terror of the Vervoids') were positioned in the same display case as Drathro.

The 'Hall of Monsters' finally concluded with a display consisting of a Sontaran ('The Two Doctors'), a Cryon ('Attack of the Cybermen'), a Tyrannosaurus embryo in a jar ('The Mark of the Rani'), the Karfelon laser canon ('Timelash') and the Sontaran's helmet.

Gallery 3

The final gallery showcased the Sylvester McCoy era, which at the time of the exhibition's opening was of course the most recently televised. The seventh Doctor's debut story 'Time and the Rani' was represented by the Giant Brain prop, a Tetrap and the Rani's costume as worn on screen by Kate O'Mara. After this came further items from Season 24; a Cleaner robot from 'Paradise Towers', a Navarino from 'Delta and the Bannermen', an animatronic Tetrap mask from 'Time and the Rani' and the Pool Cleaner from 'Paradise Towers'. In a lone display case was the Nemesis/Lady Peinforte statue from the twenty-fifth anniversary story 'Silver Nemesis'. In a break from the seventh Doctor theme, there then came a selection of Time Lord costumes, including a number with the elaborate fibreglass ceremonial collars and one Chancellery Guard.

The tribute to the seventh Doctor's era then resumed with a number of story-specific displays, such as the Kandyman, Fifi and a Pipe Person from 'The Happiness Patrol' and a God of Ragnarok, Clown costumes and the robot Bus Conductor head from 'The Greatest Show in the Galaxy'.

The (at the time) final televised season was well represented, with exhibits such as the Control costume and a Husk from 'Ghost Light', armour from 'Battlefield' and the Master's costume plus two Cheetah People from 'Survival'. Also included, from 'The Curse of Fenric', were the trio of Haemovores that had been first displayed at Longleat in 1990, one in a naval uniform and the other two in medieval-style costumes. Another display of items dating from 1989, this time not from a televised *Doctor Who* story but from *The Ultimate Adventure* stage play, consisted of the alien creature Zog and a flying insect alien mask.

The final and most substantial display case saw the Daleks providing the exhibition's climax, just as they had at Longleat and Blackpool over the years. This exhibit included a number of artefacts from 'Remembrance of the Daleks', including an 'Imperial' Dalek (Dalek I2/I4), the destroyed Dalek skirt, the Special Weapons Dalek, the Emperor Dalek, the 'Imperial' Dalek transmat prop and the Dalek battle computer, the latter of which mistakenly had a Terry Molloy-style Davros mask placed on its seat. Another Dalek was added to represent the 'Renegade' faction; to achieve this, Dalek N1, a prop that had appeared on screen only in 'Revelation of the Daleks', was repainted in a black-and-gold colour scheme that had not actually been seen in 'Remembrance of the Daleks'. The display retained the white plastic background constructed for the MOMI exhibition.

The 'walk-in' Dalek, also previously seen at MOMI, became another memorable feature of Gallery 3. It was again placed in front of mirrors, but now a voice modulator was installed in the dome so that visitors could chant the legendary battle cry of 'Exterminate'.

Merchandise

Within the building it was also possible to observe the manufacturing process of Dapol's action figures. Trays and trays of Daleks and other monsters were a common sight as they emerged from the factory. A small shop at the end of the tour then allowed visitors to purchase some of these very figures. Other *Doctor Who* merchandise items produced by Dapol included a 1997 pocket diary available in a choice of maroon, blue or black and priced at £1.00, and an address book available in black, red or white and priced at £1.75. Both of these featured the diamond *Doctor Who* logo.[140] Other stationery items included holographic glitter pens available in gold, purple, silver, red or green and priced at £1.75, and pencils with a tip eraser available in yellow, gold, blue, green or red and priced at 45p each.[141] Other exhibition merchandise included embroidered polo shirts, car stickers and souvenir brochures.

---

[140] Howe, D J and Blumberg, A T (2000), *Howe's Transcendental Toybox*.
[141] Howe, D J and Blumberg, A T (2000), *Howe's Transcendental Toybox*.

The shop also stocked some popular non-Dapol *Doctor Who* merchandise, including the BBC video range and the latest book titles. A separate and much larger section of the shop was dedicated to Dapol's model railway products.

Events

Like Longleat, the Llangollen exhibition became a popular venue for actor appearances and signings. Those visiting over the years included Peter Davison, Colin Baker – who had attended the opening in 1995 – and Sylvester McCoy. On one memorable occasion, on 22 February 1997, Davison was accompanied by former companion Sophie Aldred (Ace) and producer John Nathan-Turner, all meeting fans and signing autographs.

Such events were, and remain to this day, a successful way of boosting exhibition attendance figures and revenue. At Llangollen, though, things were taken a step further with the innovation of 'Travellers in Time' packages. Fans who paid to participate in these could join an actor who had appeared in *Doctor Who*, enjoy a meal with them at their shared hotel, visit the local steam railway and canal, and of course tour the exhibition itself. The events proved particularly successful, with demand outstripping availability, as organiser David Boyle proudly recalled:

'We ran about, I don't know, maybe thirty of them. We had guests including the Master [actor Anthony Ainley], K-9 [voice artist John Leeson], Peter Davison, Colin Baker, Sylvester McCoy and Sophie Aldred. In the evenings we had great fun.

'We would utilise the steam railway in Llangollen, with whose owners I was very friendly. So we had trips on the train. We even staged a Cyberman attack against the Doctor and the companion on one of the trains, which was quite wonderful! And then we had the horse-drawn boats – again, we were very friendly with the owners, so we got involved with them and they were part of the fun. As the events evolved, we got to a super point where we had a group of Cybermen attacking each boat as it was going down the canal, which was very exciting. And then we had trouble where the engine broke down, so we made everyone inside get out and pull the boat, and that was wonderful. It was a really marvellous period of time.'

These 'Travellers in Time' events were sometimes promoted in the news pages of *Doctor Who Magazine*, an example being where Sylvester McCoy, Elisabeth Sladen and John Nathan-Turner were due to attend one across 1 to 3 November 1996.[142] Sophie Aldred remembers them fondly, as she wrote in the Steve Berry-edited *Behind the Sofa* book:

'The idea was you'd have a meal in the restaurant with us – me and Sylvester or whoever – in the evening and then, the following day, we'd all go on the steam railway together. After that, we'd take a canal boat over the highest viaduct in Christendom, until, finally – the treat of all treats! – a visit to the Dapol model

---

[142] *Doctor Who Magazine* #245.

factory. There'd be a chance to make your own *Doctor Who* figure, rattling Daleks and Cybermen off the production line. All the fans would be absolutely overjoyed. And so would I. And now, here I am, yet another 20 years on. As I sit at my kitchen table, I'm looking up at my windowsill, on which sits a plastic Dapol figure of a Cyberman, a Sylvester Doctor and an Ace.'[143]

These days, it is rare that fans get to spend so much time with the actors they admire from the show. While the convention circuit still does well, Comic Con events with literally thousands of attendees result in a more detached experience.

The Legacy

The legacy of the Llangollen exhibition remains the fact that it helped to keep *Doctor Who* in the minds of fans and the general public at a time when it was not so highly-thought-of by the Corporation that created it. More so, it rescued many unique and rare artefacts from disappearing forever. As David Boyle noted, 'At that time we were quite well aware that if we hadn't done something with the costumes, there was a good chance that they would all be sold off.' As well as providing a semi-permanent home for many *Doctor Who* artefacts, the exhibition and its associated merchandise served to maintain *Doctor Who* 'in the quietest period of its existence', as Boyle phrased it.

Dapol owners David and Pauline Boyle parted ways around the turn of the decade, and David moved to Blackpool while Pauline remained in Llangollen. In January 2002, Dapol's license to manufacture the action figure range ended and, as Martin Wilkie explains, 'We couldn't maintain the exhibition alongside the unlicensed toys, so our involvement [also] came to an end.'[144] With no *Doctor Who* toys now being made, the Dapol factory tour naturally became less attractive to the show's fans, and this contributed to a steady decline in visitor numbers. When it was announced that the exhibition was finally to end, Dapol managing director George Smith acknowledged that attendance had gradually dwindled from 40,000 a year to 15,000 a year.[145]

The attraction closed its doors for the final time on 30 December 2003. This, coupled with the closure of the Longleat exhibition earlier the same year, was a great disappointment to many fans, and once again cast a shadow of doubt over the future of all the props and costumes that had been on display. However, better news came with the announcement that *Doctor Who* would soon be returning for a new television run. Not only that, but artefacts from the show were about to go on public display in Blackpool for the first time in nearly twenty years.

---

[143] Berry, S (2013), *Behind the Sofa*, P79-80.
[144] *Doctor Who Magazine* #361.
[145] news.bbc.co.uk/1/hi/wales/north_east/3223370.stm

Chapter 7
Blackpool II (2004-2009)

In 2004 the Doctor returned to an old haunt: Blackpool in the North West of England. Once again, David Boyle was the driving force behind this new venture. Following his split from wife Pauline and move to the seaside town, and the subsequent downturn in fortunes of the Llangollen exhibition, Boyle had made enquiries regarding the status of the *Doctor Who* artefacts. 'I received a phone call from Lorne Martin,' he recalled, 'telling me about the costumes and what we'd accumulated – because quite a lot of what had been on display in Llangollen was actually my product, that I'd bought and paid for over the years, including the Bessie car outside. While we were discussing it, I said, "Well, why don't you bring it to Blackpool?" He said, "Well, there's nowhere in Blackpool to put it." I said, "I just happen to have all the premises where the *Doctor Who* exhibition was originally."'

These premises were not the only ones in Blackpool that Boyle had acquired, and although the idea of a return to the original *Doctor Who* venue had a romantic appeal to it, the use of a larger building was eventually considered preferable in view of the quantity of potential exhibits. The viability of this new endeavour was, however, dependent on Pauline Boyle, as proprietor of the Llangollen site, agreeing to the move. As David Boyle explained: 'I said to Lorne, "I've actually got better premises farther down the road, on the sea front." So he then said to me, "What's the situation?" I said, "Well, if Pauline wants to let the exhibition go, not a problem." So I rang and spoke to Pauline and she said she would be delighted to let it go, because the *Doctor Who* items were filling the exhibition space and it wasn't turning over the amount of money that was necessary to justify its square footage in the factory. And she'd got lots of work for the factory. She couldn't make enough model trains and components. She said if we wanted it, she wouldn't stand in our way. So we went back to Lorne, discussed it with Experience Design & Management, and the agreement was that the exhibition would come to Blackpool.

'That's how the new exhibition came about; by the courtesy of Pauline allowing it to go from Llangollen and the BBC of course wanting a better income from it than it had been generating before.'

Blackpool was arguably a perfect location for the exhibition to move to, given the long history the town shared with the show. For many fans, Blackpool and *Doctor Who* share a special bond. Christopher Daniels, who had visited the original exhibition, was one of those delighted to see it back: 'I thought it was so good that it [had] come back to Blackpool. I still think to this day that Blackpool was a good place for it.' David Boyle agreed, and was delighted to be able to bring the exhibition back to the town:

'I'm looking forward to a day when they realise that it should [still] be in Blackpool. Its original spiritual home. This is where it had so many years of money being produced for the BBC, when the show was not on the highest levels [of popularity]. Right now it's at the apex of its life, it's at the highest levels, and of course it really should have an exhibition in Blackpool.'

The new venue, much like Llangollen at the start of the 1990s, needed display facilities installed in order to house the exhibits. Once again this required significant investment by David Boyle: 'I had to do the same thing again. I had to buy the cabinets, the big cases, all the aspects again. It cost me a fortune; money I had to borrow, because I was really down on my uppers at the time. I had to borrow a vast amount of money to be able to bring it to Blackpool, and I did.'

The financial investment also extended to money that had to be paid to the BBC in order to acquire their artefacts once again. Boyle clarified: 'We paid the BBC a considerable amount of money, and it's probably the only time they actually made a good profit, because all the expenses were down to me.' A similar agreement had of course been reached previously for the Llangollen exhibition. Boyle and Experience Design & Management once again split the set-up costs, with percentages of the admission takings going to both parties plus the BBC. 'I'm not allowed to tell you what it was,' said Boyle, 'but it was a high percentage that we paid to the BBC; much higher than anyone else who was doing this type of deal.' This contributed to making *Doctor Who* a profitable brand for the BBC even during the show's so-called 'Wilderness Years'. Dapol and David Boyle therefore not only saved historic *Doctor Who* items from being destroyed or sold off, but also incentivised the BBC to allow them to be placed on display. As Boyle stated, 'The BBC earned a lot of money from it; so in all the time it was under my care, both in Llangollen and in Blackpool, a lot of money was made from *Doctor Who*.'

The exhibition was actually titled the *Doctor Who* Museum, reflecting the archive nature of the pieces included. It opened to the public on Friday 9 April 2004 – the start of that year's Easter Bank Holiday weekend – with admission for adults costing £6, for children and OAPs £4, and a family ticket priced at £18.[146] A lot of the items on display had been simply transferred across from Llangollen, but others derived from the Longleat exhibition, which had also closed the previous year. These included Tony Oxley's TARDIS console, which had been on display at Longleat ever since 1974. 'It was an amalgamation of items from Longleat and from the Dapol exhibition at Llangollen,' confirms Christopher Daniels. 'You had the console room from Longleat, and a lot of the other stuff was from Llangollen when that closed down.' This combination of artefacts resulted in what was, at that time, the biggest exhibition of *Doctor Who* costumes and props there had ever been.

---

[146] *Doctor Who Magazine* #344.

DOCTOR WHO EXHIBITIONS

The Exhibition

The Museum's displays remained largely the same over the course of its five-year run, although they underwent some minor alteration and rearrangement. The artefacts transferred from Llangollen included the 'Behind the Sofa' tableau originally created for MOMI; this was again the only exhibit to recreate a scene from outside the on-screen *Doctor Who* universe, although there was also a case containing a variety of tie-in merchandise, including the latest offerings generated by the 21st Century episodes. Other cases transferred from Llangollen included photographs, book covers, and a Haemovore mask squashed against the glass.

Each case was individually numbered, with an A4-size sign explaining what the exhibit was, the story it had appeared in and the relevant transmission dates. These signs would have been particularly useful for new fans unfamiliar with items seen on screen during the 1970s and 1980s. Christopher Daniels, who would later work at the venue, was one of many visitors pleased to see these vintage artefacts: 'The first time I went in, I thought, "I can't believe they've still got some of this stuff." I thought a lot of it had gone to the great dustbin in the sky a long time before.'

Many of the items on display had also been part of the original Blackpool exhibition. As someone who had attended that exhibition too, Daniels was delighted to see them again: 'When the new one opened, in a way it was like being reunited with old friends.' Unfortunately some of those older pieces were beginning to show signs of deterioration that couldn't be hidden simply by lower-level lighting.

On entering the exhibition, the TARDIS control room provided an opening thrill. John Molyneux, reviewing the attraction for *Doctor Who Magazine*, praised the console in particular: 'The inaccurate, retro instrumentation remains more visually exciting than its TV counterparts, while the time rotor's operation is still smooth and silent despite being over 30 years old.'[147] The ship's exterior police box shape was represented by the familiar model on a starry background, as first displayed at MOMI and then at Llangollen. In the roundels of the control room were once again displayed images of all the Doctor's incarnations, updated to include the ninth and tenth. Surrounding the control room, as was traditional, a number of viewing windows held various monster costumes. These included a Yeti ('The Web of Fear'); a 'blobby' Axon ('The Claws of Axos') and a Silurian ('Warriors of the Deep'). A replica Dalek, previously seen at Llangollen, was occasionally also found in the control room or in the shop area. In a black-and-silver colour scheme, it was used largely for promotional purposes.

On leaving the control room, the first exhibit on the left was initially the Magma beast from 'The Caves of Androzani', although this was regularly rotated with other items. On the right-hand side, a display featuring a number of Cyberman pieces was installed. Alongside a selection of suits, gloves and boots

---

[147] *Doctor Who Magazine* #344.

were Cyberman helmets from 'The Wheel in Space' and 'The Invasion', the Cyber Leader helmet from 'Revenge of the Cybermen', and the Cyber Controller helmet plus a chest unit from 'Attack of the Cybermen'. At some point, a helmet from the redesigned 'Cybus' Cybermen first seen in 'Rise of the Cybermen'/'The Age of Steel' was added.

The Cybermen designed by Dinah Collin initially for 'Earthshock' were afforded a significant display of their own, with six complete 1980s costumes being included. Four of these were stood upright, with the majority of the components coming from their final classic series appearance in 'Silver Nemesis'. Two destroyed Cybermen were placed on the floor; these dated from 'Earthshock' and 'The Five Doctors' respectively. Behind the costumes was an illustrated backdrop depicting numerous other Cybermen of the matching design against an orange background. To complete the scene, the Cyberscope prop from 'Silver Nemesis' was added. A Cryon costume from 'Attack of the Cybermen' was sometimes placed in this display as well, but occasionally featured as a separate exhibit elsewhere in the exhibition, accompanied by one of the destroyed Cybermen.

Continuing along the right-hand side of the corridor, the next exhibit was a Husk ('Ghost Light'). This was followed by the large Malus face from 'The Awakening'. The smaller Malus puppet was also mounted into a display case, with its red eyes illuminated and a left-to-right head movement. Then came a pair of Tractators from 'Frontios'. One of these still remained motorised, with the lower lip moving up and down; unfortunately the other's jaw was in a less functional state, with the left side completely dislocated and separated.

Additional exhibits seen in the early part of the exhibition over time, having previously been located elsewhere in the Museum, included a Tetrap ('Time and the Rani'), a Navarino ('Delta and the Bannermen'), an Ice Warrior ('The Ice Warriors') and the large Kroll miniature ('The Power of Kroll'). An older piece in the Museum was a sarcophagus prop from 'Pyramids of Mars'; but the oldest piece of all was the 'walk in' Dalek 1-7, with the upper section originally constructed in 1963. Unlike at the MOMI and Llangollen exhibitions, this time it was placed behind glass in a cabinet. By this point it had been given a silver-and-blue livery akin to that of its first on-screen appearance.

In another display cabinet a Tetrap hand was placed on top of the Sea Devil cutting device seen in 'Warriors of the Deep', along with a knee- or elbow-pad worn by a guard in 'Snakedance'. The next cabinet held a Time Lord robe, minus the collar. Other display cases presented miscellaneous items such as Soldeed's staff ('The Horns of Nimon'); the Caretakers' tracking device ('Paradise Towers'); a Tetrap miniature ('Time and the Rani'); and a guard helmet from 'The Pirate Planet'. A further case held both a black Time Lord-style robe and the chest piece worn by Lytton when undergoing Cyber-conversion in 'Attack of the Cybermen'.

A long display case housed what was referred to in advertising leaflets as the 'Robot Zone'. Exhibits here included the Gundan robot ('Warriors' Gate') still wielding its axe; the Pool Cleaner robot from 'Paradise Towers'; and the Garm

('Terminus'). At some point while on display, the Garm lost its right arm, which partly disintegrated due to age; subsequently the costume was angled to try to hide this fact. Crammed into a corner next to the Garm were the K1 Robot ('Robot'), the Giant Brain prop from 'Time and the Rani' and a K-9 replica. Next to these were the Drathro L3 robot from 'The Trial of a Time Lord': 'The Mysterious Planet' and, added a little later, a Sontaran from 'The Two Doctors', complete with weapon. Despite their poor condition, a number of damaged survivors of the Longleat fire were also on display in the Museum; these included the Android from 'The Visitation' and a Cleaner Robot from 'Paradise Towers'.

Continuing along the displays, visitors came to one of the most colourful exhibits: the Kandyman from 'The Happiness Patrol', accompanied by the Fifi puppet from the same story. Still seated in a leather desk chair was the Pirate Captain, complete with Polyphase Avatron, from 'The Pirate Planet'. Then came the L1 tracker robot from 'The Trial of a Time Lord': 'The Mysterious Planet'. Opposite these items was the light silver K-9 replica and the remnants of the prop damaged in the Longleat fire. On a nearby TV monitor was played a *Pebble Mill at One* interview with Patrick Troughton and Bernard Wilkie, originally broadcast in 1973. Transferred from Llangollen was David Boyle's replica of the Doctor's roadster Bessie.

Through a round viewing window, the materialising and dematerialising TARDIS display first installed in Longleat in 1987 could now be seen in Blackpool. It featured an interactive element, with a button allowing the visitor to materialise the TARDIS. Another display case featured items used by seventh Doctor Sylvester McCoy in 'Time and the Rani', including a Panama hat, two paisley handkerchiefs and a knitted blue-and-mauve-striped scarf. Peter Davison's first season as the Doctor was represented with a cabinet featuring hunting spears and masks from 'Castrovalva' and the Trickster mask from 'Kinda'. Further cabinets held a variety of costume pieces and a Minyan guard helmet from 'Underworld'; a Horda from 'The Face of Evil'; a Guard helmet from 'The Pirate Planet'; and Haemovore hands from 'The Curse of Fenric'.

The Melkur statue from 'The Keeper of Traken' was accompanied by a costume worn on screen by Anthony Ainley as the Master. Another villainous Time Lord was represented in the exhibition in the form of Kate O'Mara's costume from 'Time and the Rani'. The latter was accompanied by another Anthony Ainley Master costume: this time the one worn in 'Survival'. A pair of Time Lord costumes were also mounted together, namely a Chancellery Guard uniform, and one comprising the traditional robes, collar and skullcap as seen in 'The Deadly Assassin'. The Doctor's companions were also well represented, via costumes for Ace, Turlough, Adric and Nyssa, as had been seen previously at Longleat. These comprised the filling of a Time Lord sandwich, as on the other side of them were another Chancellery Guard uniform, complete with Captain's helmet, and another robe, collar and skullcap from 'The Deadly Assassin'.

Further items used on screen by actors playing the Doctor had been transferred from Llangollen. These included walking canes wielded by William

Hartnell, a pair of trousers and braces worn by Patrick Troughton, and a shirt and waistcoat worn during 'The Two Doctors' by Colin Baker. Jon Pertwee's burgundy jacket from 'The Time Monster' and 'The Three Doctors' was positioned next to his cape and Elisabeth Sladen's costume from 'The Five Doctors'. Fourth incarnation Tom Baker's Season 18 costume, seen on screen from 'The Leisure Hive' to 'Logopolis', was displayed, complete with hat and iconic scarf, alongside a long, white Time Lord-style gown. Concluding a chronological journey through the classic-era Doctors were complete costumes worn by Peter Davison, Colin Baker and Sylvester McCoy. Just prior to the latter's seventh Doctor outfit, which came complete with question-mark umbrella, was presented the costume worn by Nicola Bryant as Peri during 'The Mysterious Planet' section of 'The Trial of a Time Lord'.

The 'Wilkie' Dalek 2-8 had also made the move from Llangollen and was displayed in the centre of a horseshoe-shaped room inside an individual case, surrounded by toy replicas of the bronze Daleks from the 21st Century episodes. A full-size bronze Dalek was positioned atop the case, allowing an interesting comparison of Dalek props separated by over 40 years. This horseshoe-shaped room would later feature other props from recently-televised episodes. Prior to their introduction, however, the walls were ringed by a variety of classic-era creations. These included Omega ('Arc of Infinity'); a Foamasi ('The Leisure Hive'); the adapted Terileptil costume seen as an Alien Delegate in 'The Trial of a Time Lord': 'Mindwarp'; a Time Lord Chancellery Guard Captain costume ('The Deadly Assassin'); Mestor the Gastropod ('The Twin Dilemma'); a Pipe Person ('The Happiness Patrol'); and a Marshman ('Full Circle'). Further items seen here were four clown costumes, including the Chief Clown, from 'The Greatest Show in the Galaxy', plus two out of the three seated Gods of Ragnarok from the same story; a Mogarian ('The Trial of a Time Lord': 'Mindwarp'); Control ('Ghost Light'); the Nemesis statue ('Silver Nemesis'); and a Nimon head ('The Horns of Nimon'), curiously attached to the body of a Krarg from the unfinished story 'Shada', minus its diamond-shaped pieces.

An impressive Dalek exhibit was mounted over two levels and across two display cases. At the front were positioned the Special Weapons Dalek, the destroyed Dalek skirt and the Dalek battle command chair from 'Remembrance of the Daleks'. The Special Weapons Dalek had been repainted at some point, and now appeared more 'dirtied down' than it had on screen. Dalek L1, previously seen only at Longleat, had also been transferred up to Blackpool, and retained its internal movement mechanisms. Although in the gun metal grey-and-black colour scheme, it still had the 'Imperial'-style plunger attachment.

Davros was also represented in the display, with a Michael Wisher-style mask on a Terry Molloy-style chair. As Christopher Daniels recalls, 'When they had Davros at Blackpool they'd got the wrong head on him, and no hand; and the dashboard [on the chair], I don't know what the heck they'd done to it, but it was nothing like the one in the TV series.' On the upper level of the combined double display were positioned the Supreme Dalek from 'Remembrance of the Daleks', still against the white, vacuum-formed plastic background originally constructed for the MOMI exhibition, and the transmat device from the same story. Dalek N1 – the one that had missed out on an appearance in 'Remembrance of the Daleks' because it was part of the USA Tour – was also placed on the upper level, painted in black with gold features. Elsewhere in the exhibition was Dalek I2-I4, in the 'Imperial' white-and-gold livery.

A display cabinet with a wave-shaped edge included Christopher Daniels' favourite item in the Museum: the Brontosaurus model that had featured in 'Invasion of the Dinosaurs'. After all these years, the model's legs had collapsed and were no longer able to support its body weight. Despite this, the dinosaur brought back Daniels' very first memory of *Doctor Who*: 'My earliest memory is of "Invasion of the Dinosaurs", and it was nice to have the Brontosaurus in the exhibition; that's why I liked it so much. That model was probably the most decayed thing we'd got, when I helped out in there. It was in such a terrible state.'

In a similar display cabinet were placed two snake props used to represent the Mara in 'Snakedance'; and through another window were the Sil and Kiv Mentor costumes from 'The Trial of a Time Lord': 'Mindwarp'.

To create more immersive exhibits, in keeping with Blackpool tradition, a number of monsters were placed in bespoke environments. For example, a graveyard was the home for the Ancient One and two Haemovores, one in a padded gilet and the other in a naval uniform, plus Ace's grey dress, all from 'The Curse of Fenric'. Similarly, two Vervoids ('The Trial of the Time Lord': 'Terror of the Vervoids'), three Cheetah People ('Survival') and two Mandrels ('Nightmare of Eden') were placed in a jungle environment. The Morbius monster and a mocked-up Professor Solon in his laboratory, which had been on display in Longleat during 2003, was another exhibit transferred to Blackpool. Two Sea Devils from 'Warriors of the Deep', one with the samurai-style helmet and one without, were placed in a display case with plastic seaweed dangling from the ceiling.

Two sizeable cases were used to display a wide variety of masks and helmets, a series of shelves being added at a later date to make the individual items easier to view. Those included in the first case were: Sharez Jek ('The Caves of Androzani'); lion mask ('The Masque of Mandragora'); the Hecate priestess (*K-9 and Company*); a Silurian ('Warriors of the Deep'); a Solonian mutant ('The Mutants'); a Vanir ('Terminus'); a Sea Devil ('Warriors of the Deep'); the Terry Molloy-style Davros, later replaced by the scarred Terileptil ('The Visitation'); a replica Exxilon ('Death to the Daleks'); a Voc robot ('The Robots of Death'); the Ergon ('Arc of Infinity'); the Queen Bat ('The Caves of Androzani'); and a Marshman ('Full Circle'). Heads and masks in the second display cabinet were: an insect alien from stage show *The Ultimate Adventure*[148]; Mara banishment mask ('Snakedance'); Jacondan headpiece ('The Twin Dilemma'); the Bus Conductor robot from 'The Greatest Show in the Galaxy'; Haemovore ('The Curse of Fenric'); Mawdryn headpiece ('Mawdryn Undead');

---

[148] twitter.com/who_fx/status/542740158144348160

Nyssa's mask from 'Black Orchid'; White Guardian headpiece ('Enlightenment'); and a Vervoid ('The Trial of a Time Lord': 'Terror of the Vervoids'). Other pieces on display included caps worn by Lakertyans ('Time and the Rani'); the robot Dragon head from 'Dragonfire'; and a Morlox ('Timelash').

Also mounted in a display case was a weapon assortment that included a Karfelon laser canon, laser rifle and Krontron crystal deflector gun ('Timelash'); a rifle from 'The Sun Makers'; a handgun from 'Dragonfire'; and a Dalek trooper helmet ('Resurrection of the Dalek').

As in Llangollen, a clothes rail of miscellaneous costumes was also included in the exhibition. Other exhibits from the five year run included an animatronic Tetrap head with exposed inner workings from 'Time and the Rani'; Zog from *The Ultimate Adventure*; and the animatronic Terileptil head from 'The Visitation' that previously, while at Llangollen, had been paired with the red Terileptil body. Toward the end of the Museum's run, a replica Mechanoid, modelled on those that appeared in 'The Chase', was added. Given that, later, after the Blackpool exhibition closed, three Plasmatons from 'Time-Flight' were auctioned at Bonhams, it seems likely that they were also displayed at some point during the five-year run.

The Blackpool exhibition also provided a useful resource for the team working on bonus features for the *Doctor Who* DVD range. Shots of the K1 Robot were recorded there for use in the *Are Friends Electric* documentary on the 'Robot' DVD. Similarly, in *The Cyber Story* feature on the 'Attack of the Cybermen' DVD, Cyberman exhibits provided backgrounds and close-ups as costume designer Dinah Collin and actor Mark Hardy described the costumes; and a shot of the Cyber Controller helmet was shown as script editor Eric Saward discussed the character's reappearance in the story.

After the transmission of new *Doctor Who* episodes for the first time since 1996, additional props and costumes were added to the exhibition over time. In 2005, exhibits from Christopher Eccleston's only series as the Doctor included an Auton ('Rose'); a Slitheen suit and Annette Badland's costume from 'Aliens of London'/'World War Three'; and the Anne Droid ('Bad Wolf'). 'The End of the World' provided a number of exhibits, including the Steward's costume, an Adherent of the Repeated Meme, Hop Pyleen, a Tree of Cheem and Jabe's costume. Some smaller props were mounted to the wall in protective bubbles; these included Captain Jack's sonic blaster with holster and a gas mask from 'The Empty Child'/'The Doctor Dances'. Later additions included an Auton Bride ('Rose'), the Face of Boe ('The End of the World'), Simmons' costume from 'Dalek', plus Novice Hame and Chip costumes from 'New Earth'.

Unfortunately, the modern props and costumes, in fine and fresh condition, made the older artefacts look more threadbare by comparison. Fans were nevertheless grateful that in the 21st Century these items still existed. As Christopher Daniels observes, 'It was great to see there was so much [older] stuff still there at that time. Okay, the Cyberman suits were looking quite shonky. But it was good to be there and see [all these things].' There was, though, no getting away from the fact that certain items were beginning to look their age. For example, the K1 Robot was starting to lose its foam and structure. As Daniels again remembers, 'The latex was starting to crack on some of the things. The Kandyman was also starting to perish. It was a blessing the series came back when it did, because everything [from the earlier stories] was getting old and tired, really.' The poor condition of the older items probably contributed to the fact that the majority were later sold off by the BBC. Happily some were salvaged and have since been restored to their former glory.

As with all such ventures, things at the *Doctor Who* Museum didn't always go smoothly. One of the most significant issues arose from the growth of the internet, and social media in particular. Over the years, visitors to the various *Doctor Who* exhibitions had often taken photographs of the exhibits. As many of these images started to become freely available to view online, the attraction of seeing the props and costumes in person was somewhat diminished, and this dented admission numbers. David Boyle explained: 'I asked the BBC what they thought, and I was immediately instructed not to allow photographs to be taken, because [they] were turning up on the internet and other places. And, as the BBC said, if they're on the internet, people don't need to visit the exhibition, because sooner or later you'll get somebody picturing everything.'

The consequent introduction of a policy of gently asking visitors not to take photographs led to an enforcement problem, as Boyle again described: 'There were a couple of people who worked for us who were a bit over-zealous on that. And some of the things that are supposed to have happened, that I'm supposed to have done, were actually done by these other people and not by me. I felt very aggrieved about that, because people started to put [adverse comments online], basically criticising me and [calling for me to be sacked].'

As with the controversy over the inaccuracy of some of the Dapol action figures, David Boyle, despite all his efforts and financial expenditure, once again became the subject of negativity from some fans. As he phrased it, 'That resulted in certain people thinking the exhibition was being run by an idiot in Blackpool.' Fortunately, these attitudes were very limited; overall, Boyle considered his new Blackpool venture a 'wonderful' experience.

Long-time fan Christopher Daniels made a family visit to the *Doctor Who* Museum on its opening weekend, and could barely contain his excitement: 'We went up on, I think it was the Saturday or the Sunday, and we were some of the first people to go in there. I couldn't wait, and virtually ran up the seafront.' The new attraction managed to recapture the magic created for over a decade between 1974 and 1985. As Daniels again explains, 'It had an atmosphere all of its own, once you were in there, out of the sunlight, in the dark, standing by the TARDIS console or walking around.'

Although Daniels first visited the Museum as a paying customer, he was later invited to help out there, as he explains: 'One of the gents who worked there, he dressed as Jon Pertwee's Doctor, and I got to know him because I used to visit a lot with my family. It came into the conversation that I had a Colin Baker costume, and he said, "Would you like to come and dress as the Doctor for the day and spend the day with us?" And I said, "Absolutely".'

Daniels also came into contact with David Boyle and speaks highly of the man: 'I knew him a little. I got on all right with him. He was kind enough to give me the opportunity, and I'll always be grateful to him for allowing me to do it.'

Dressed as the Doctor's sixth incarnation, Daniels acted as an exhibition guide, enlightening visitors and answering their questions. As he phrases it himself, 'I would turn up as the sixth Doctor, and used to play the part to a degree. People asked questions about what was in the exhibition, what story a particular exhibit was from, where it was made, and things like that.' Taking on this role in 2008, Daniels continued volunteering at the exhibition right up until its final day: 'It was only on an amateur basis, nothing contractual or anything, but I knew I had to behave myself. I was there a) to make the exhibition fun and b) to make *Doctor Who* look good, and to make the sixth Doctor look good.'

In the latter regard, Daniels felt a responsibility to put right a sometimes-negative public perception of the sixth Doctor. He recalls one particular know-it-all visitor: 'He was telling his girlfriend, "Oh that's the sixth Doctor; he was the one that got sacked because he was no good".' Although initially nervous, Daniels quickly grew in confidence as he became accustomed to dealing with such situations and relaying his knowledge of the show: 'We wanted to give people that extra pizzazz, for the want of a better expression; to give them something positive to remember.'

The later *Doctor Who* Experience exhibitions operated by BBC Worldwide would employ professional hosts to perform a similar role and guide visitors through their interactive walk-through adventures. In Blackpool, the arrangement was more informal, but delivered by an enthusiastic team. As Daniels remembers, 'When I helped the guys out at Blackpool, they were a dedicated little team who actually liked the series.' Even those who initially were not as *au-fait* with *Doctor Who* history were keen to pick up more information from Daniels. This enthusiasm led to him and other team members creating little sketches to perform, further enhancing the visitor experience.

'A guy worked in there who used to dress as a Cyberman,' recalls Daniels. 'They had a costume in the back that he used to put on; it was a "Silver Nemesis" one. And in the section of the exhibition where the robots were, there was a piece of blank wall where the two cabinets joined in the alcove, and he used to stand there stock still. People used to walk up to him, and all of a sudden he'd just twitch and start moving. Then I'd come from nowhere [in my sixth Doctor costume], and ward the Cyberman off with my sonic screwdriver, or pretend to throw gold dust at him or something. I'd fight him off and tell the visitors something like, "I'm sorry about that, but do enjoy the rest of your stay. The rest of it is under control, as far as I know". For a minute, you could lose yourself in the action. In a safe way. Just a few feet outside was Blackpool seafront.'

Any concern that younger members of the viewing audience might no longer find the Daleks and other monsters scary was proved unfounded in Blackpool. Daniels however was on hand to help allay junior visitors' fears – a task made easier by being a father himself: 'There were some children who were scared stiff in there, and they actually looked up to me as the Doctor to look after them. It was quite a big responsibility; bigger than people realise.'

Having the Doctor, or 'Doctor Who' as they so often called him, guiding them around the exhibition reassured many children, and left Daniels with some of his fondest memories: 'There was this one little kid, he was absolutely frightened to death, and his Mum and Dad could not pacify him. They saw me and said, "Oh, the Doctor's here." And I went up to him, crouched down to his level and said, "Hello young man, why are you so scared? Which one is frightening you? Do you want to show me?" He held my hand and took me up to where the Tractator was. And I knelt down by him, so I was at his level looking up at it, and said, "He's a bit of an ugly brute, isn't he? You know he's just a big caterpillar, don't you? Don't worry, I've beaten him. Just think of him as a big caterpillar." Anyway, the boy was pacified after that. I stayed with the family and took him round the exhibition, because his Dad said, "Do you want me to take you round, or do you want Doctor Who to take you round?" And he said, "I want Doctor Who to." So I took him round. The next day, I was in the lobby and the same family came in again; they were obviously staying up there for the weekend. And the boy's Mum said, "We've got to come in and say thanks. He has not shut up all night about Doctor Who taking him round the exhibition, and how much he enjoyed it. He'll never forget it."'

Moments like this account for why Daniels enjoyed his role so much and was so grateful for the opportunity he was given. Another anecdote illustrates it further: 'I took round one family who had a little girl with them. She was probably only about three or four, bless her heart. She looked up at me and said, "Doctor Who?" and I bent down and said, "Yes, my dear, what is it?" She looked up at me with her little blue eyes and said, "Doctor Who, when I grow up I want to be your companion." And that epitomised why I did it, really.'

Daniels looks back on the time with tremendous fondness. 'David [Boyle] and his crew, they were kind enough to let me do it. They gave me an opportunity that I seized with both hands, and those memories will be with me forever. That's something that money simply cannot buy.'

Unfortunately all good things must come to an end.

The End

When the Museum opened in 2004, anticipation had been starting to build for *Doctor Who*'s return to television. Five years on, the show was thriving, delivering viewing figures that matched those achieved 20 years earlier, even though the ratings landscape had changed dramatically in the interim. The Museum, however, had to close in the latter part of 2009, once the building's lease expired. As Christopher Daniels reflects, 'At first when the exhibition was going to go, I was sad. I didn't know the reason behind it, I just realised that a bloody good time was coming to an end.'

David Boyle explains: 'Our lease was originally for five years, and at the end of five years it was agreed that the costumes would be returned to

Cardiff.' Initially, the closure was due to occur at one of the busiest times of the year, during the Blackpool holiday season. However, having realised this, Boyle managed to negotiate a short extension, allowing it to remain open until toward the end of the year instead.

Daniels was invited to attend the final weekend, wearing his sixth Doctor costume, just as he'd done on so many occasions before: 'David said "Is there any chance at all you could come back for the final weekend?" And I said, "I don't know, I'll have to see, because of finances." Anyway, the landlady at the place where my family usually stayed said, "I'll do you the room half price so you can come back." And bless her heart, she did.'

The Museum finally closed on Sunday 8 November 2009. That final day saw a lot of visitors attend for the last time. 'It was a bittersweet weekend, that last one,' says Daniels. 'I felt sorry for David [Boyle] and the people, especially the guys that were working in there, because it was their livelihoods. I mean, I was okay, the next week I went back to work fixing computers. It was a bittersweet time, but I wouldn't have missed it for the world.'

Most of the *Doctor Who* artefacts remaining were then returned to BBC Worldwide. Those considered suitable for restoration were retained for the new *Doctor Who* Experience attraction due to open the following year. Those considered beyond repair or unworthy of retention were auctioned off; a logical move, given that BBC Worldwide needed to fund their new venture. Dalek N1, for example, was sold for over £20,000, and now resides in a private collection in the USA. Some of those present on the Museum's final day have claimed that the cataloguing of artefacts was already in process while visitors were still in the building.

However, during the Museum's five year run, *Doctor Who* had been thrust back into the public imagination, and this had spawned a whole new series of exhibitions across the UK, the like of which had not been seen before.

Chapter 8
Doctor Who – Up Close

In 2005, *Doctor Who* had returned triumphantly to television screens, capturing the imaginations of a whole new generation and delighting those long-term fans who had feared it was gone for good. Having invested a significant budget in the new episodes, the BBC were very proactive in promoting the show. Daleks, the TARDIS police box and later Cybermen were popular choices for making publicity appearances. BBC Worldwide were also quick to capitalise on the show's newfound success; and once again, exhibitions of costumes and props proved a very useful tool for promotion and audience engagement.

New exhibitions were organised in venues across Britain, the first of them opening while the 2005 series was still being broadcast. Generally given an 'Up Close' branding, these allowed new fans to get literally up close to the exciting world of *Doctor Who*. While the Museum in Blackpool presented items predominately from the show's so-called 'classic era', these new exhibitions focused on the modern episodes, featuring the latest costumes and props shortly after they had appeared on screen.

Long-term exhibitions were set up in Cardiff, close to where *Doctor Who* was now being made, and at Land's End in Cornwall. Smaller, short-term exhibitions alternated between two established attractions, the National Space Centre in Leicester and the Spaceport on Merseyside. Larger exhibitions were then installed in Manchester, at Earl's Court in London, and at the Kelvingrove Museum in Glasgow. Further locations were later added in Coventry and Newcastle. As the exhibitions were to appear at a variety of different venues, they were designed and constructed to enable easy transportation and reinstallation. For instance, attractive backgrounds and information boards were attached to metal girder structures to which lights could also be fitted. This task was once again undertaken by Experience Design.

In 2008, an episode of British soap opera *EastEnders* featured two characters, Stacey Slater and Bradley Branning, visiting a *Doctor Who* convention for Valentine's Day. These scenes were actually recorded at one of these Up Close *Doctor Who* exhibitions.

Brighton Pier

The first of the new exhibitions was installed under the Dome of Brighton Pier on England's south coast.[149] It opened on 14 May 2005, the day that the episode

---

[149] news.bbc.co.uk/cbbcnews/hi/newsid_4540000/newsid_4541800/4541857.stm

'Father's Day' was broadcast. Four replica classic-series-style Daleks were in attendance for the occasion, posing for photographs with their new series counterparts and patrolling the pier outside. Although the exhibited items came mainly from the recently-produced episodes, *Doctor Who's* history prior to 2005 was not forgotten. The eight previous incarnations of the Doctor were represented in four displays, two to the left, two to the right, set within curved alcoves. Above images and information about the William Hartnell and Patrick Troughton incarnations, a large screen played a loop of all the show's title sequences from over the years. Illuminated through the display board behind was an original Ice Warrior. This particular Martian had last been seen at Longleat prior to the closure of that exhibition.

The paired photographs of the Doctors were accompanied by images of some of the Time Lord's classic foes. For instance, those of the Hartnell and Troughton Doctors were accompanied by images of a Dalek, an Ice Warrior, a Yeti and a Cyberman. For the Jon Pertwee incarnation, there were a Silurian – although, oddly, in a shot from the Peter Davison story 'Warriors of the Deep' – and Linx the Sontaran from 'The Time Warrior'. The Tom Baker era was illustrated with images of the Morbius monster from 'The Brain of Morbius' and, erroneously, a Sea Devil from their 1972 debut story. For the Colin Baker era, an image of Davros was used – although, again erroneously, it was one of the Michael Wisher-portrayed version from 'Genesis of the Daleks'.

A 'Warriors of the Deep' Sea Devil costume was incongruously placed behind the display board for the Pertwee and Tom Baker Doctors. Behind the board for the Peter Davison and Colin Baker incarnations was an 'Earthshock'-style Cyberman, lit from above.

Above the Sylvester McCoy and Paul McGann display, a monitor screen played a loop of all the regeneration sequences seen in the show up to that point.

However, while the 1963-1996 episodes were not forgotten, the focus was very much on the 21st Century series. Central to the exhibition, positioned just up from the classic era display, were Christopher Eccleston's ninth Doctor costume, complete with green sweater, and Billie Piper's costume from 'Rose', the introductory episode named after her character. These were illuminated from above inside a steadily-rotating version of the TARDIS police box exterior with two transparent walls. Also included inside this large display were two of the original costume design sketches. The TARDIS interior was represented by photographs and pieces of the interior wall, complete with the roundel-inspired circular design. Also present for visitors to see were some alternate console designs and a set model.

One of the strangest exhibits in the history of *Doctor Who* exhibitions was a commonplace wheelie bin, similar to that seen in 'Rose' (2005). Visitors who lifted the lid and peered inside could view the relevant scene from the episode, of a wheelie bin 'eating' Rose's boyfriend Mickey Smith (Noel Clarke).

Also on display from 'Rose' were a male Auton; a recreation of the 'Auton brides' scene, with three brides attempting to break out of a shop window; the prop anti-plastic test tube; and a plastic duplicate of Mickey's head.

As the Gelth from 'The Unquiet Dead' had been a CGI creation on screen, they were represented simply by a body beneath a shroud on a table in an eerie crypt set – somewhat akin to a scene from a classic *Frankenstein* movie. 'The End of the World', by contrast, had featured a number of physical creatures, and on display in Brighton were the Moxx of Balhoon; Jabe and Lute from the Forest of Cheem; a couple of the episode's other alien ambassadors; one of the Crespallion Platform 1 staff; and, inside a glass case, the prop of Cassandra. A further display case included some of the prop orbs given by Cassandra, and one of the Moxx's prosthetic face-pieces.

For many visitors, the highlight of the exhibition was a chance to see one of the new Daleks, which was humorously positioned at the top of a flight of steps. However, just as had been the case in 1972 with the BBC TV Special Effects Exhibition, the *Doctor Who* production team had been unwilling to release one of the screen-used props, so a replica had to be specially made for display purposes. This task had fallen to Specialist Models, who had built two of the three genuine props, and consequently the replica was a particularly accurate one, constructed using the same methods. It was also in pristine condition, having not had to endure the rigours of television production. Visitors who dared to press a nearby button clearly labelled 'DO NOT PUSH' could activate the Dalek. The dome lights would flash, the dome would rotate, and a light would shine out of the Dalek's weapon. Assistance in achieving these animated elements was provided by Mike Tucker of the Model Unit.

A second new-series Dalek prop from was also included in the Brighton exhibition. This was made up of a distressed, damaged skirt section and the upper half with the Dalek mutant exposed, as seen during the closing scenes of 'Dalek'. Both these items were screen-used, although they had not been paired together during the actual episode. In a display bubble on the wall was the prop weapon that Christopher Eccleston's Doctor had wielded during those closing scenes.

The classic-era Wilkie Dalek 2-8 also spent some time on display in Brighton, chalking up another exhibition appearance.

From 'Aliens of London'/'World War Three', two Slitheen and the Space Pig were accompanied by the prosthetic mask with forehead zip worn by Annette Badland. Later, the architect's model of Cardiff Power Station from 'Boom Town' was added.

One of the creepier items on show was from 'The Long Game', consisting of the head of a deceased individual from Satellite 5, complete with info-spike technology.

The Steven Moffat-written two-parter 'The Empty Child'/'The Doctor Dances' was represented by an enclosure of sandbags lined with barbed wire, inside which was the prop of the large bomb on which Captain Jack (John Barrowman) had sat during the action. A prop gas-mask from the story was mounted in another display bubble on the wall.

Two items created for the show by the Model Unit were also on display, namely the destroyed Big Ben clock face from 'Aliens of London' and the Emperor Dalek from 'The Parting of the Ways'. The latter was a later addition to the exhibition, after the series had finished transmission on BBC One. Other later additions, not on display when the attraction first opened, were the Trin-E and Zu-Zana robots from 'Bad Wolf'.

A low plinth bore a caption thanking people for visiting the exhibition and was also daubed with the words 'BAD WOLF'. Public Relations, Marketing and Events Manager Vicki Whitmore noticed this one morning, and unaware that it was an intentional nod to the action of 'The Parting of the Ways', believed that the exhibition had fallen victim to graffiti vandals. 'I was really worried', she told *Doctor Who Magazine*. 'I honestly thought that someone had defaced our exhibition. The General Manager called our cleaning team! They stood there scrubbing at it for ten minutes until we finally realised.'[150] Also interviewed by *Doctor Who Magazine* were Whitmore's colleague Jason Mannix and Martin Wilkie of Experience Design, and the resulting article offered some interesting behind-the-scenes insights into the Brighton exhibition. Amongst these were the fact that the attraction was assembled over the period of a month by sixty people; and that Experience Design had been responsible for the design, by Martin Wilkie and Stuart Wescombe, and then the construction, which had involved transporting various monsters along the pier and installing them in the venue. As Wilkie commented:

'We didn't drop anything over the edge of the pier, although we did have a cherry-picker crane go through the floor. And then, when we removed a mat beneath it, we could see the sea, which was quite surreal. Luckily the pier is able to take all the weight we could possibly get on it. Other than that, the main problem was fending off seagulls and pigeons.'[151]

The exhibition attracted a healthy total of 38,000 people in the first two months, with daily attendances of between 250 and 1,700 people.[152] As usual, an in-venue shop provided the opportunity for fans to purchase some of the latest *Doctor Who* merchandise, as well as some exclusive items including a brochure and postcards. The attraction closed in Brighton on 6 November 2005 but was then relocated to the National Space Centre in Leicester.[153]

Up Close – National Space Centre, Leicester

With items transferred directly from Brighton, the National Space Centre exhibition was open for a relatively brief period, from 22 November 2005 to 8 January 2006. It was free of charge to all National Space Centre ticketholders.

Once again the centrepiece was the ninth Doctor's costume, complete with green sweater, and Rose Tyler's outfit from 'Rose'. As before, these were displayed inside the TARDIS police box with transparent walls and

---

[150] *Doctor Who Magazine* #361.
[151] *Doctor Who Magazine* #361.
[152] *Doctor Who Magazine* #361.
[153] www.doctorwhonews.net/2005/10/brighton-exhibition-moves-to-leicester_9924.html

illuminated from above. Other items retained from the 2005 series' opening episode were the male Auton and the test-tube of anti-plastic. From 'The End of the World', the Moxx of Balhoon and the Crespallion Platform 1 staff member featured. Further items on display included the Slitheen, the Space Pig and Annette Badland's prosthetic with forehead zip from 'Aliens of London', the model of Cardiff Power Station from 'Boom Town' and the World War Two bomb surrounded by sandbags from 'The Empty Child'/'The Doctor Dances'.

The destroyed Big Ben clock face from 'Aliens of London' and the Emperor Dalek from 'The Parting of the Ways' were also transferred to Leicester, as was the replica bronze Dalek. After the transmission of the 2005 Christmas special, 'The Christmas Invasion', its Robot Santas were put on display for the first time.

This successful venture was repeated when the *Doctor Who* items were reinstalled at the National Space Centre for another brief run from 12 November 2007 to 6 January 2008; between 2006 and 2009, the exhibition effectively alternated venues between here and the Spaceport on Merseyside.

Up Close – Cardiff

Cardiff, as the effective new home of *Doctor Who* since production had recommenced in 2004, was an obvious location to host an exhibition celebrating the show. Opening on 22 December 2005 in the Red Dragon Centre in Cardiff Bay, the Up Close exhibition established the city as a must-visit location for fans. It was impressive to note the alacrity with which BBC Worldwide and Cardiff Council had moved to exploit the show's newfound success in this way, as fan and journalist David Prince comments: 'I was surprised how quickly they capitalised on it.' The exhibition was initially due to run until 26 February 2006, but such was its success that it remained open until March 2011, the displays being regularly updated to feature items from the latest episodes. Part of this popularity was due to an initial free entry policy; but another draw for fans was the opportunity to combine a visit to the exhibition with a walk around some of the many Cardiff locations where *Doctor Who*, and later the spin-off shows *Torchwood* and *The Sarah Jane Adventures*, had been recorded.

The Brighton exhibition having closed the previous month, its four substantial displays celebrating the Doctor's first eight incarnations were transferred to Cardiff in time for the new venture's opening. The Ice Warrior and the 'Earthshock'-style Cyberman also made the move. In fact, the first version of the Cardiff exhibition largely replicated the Brighton one. Exhibits included the male Auton and Auton bride tableau from 'Rose'; the Moxx of Balhoon, Jabe and Lute from the Forest of Cheem and a couple of the other alien ambassadors from 'The End of the World'; and the Trin-E and Zu-Zana robots from 'Bad Wolf'.

A rotating TARDIS with transparent walls, displaying ninth Doctor and

Rose costumes, was also present, although curiously positioned behind a fabric screen. This is likely to have been a replica of the one created for Brighton, as the latter had been transferred to Leicester and would later go on to Merseyside.

The Daleks were naturally represented too. As the replica originally made for Brighton was now in Leicester, a second replica was commissioned from Specialist Models. This time, instead of having the immaculate appearance of the one first seen in 'Dalek', it had a more weathered finish as featured in 'Bad Wolf'/'The Parting of the Ways'. Alongside this was positioned the Dalek with the exposed mutant, as previously displayed in Brighton. The classic-series Wilkie Dalek 2-8 is also thought to have had a short run in Cardiff, and the Brighton replica was briefly transferred there too when the Leicester exhibition closed, prior to it being relocated to Merseyside in time for the opening of that exhibition in 2006.

Other exhibits mounted into display bubbles included the prop gas mask from 'The Empty Child'/'The Doctor Dances'; the prop weapon from 'Dalek'; the info-spiked head from 'The Long Game'; a 'Rose'-style wheelie bin, complete with Cardiff council logo and a clip of the relevant scene playing on the monitor inside; and a prosthetics display.

Further exhibits were added after the closure of the Leicester exhibition. These included the 'Aliens in London'/'World War Three' items; the sandbags and World War Two bomb from 'The Empty Child'/'The Doctor Dances', along with a barrage balloon miniature; and the Emperor Dalek miniature from 'The Parting of the Ways'.

On the exhibition's opening, a sign read 'ITEMS FROM "THE CHRISTMAS INVASION" WILL BE ON DISPLAY AFTER CHRISTMAS.' This indeed proved to be the case. The items in question included the tenth Doctor's pyjamas and dressing gown; two Robot Santas; the Sycorax Leader costume; and a Christmas tree.

Further new additions were made after the broadcast of David Tennant's first full series as the tenth Doctor. For example, a number of items made up a display representing the episode 'New Earth', replacing the Auton bride shop window exhibit. These included one of the tenth Doctor's brown suits; medicine packs; the static Cassandra prop; a Catkind costume; and the Face of Boe head, outside of its case and mounted on the wall.

One of the new, Cybus-style Cybermen from 'Rise of the Cybermen'/'The Age of Steel' also made its exhibition debut, positioned beside a fake window with shattered glass on the ground, replicating the action of one of the scenes seen on screen. It was accompanied by a maid's uniform costume similar to the one worn by Billie Piper in the story; John Lumic's chair; and a technician's uniform costume.

The Dalek display was also updated to reflect the Series 2 finale 'Army of Ghosts'/'Doomsday'. The bronze Dalek with flashing lights, dome and eyestalk movement was now accompanied by a gas-masked soldier costume and the prop control levers that opened the hole into the void.

Further updates to the exhibition were made in 2007. Notably, the central focal point became a large transparent globe with the *Doctor Who* logo and a Welsh dragon inside. Later still, after the January 2008 closure of the Manchester exhibition (discussed later), this was replaced by the large machine from 'The Lazarus Experiment'. Positioned around these central features were costumes representing new-series Doctor-and-companion combinations. These included the ninth Doctor and Rose Tyler costumes from 'Rose'; and the tenth Doctor and Martha Jones costumes from 'Smith and Jones'. The fabric screen previously placed around the TARDIS exterior box was removed at this time, so that the box was now clearly visible in one corner of the exhibition. Other additions from the 2007 series included a helmeted Judoon from 'Smith and Jones'; and the black Dalek Sec prop, the Dalek Sec Hybrid and a Pig Slave from 'Daleks in Manhattan'/'Evolution of the Daleks'.

An interview with *Doctor Who*'s then Executive Producer and head writer Russell T Davies, clips from which can be found in 'The Journey (So Far)', a bonus feature on the *Complete Fourth Series* DVD and Blu-ray sets, was recorded around 2008 at a *Doctor Who* exhibition, thought to have been the Cardiff attraction. Davies is seen sat beside the machine from 'The Lazarus Experiment', with a tenth Doctor suit in the background. A wider shot reveals other exhibits, including the Anne Droid and Trin-E from 'Bad Wolf', plus an Auton bride from 'Rose'. Also seen mounted on the Lazarus machine is the iconic Martha Jones costume of red leather jacket and denim jeans.

It was Davies who, on 30 October 2008, reopened Up Close – Cardiff after it underwent a full refurbishment in the latter half of that year. A fake wall was installed in the entranceway, and on the signal of the head honcho, the wall exploded and two Cybermen stomped out to terrorise the gathered crowd.

One consequence of the refurbishment was that the direction of passage through the exhibition was changed, as entry was now to the left of the ticket desk rather than the right. Some of the first items visitors encountered included a ninth Doctor costume; and the tenth Doctor's dressing gown and pyjamas from 'The Christmas Invasion', his blue suit combination and, in a display case, his Converse trainers. A nearby interactive screen displayed information and facts about the Time Lord's various incarnations. Companion costumes for Billie Piper ('Rose') and Freema Agyeman ('Smith and Jones') were also exhibited.

A TARDIS exterior prop was placed on a green-screen landscape. Visitors would step onto the landscape and, via electronic effects, see themselves on a TV monitor standing on the surface of the Ood Sphere. The effect was not that effective, with a lot of fringing occurring, as fan David Prince confirms: 'The green-screen was terrible. It was atrocious.'

Continuing through the exhibition, the first monster encountered was a Sontaran, with helmet on a separate plinth, accompanied by a UNIT soldier and pieces of the set used for the two part story 'The Sontaran Stratagem'/'The Poison Sky'. Items from 'The Fires of Pompeii' were also exhibited, including garments worn by the Sisters of the Sibylline, Donna Noble and Metella. These were complemented by set elements and props, including a marble circuit-board piece.

Other monsters on display included a male Clockwork Droid, in dark navy costume, from 'The Girl in the Fireplace', and a Hath from 'The Doctor's Daughter'. Opposite the Hath, an impressive Cyberzone was positioned in the far left corner of the exhibition. Two of the Cybus-style Cybermen were displayed, one of which had a movement mechanism installed to make it twitch, and a voice track would play on the pressing of a button. The area was supplemented by other items from 'Rise of the Cybermen'/'The Age of Steel': John Lumic's chair and a maid outfit seen during Jackie Tyler's birthday party scenes, or possibly the costume worn by Billie Piper .

'Silence in the Library'/'Forest of the Dead' was also well represented, with set pieces including an information portal, a desk topped with books, a Vashta Nerada-inhabited spacesuit and a prop information node.

Moving forward, visitors embarked on a Dalek encounter, with a number of stories represented, including 'Daleks in Manhattan'/'Evolution of the Daleks'. On the left were exhibited the Dalek Sec Hybrid, complete with headpiece, and Diagoras's suit; opposite these were a Pig Slave and the showgirl costume worn by Tallulah; and mounted on the wall in a display bubble was one of the tommy-gun Dalek weapons seen during the story's closing scenes.

Series 4's epic finale 'The Stolen Earth'/'Journey's End' was marked with costumes of Captain Jack Harkness, Martha Jones, Donna Noble and Rose Tyler. Opposite these was the refurbished exhibition's most significant installation. Three different Daleks were showcased: from left to right, the black Dalek Sec; the Supreme Dalek; and a bronze Dalek, complete with Crucible equipment attachment. On pressing a button, the visitor could trigger the Supreme Dalek to rise up and Dalek Sec to swing forward. Lasers would fire, lights would flash and a voice track would bark out Dalek messages of conquest. Prop weapons and even Harriet Jones's passport from the story were placed in display cases nearby.

Moving on from the Dalek zone, next up were two Ood and Donna Noble's costume from 'Planet of the Ood'. In a display case sat a Robot Santa mask from 'The Christmas Invasion' and a remote control unit from the Santas' second appearance in 'The Runaway Bride'. A single leg from the latter story's Empress of the Racnoss was also positioned nearby. From 'Human Nature'/'The Family of Blood' came costumes for Brother and Sister of Mine and John Smith; Martha Jones's maid outfit; and a Scarecrow. Donna Noble's costume from 'Turn Left' was complete with Time Beetle attached to its back and positioned within an arrangement of mirrors, as seen during the episode.

A mock-up of the seated host who metamorphosed into a werewolf in 'Tooth and Claw' had previously been displayed here during 2006; toward the end of the exhibition's run it made a reappearance, this time without the surrounding cage seen previously. The large Lazarus machine took up a significant section of the exhibition and was used as a display area for costumes from the unrelated Christmas special 'The Next Doctor', including those of Jackson Lake, Mercy Hartigan and a Cybershade. Opposite this, items on show from another Christmas special, 'Voyage of the Damned', included a Heavenly Host robot, Astrid Peth's costume and Banakafalatta, accompanied by set elements such as loungers and windows. High above, overlooking the exhibition, a Weeping Angel from 'Blink' rotated, accompanied by a Monk costume from 'Tooth and Claw'.

The last section of the exhibition, prior to the little shop, saw a variety of items rotated onto display. The Anne Droid and Trin-E robots from 'Bad Wolf' made return appearances here. Other exhibits included another Captain Jack Harkness costume, a distressed K-9 prop from 'School Reunion', and the cloud-bursting machine used by Sarah Jane Smith and Maria Jackson in the 2007 *The Sarah Jane Adventures* episode 'Warriors of Kudlak'. In one of the more interesting additions, a recreation of the character Tarak Ital's head as infected by the Flood in 'The Waters of Mars' was placed inside a waterproof tank. Visitors could press a button on the outside of the tank and water would trickle from the mouth and down the chin. Positioned nearby was Ital's costume from the episode.

Following Matt Smith's first season as the Doctor, further new exhibits were added to the exhibition. For example, the Elder Ood seen in 'The End of Time: Part One' was positioned with a standard Ood counterpart. From 'Victory of the Daleks' came an Ironsides Dalek and the Winston Churchill, Bracewell and Amy Pond costumes; these items were positioned in front of the set from which the 'new paradigm' Daleks emerged during the episode, although none of those redesigned Daleks was present. Other items from the 2010 series included the 'frozen' eleventh Doctor's costume from 'Amy's Choice', a Vampire girl's dress from 'Vampires of Venice' and a Smiler cabinet, with angry Smiler mask placed inside, from 'The Beast Below'.

After the January 2010 closure of the exhibition at the Kelvingrove in Glasgow (discussed later), a Tritovore and Lady Christina de Souza's costume from 'Planet of the Dead' were also moved to Cardiff. Another costume from that episode was put on display here too: that worn by comedian Lee Evans as Malcolm, the UNIT scientist.

Sunday 27 March 2011 saw the exhibition's doors close for the final time, the major *Doctor Who* Experience having opened in London the previous month. Exhibition manager Graham Jones, speaking to the *South Wales Echo* at the time, said of the closure: 'It is damaging to the economy of Wales and the economy of Cardiff. We thought that [BBC Worldwide] would have respect and regard for their fans. It does seem that this decision has been made in a way that is not very compassionate toward Cardiff.'[154] The article also claimed that the exhibition had drawn more than half a million visitors over the years. Jones's disappointment was clear, as he suggested that kids visiting the Red Dragon Centre during the upcoming Easter holidays would be reduced to

---

[154] www.walesonline.co.uk/news/wales-news/time-up-doctor-who-exhibition-1847875

tears on learning that the exhibition was now closed.

The closure also caused a level of disquiet amongst *Doctor Who* fans in the city, as David Prince remembers: 'The feeling generally around the fans was that [BBC Worldwide] had shot themselves in the foot by closing it at that time.' It would be over a year before the *Doctor Who* Experience eventually transferred from its initial London home to Cardiff Bay. That left a long gap with no official *Doctor Who* attraction in the city where the show was actually being made. Prince adds: 'What I heard from [local] fans at the time was, "Why is London getting it first?" I know we obviously had to wait for the building to be constructed, I can understand that, but there was that feeling of, "Why don't they just leave [the Up Close exhibition] open, then?" Perhaps at a smaller level. Or even just [keep] the shop.'

This fan discontent about the closure persisted for some time, because – aside from one convention held over a weekend in 2012 – there followed a long absence of a Cardiff focal point for *Doctor Who* fan activity. There was no longer even the option of visiting what had previously been the closest exhibition outside of Cardiff – the one in Land's End, Cornwall – as that had also closed by this time.

Up Close – Land's End

The Land's End Up Close exhibition opened on 7 April 2007 and ran for nearly four years. Its entrance really could not be missed; following tradition, an oversized TARDIS exterior marked the position, but the scale on this occasion was unlike anything seen before: the whole of the building that housed the exhibition had the familiar police box image painted onto it, dominating the courtyard in which it stood. During its extended run, the exhibition enjoyed regular updates of its displays as new items became available. The following description gives a flavour of some of the props and costumes seen there.

Many of the exhibits had also been on display at one time or another in Brighton, Leicester, Cardiff or Merseyside. These included an Auton bride from 'Rose', along with a mannequin intended to represent a male Auton but lacking an accurate mask; Jabe, the Moxx of Balhoon, an Adherence of the Repeated Meme and another of the alien ambassadors from 'The End of the World'; and the Slitheen and Space Pig combination from 'Aliens of London'/'World War Three'; the miniature barrage balloon from 'The Empty Child'/'The Doctor Dances'; the Face of Boe, the Cassandra prop and a Sister of Plenitude from 'New Earth'; plus the rusted K-9 prop used in 'School Reunion'. Further exhibition stalwarts taking their turn in Land's End included an Ood; a Scarecrow; a showgirl costume from 'Daleks in Manhattan'/'Evolution of the Daleks'; David Tennant's blue suit combination; and guest star Kylie Minogue's Astrid costume plus a Heavenly Host from 'Voyage of the Damned'.

Further notable exhibits in Land's End included a Weeping Angel, curiously labelled 'Stone Angel' on the accompanying signage; a female

Clockwork Droid in pink costume from 'The Girl in the Fireplace'; and two Cybermen in a small, mocked-up snow-covered graveyard like that seen in 'The Next Doctor'. Other, later additions to the exhibition included a Roboform Santa accompanied by a tuba and one of the legs from the Empress of the Racnoss ('The Runaway Bride'); a helmeted Sontaran ('The Sontaran Stratagem'/'The Poison Sky'); a Smiler ('The Beast Below'); a Vampire girl dress ('Vampires of Venice'); and pregnant Amy's costume ('Amy's Choice'). As in Cardiff, a TARDIS police box was also positioned on a green-screen zone, giving visitors a chance to experience first-hand the electronic effect.

Unsurprisingly, a bronze Dalek also featured; and at some point a seemingly unique exhibit was added. This featured an open Dalek casing revealing a Kaled mutant that moved up and down. This was in fact the prop used for Dalek Caan in the Series 4 finale 'The Stolen Earth'/'Journey's End' and, as such, differed from the similar exhibit seen in Brighton during 2005, which had utilised the damaged lower half of a Dalek casing.

The exhibition closed on 3 January 2011, with a party held to mark the occasion and free entry for younger visitors who dressed up as their favourite *Doctor Who* characters.[155]

While the long-term Up Close exhibitions in Cardiff and Land's End were in progress, shorter but similar attractions were installed in cities across the UK. Venues in Manchester, London, Coventry, Glasgow and Newcastle all hosted such ventures. As mentioned previously, a further exhibition also alternated between the National Space Centre in Leicester and the Spaceport on Merseyside.

Spaceport – Merseyside

The Spaceport visitor attraction in Liverpool twice played host to a *Doctor Who* exhibition.[156] The first of these ran from 30 September 2006 to 4 January 2007. Its displays were largely similar to those seen previously in Leicester. They included the male Auton with the test tube of anti-plastic from 'Rose'; selected aliens from 'The End of the World'; and the Zu-Zana robot from 'Bad Wolf'/'The Parting of the Ways'. The rotating TARDIS with transparent walls, previously featured in both Brighton and Leicester, had also now been moved to Merseyside. However, the Spaceport exhibition had an added advantage over the preceding National Space Centre attraction, in that it was able to include numerous items from the recently-transmitted 2006 series.

Inside the rotating TARDIS resided a tenth Doctor costume, complete with brown coat and brown suit combination, and a more recent Rose costume, from 'New Earth'. Other new exhibits from 2006 included a Sister of Plenitude ('New Earth'); a Monk with the Koh-I-Noor diamond ('Tooth and Claw'); the rusted K-9 prop ('School Reunion'); a male Clockwork droid

---

[155] www.doctorwhonews.net/2010/12/dwn171210112508-lands-end-exhibition.html
[156] web.archive.org/web/20090404045242/www.doctorwhoexhibitions.com/09/previous.html

in dark navy costume ('The Girl in the Fireplace'); Rose Tyler's 1950s-style dress ('The Idiot's Lantern'); Victor Kennedy's cane ('Love and Monsters'); and an Ood with glowing red eyes ('The Impossible Planet'/'The Satan Pit'). A bronze Dalek was present too, as was one of the new-style Cybermen. After the exhibition's closure, these items were all then transferred to the nearby city of Manchester.

The second exhibition at the Spaceport venue was named The Art of *Doctor Who* and ran from 23 May 2008 to 1 March 2009. A poster advertising it as the 'Script to Screen Exhibition' proclaimed, 'NEW FOR 2008: TWICE THE SIZE OF LAST TIME.' On this occasion there was a focus on the practical side of television programme-making. Features included a mock-up of the *Doctor Who* production office; set models; and examples of the show's concept art and costume design work. A typical exhibit was the blue version of the tenth Doctor's suit accompanied by a Costume Department item demonstrating the fabric samples used to make it. Similarly, a TARDIS exterior police box was paired with a set model of the interior; and an Ood was coupled with a demonstration of the mask construction process.

A single display board showed images of the Doctor's nine previous incarnations. Further exhibits included the rusted K-9 prop ('School Reunion'); a Sontaran without a helmet ('The Sontaran Stratagem'/'The Poison Sky'); a Judoon with a helmet ('Smith and Jones'); a Sycorax warrior ('The Christmas Invasion'); a Scarecrow ('Human Nature'/'The Family of Blood'); and a Hath ('The Doctor's Daughter'). In a surprising addition, a classic-era Sontaran from 'The Two Doctors' was placed alongside its new-series counterpart. Other old favourites, the Daleks and the Cybermen, were also represented, with one of each of their modern variants on display. The Astrid Peth ('Voyage of the Damned') and showgirl ('Daleks in Manhattan'/'Evolution of the Daleks') costumes were also exhibited.

Props on display included the ninth Doctor's bomb ('Rose'); a gas mask ('The Empty Child'/'The Doctor Dances'); a Robot Santa mask ('The Runaway Bride'); the Master's laser screwdriver ('The Sound of Drums'/'Last of the Time Lords'); a Dalek tommy-gun ('Daleks in Manhattan'/'Evolution of the Daleks'); the Chameleon Arch and a weapon ('Human Nature'/'The Family of Blood'); and the Doctor's timey-wimey detector prop ('Blink'). Development pieces used as a part of the construction of the first new-series Dalek were also placed in a display case for visitors to see.

To celebrate the exhibition's extension, a competition was run to win a Cybershade head.[157] This is likely to have been one of the Millennium FX replicas being produced at that time.

---

[157] www.liverpoolecho.co.uk/news/liverpool-news/heads-roll-spaceport-doctor-who-3458606

DOCTOR WHO EXHIBITIONS

Up Close – Manchester

The Museum of Science and Industry in Manchester hosted a *Doctor Who* exhibition of significant size. Opening on 31 March 2007, the same day as Series 3 began on BBC One with 'Smith and Jones', it was initially set to run until 5 November, but was eventually extended until the beginning of the following year. Described as one of the biggest *Doctor Who* exhibitions ever, it featured lots of new costumes and props not previously displayed.

One of the major items making its exhibition debut in Manchester was the huge Empress of the Racnoss creature from the Christmas special 'The Runaway Bride', broadcast only a few months earlier. Other items from the special included Donna Noble's wedding dress, a Robot Santa and, arranged in a display case, props such as the remote control, a Roboform mask, baubles and an axe. Actor Don Gilet, who had played Lance in the story, at one point made a guest appearance at the exhibition and posed for photographs with the Empress.

Previous incarnations of the Doctor, from William Hartnell to Paul McGann, were represented by way of a wall-mounted infographic. The rotating TARDIS with transparent walls, which had already been seen in Brighton, Leicester and Merseyside, had now also been moved to the Manchester exhibition. Inside once again were the tenth Doctor's suit and Rose's costume from 'New Earth'.

Other items familiar from earlier exhibitions included a male Auton from 'Rose'; various aliens from 'The End of the World', including Lute from the Forest of Cheem and one of the Crespallion Platform 1 staff; a Slitheen together with the Model Unit's destroyed Big Ben miniature from 'Aliens of London'/'World War Three'; the Cardiff Power Station model from 'Boom Town', as last seen in the Cardiff exhibition; and the Zu-Zana robot from 'Bad Wolf'. Displayed for the first time, though, was the Powell Estate model also created by the Model Unit and used during production of 'The Christmas Invasion'.

Another of the major new exhibits featured an array of items from 'Tooth and Claw': Queen Victoria's costume, as worn by Pauline Collins; the large telescope/light chamber prop; the boxed Koh-I-Noor diamond prop, in a display case and surrounded by a mistletoe necklace; and a hooded Monk costume.

Representing the previous episode, 'New Earth', were a Catkind Sister of Plenitude and the Face of Boe. Other exhibits from the 2006 series included a male Clockwork droid in the dark navy costume ('The Girl in the Fireplace'); the distressed K-9 prop from 'School Reunion'; and Rose Tyler's 1950s-style outfit ('The Idiots Lantern').

Two further sizeable installations also came from the 2006 series. 'Rise of the Cybermen'/'The Age of Steel' was represented by a Cybus-style Cyberman and, seated on his impressive throne prop, the Cyber Controller. From 'The Impossible Planet'/'The Satan Pit' came a section of the Sanctuary Base 6 set, generally accompanied by an Ood, although the latter was absent when needed for production of 'Planet of the Ood' in August and September 2007.

The Daleks naturally made an appearance too. As in Cardiff during 2006, their display reflected the Series 2 finale 'Army of Ghosts'/'Doomsday': a bronze Dalek with flashing dome lights and dome and eyestalk movement was accompanied by a gas-masked soldier costume from that story.

During 2007, items from the newly-transmitted series went on display. These included a helmeted Judoon ('Smith and Jones'); a Carrionite with cauldron ('The Shakespeare Code'); the large Lazarus machine ('The Lazarus Experiment'); the tenth Doctor's frozen spacesuit ('42'); and a Weeping Angel ('Blink'). Added to the Dalek display area were the Pig Slave and showgirl costumes from 'Daleks in Manhattan'/'Evolution of the Daleks'.

The Manchester exhibition apparently attracted an impressive total of some 250,000 visitors[158], which may explain why it was extended until 6 January 2008. During its final few weeks, Astrid Peth's waitress costume and a Heavenly Host were added, shortly after their on-screen appearance in the 2007 Christmas special 'Voyage of the Damned'.

Following the exhibition's closure, many of its featured items were prepared for another public appearance, this time at Earl's Court in London.

Earl's Court, London

Earls Court Exhibition Centre in Earl's Court, London was the venue for what was declared to be the largest-ever UK exhibition of *Doctor Who* costumes, props and monsters. A press launch event was held on 18 March 2008, with fourth Doctor Tom Baker the guest of honour. The attraction opened to the public two days later and ran through to 7 January the following year. It is thought to have attracted nearly 200,000 visitors in total.[159] Experience Design were once again responsible for setting things up, continuing their long association with *Doctor Who*; and, as previously mentioned, many of the items on display came direct from the recently-closed Manchester exhibition.

Visitors followed in the footsteps of Rose Tyler, navigating through an area designed to resemble the basement of Henrik's department store as seen in 'Rose' (2005). On either side of the route were positioned a number of Autons from that episode.

Doctor Who's incumbent star David Tennant recorded a short piece for the exhibition. A mannequin, stood next to a TARDIS exterior prop and dressed in the tenth Doctor's blue suit, red tie and brown coat combination, had Tennant's face projected onto it, and his dialogue served as a warning for visitors: 'The TARDIS was drawn to this point in time and space. There must be a reason. These readings, these don't make any sense. Well, Earth sense. They're off the scale, and readings this far off the scale usually mean there are

---

[158] Earl's Court Exhibition Press and Preview event invitation.
[159] Hearn, M (2013). *The Vault*. BBC Books.

DOCTOR WHO EXHIBITIONS

Daleks in the vicinity, right here in London!'

The next exhibits featured were from 'The End of the World', including those seen in Manchester, namely Lute from the Forest of Cheem, one of the Crespallion Platform 1 staff, plus two other aliens. Other previously-seen displays included a Slitheen from 'Aliens of London'/'World War Three'; a gas mask from 'The Empty Child'/'The Doctor Dances'; the Trin-E robot from 'Bad Wolf'/'The Parting of the Ways'; the Cardiff Power Station model from 'Boom Town'; and the Powell Estate flats miniature, a Robot Santa and (with a replica headpiece, as the original would have been fitted directly to the actor) the Sycorax Leader from 'The Christmas Invasion'. The miniature destroyed Big Ben clock face from 'Aliens of London'/'World War Three' also returned, and was placed on a rotating plinth to allow visitors to examine its intricate detail from all sides.

Continuing the chronological journey through the show's recent history, from 'New Earth' came two of the Catkind nurse costumes; the Cassandra prop, with a static model installed in place of the CGI creation seen on screen; a pair of prop pods; and, in front of the latter, one of the garments worn by the infected hospital patients.

The Face of Boe, seen in multiple episodes, was also present in the exhibition, complete with all its supporting machinery. Displayed for the first time, though, were the Victor Kennedy and Abzorbaloff costumes from 'Love and Monsters'.

The exhibition's next section gave an insight into the making of one of the show's monsters. A series of display cases contained clay models of Ood masks, demonstrating such techniques as the creation of the moulds; the insertion of controls to make the eyes blink; and the fitting of the mask to the actor's head. The final result was demonstrated by way of a complete Ood in costume as seen in 'The Impossible Planet'/'The Satan Pit'.

Also on display were a pair of prosthetics created by Millennium FX, one worn by Mark Gatiss as the older Professor Lazarus in 'The Lazarus Experiment' and the other by David Tennant as the aged John Smith, the Doctor's human *alter ego*, in 'The Family of Blood'.

A second Robot Santa and a cloaked Roboform from 'The Runaway Bride' served as an introduction to one of the exhibition's highlights: the full-size Empress of the Racnoss creature. Donna Noble's wedding dress from the same story was displayed alongside. Again, these had all been seen before on Merseyside, as had another large exhibit: the telescope prop from 'Tooth and Claw', accompanied by Queen Victoria's and Father Angelo's costumes and, in a display case, the Koh-I-Noor diamond in a box surrounded by mistletoe.

From 'The Impossible Planet'/'The Satan Pit', two further Ood were displayed on the Sanctuary Base 6 set section created for the Merseyside exhibition. The Doctor's faithful electronic dog K-9 was given his own plinth; on the activation of a button, he could be made to light up and raise his head. The episode 'Fear Her' was represented simply by a few of Chloe Webber's drawings from the episode, including one of her father and one of a boy in a

Union Jack T-shirt.

Rose Tyler's 1950s-style dress and jacket combination from 'The Idiot's Lantern' was presented along with the Doctor's tape recorder prop and the recreation of the Alexandra Palace transmitter used to record that episode's dramatic conclusion. Another Series 2 episode, 'The Girl in the Fireplace', was represented by a large dissecting table and a male Clockwork Droid.

A Scarecrow from 'Human Nature'/'The Family of Blood' provided an insight into the world of pyrotechnics, with one of Real SFX's firing devices accompanying the costume. Further behind-the-scenes items on display included a wind machine, and costume designs with fabric samples. By entering a blue-screen-walled pod, visitors could see themselves on the TARDIS interior set, via the familiar electronic effect.

Entering the Cyberzone through a PVC strip curtain, visitors first encountered, on the right, the impressive Cyber Controller seated on his equally imposing throne from 'The Age of Steel'. A pair of the modern, Cybus-style Cybermen were also on display. These two were static, but occasionally another Cyberman could be found roaming the zone, the costume having been donned by an actor.

Also to be found in the exhibition were a selection of costumes from the 2007 series, including companion Martha Jones's memorable red leather jacket and jeans combination. Doomfinger the Carionnite from 'The Shakespeare Code', complete with prosthetic mask, was displayed along with a witch's cauldron and the sign from the Elephant pub. Additional 2007-series exhibits were a helmeted Judoon from 'Smith and Jones'; Martha's maid costume and two suits, brown and blue, worn by John Smith in 'Human Nature'/'The Family of Blood'; a Weeping Angel ('Blink'); and costumes for Professor Yana and two Futurekind ('Utopia').

The Daleks as usual featured in a spectacular exhibit. A specially-constructed set featured two bronze Daleks and the black Dalek Sec. These all had flashing dome lights and lasers firing from their weaponry. The two bronze Daleks enjoyed some forward and backward movement too, while an accompanying audio track proclaimed the extermination of the humans. The same audio track, recorded by regular Dalek voice artist Nicholas Briggs, would later be reused in Cardiff when the exhibition relocated there in October 2008.

After the broadcast of 'The Stolen Earth'/'Journey's End', Davros was also added to the display. Further Dalek-related exhibits included the Dalek Emperor miniature from 'The Parting of the Ways' and – specially created for this exhibition – a static 'walk-in' bronze Dalek. Similar to the classic-series equivalent, Dalek 1-7, first seen at MOMI, the latter gave children and adults the chance to peer inside, move the arm and weapon and gain an appreciation for the work done by Dalek operators. The Pig Slave and showgirl costumes from 'Daleks in Manhattan'/'Evolution of the Daleks' were also exhibited.

The most recent episode to have been broadcast before the exhibition opened was the 2007 Christmas special 'Voyage of the Damned', so items from that story were added. These included Astrid's costume, Max Capricorn's life support machine, two Heavenly Hosts, the costumes of Foon and Morvin Van Hoff and Banakafalatta, plus a *Titanic* lifebuoy.

During the exhibition's run, the 2008 series was screened, and additional items could then be added. These included Donna Noble's costume from 'Partners in Crime', a Sontaran from 'The Sontaran Stratagem'/'The Poison Sky', a Vashta Nerada-inhabited spacesuit from 'Silence in the Library'/'Forest of the Dead' and a Hath from 'The Doctor's Daughter'.

To promote the 2009 Christmas special 'The Next Doctor', costumes for Miss Hartigan and Jackson Lake, plus a Cybershade, were installed a few days before the episode was broadcast.

A small shop completed the visitor's journey and offered the chance to pick up some of the latest *Doctor Who* merchandise. During the Halloween weekend of 31 October to 2 November 2008 organisers allowed free entry to the exhibition to those younger fans keen to dress up. The Earls Court exhibition finally closed on 7 January 2009, following which some of the displayed items were transferred to a new venue at the Transport Museum in Coventry and others to the Kelvingrove Art Gallery in Glasgow.

Up Close – Coventry

The Coventry Transport Museum hosted this city's *Doctor Who* exhibition, which was open from 13 March 2009 until 10 January 2010 and largely mirrored the 2007 Manchester attraction.

The exhibition began with a blue suit worn by David Tennant's Doctor, positioned by a TARDIS exterior box. Other exhibits, most of which had also been seen in Earls Court, included Doomfinger the Carionnite from 'The Shakespeare Code'; the Sycorax Leader from 'The Christmas Invasion'; a Catkind nurse from 'New Earth'; and the hooded Roboform from 'The Runaway Bride'. Two Ood from 'The Impossible Planet'/'The Satan Pit' were again displayed on the Sanctuary Base 6 set recreation. Other displays included K-9; the Pig Slave and showgirl costumes from 'Daleks in Manhattan'/'Evolution of the Daleks; Davros from 'The Stolen Earth'/'Journey's End'; a Sontaran, complete with head prosthetic, not just helmet; plus the male Clockwork Droid in the dark navy costume from 'The Girl in the Fireplace'.

The more elaborate displays that had been popular in Manchester during 2007 once again featured in Coventry: specifically, the Empress of the Racnoss; a Cyberman with the Cyber Controller on the Cyberthrone; and two bronze Daleks.

The *Coventry Telegraph* reported that the Doctor's roadster Bessie and Jon Pertwee's costume were added to the exhibition in December 2009.[160] Also

---

[160] www.coventrytelegraph.net/news/coventry-news/new-props-costumes-doctor-who-3071264

reportedly added were items from the recently-broadcast story 'The Waters of Mars', including 'the monster Flood, Capt Adelaide Brooke's uniform and the robot Gadget'.[161] These items were displayed for only a short time before the exhibition closed in January 2010.

Kelvingrove, Glasgow

The Kelvingrove Art Gallery in Glasgow, Scotland hosted an extensive exhibition of *Doctor Who* costumes and props. At its 27 March 2009 opening, two Cybus-style Cybermen posed for photographs outside, terrorising children and two traffic wardens. This exhibition featured a combination of items from Earls Court and The Art of *Doctor Who* attraction that had been at the Spaceport on Merseyside.

The Auton display, featuring a mock-up of the Henrik's department store basement as seen in 'Rose', which had begun the exhibition in Earls Court, was one of those transferred to Glasgow. Chalking up yet another public appearance was the Moxx of Balhoon, which had now been afforded its own individual plinth. Other aliens from 'The End of the World' included two of the alien ambassadors; one of the Crespallion Platform 1 staff; the Face of Boe; and Cassandra, with the weathered frame and static prop face as seen in Earls Court. Also as in Earls Court, the pair of the prop pods featured in 'New Earth' provided a background for a Catkind nurse and garments worn by the infected flesh people.

As usual, exhibits seen at other venues across the UK remained, including K-9; a gas-mask prop from 'The Empty Child'/'The Doctor Dances'; the Zu-Zana robot from 'Bad Wolf'/'The Parting of the Ways'; the Abzorbaloff and Victor Kennedy's costume from 'Love and Monsters'; a Scarecrow from 'Human Nature'/'The Family of Blood'; a Robot Santa from 'The Christmas Invasion'; a Hath from 'The Doctor's Daughter'; and a Sontaran without helmet from 'The Sontaran Stratagem'/'The Poison Sky'.

A trio of Cybermen were positioned in front of a mirrored wall: the Cyber Leader from 'The Next Doctor' joining two of his subordinates. A button activated a voice track and some illumination within the Leader's helmet. Accompanying the men of steel, from the same story, was Mercy Hartigan's costume, complete with umbrella.

A Weeping Angel from 'Blink' was placed in front of a backdrop recreating the Wester Drumlins house wall bearing the Doctor's graffiti, warning Sally Sparrow to duck. Again the accompanying information board incorrectly called the monster a 'Stone Angel'.

In similarly impressive displays, an Ood was placed within a cage, mirroring the events of 'Planet of the Ood'; and a Vashta Nerada was positioned behind one of the curved desks topped with books seen during

---

[161] www.coventrytelegraph.net/news/coventry-news/new-props-costumes-doctor-who-3071264

'Silence in the Library'/'Forest of the Dead'.

Other costumes on display included those of Astrid Peth ('Voyage of the Damned'); Jackson Lake ('The Next Doctor'); the showgirl Tallulah ('Daleks in Manhattan'/'Evolution of the Daleks'); a soldier ('Doomsday'); and Professor Yana and a Futurekind ('Utopia'). Two companion costumes also featured, specifically Martha Jones's red leather jacket, pink T-shirt and jeans combination and Donna Noble's costume from 'Partners in Crime'. From 'The Fires of Pompeii', a costume worn by one of the Sibylline sisterhood and two of Evelina's costumes were displayed, along with a prop marble circuit board and altar set piece.

The Cardiff production office mock-up that had been at The Art of *Doctor Who* exhibition on Merseyside was also now installed in Glasgow. It came complete with schedules and Art Department designs covering every inch of wall space. Set models and an impressive miniature of the Empress of the Racnoss were visible too.

The walk-in bronze Dalek also made the trip from Earls Court, as did a complete bronze Dalek with the button activating lights and a voice track. The black Dalek Sec and a second bronze Dalek were also placed in a recreation of the environment seen in 'Daleks in Manhattan'/'Evolution of the Daleks', complete with Dalek movements, voices and lasers.

Max Capricorn's life support machine from 'Voyage of the Damned' was accompanied by other items from that episode: a painting of the *Titanic*; a prop lifebuoy; a Host; and Morvin's and Foon's costumes.

Items used by David Tennant, a proud Scotsman, were a popular attraction in Glasgow. These included his Doctor's brown coat, Converse trainers, sonic screwdriver and fob watch. The TARDIS set model and exterior police box prop were also included. After 'Planet of the Dead' was broadcast, a Tritovore and Lady Christina De Souza's costume were put on display.

The exhibition closed in January 2010, with the Up Close roadshow then rolling on to one final destination, this time in the North East of England.

Up Close – Newcastle

Running at the Centre for Life in Newcastle from Saturday 22 May 2010 – the day 'The Hungry Earth' was broadcast – until 31 October 2010, this small exhibition afforded an opportunity to see costumes and props from Matt Smith's debut series as the Doctor. These included Smith's main costume, with red trim shirt and bow tie; his raggedy Doctor costume from 'The Eleventh Hour'; and his King's Arms football kit from 'The Lodger', plus Amy's and Rory's frozen outfits from 'Amy's Choice'. A TARDIS exterior prop was placed on its back with a light shining from inside, mirroring the crashed time-and-space machine as seen in 'The Eleventh Hour'. An Ironsides Dalek from 'Victory of the Daleks' was displayed in addition to a large map prop also seen during the episode. Further exhibition debutants included a Smiler in a booth from 'The Beast Below'; Rosanna Calvieri's costume from 'Vampires in

Venice'; and two Silurians – one of them the Restac costume – plus other set pieces from 'The Hungry Earth'/'Cold Blood'.

A trio of Cybus-style Cybermen were positioned around the Cyberthrone seen during 'The Age of Steel'. The display also included the Cyber Controller from the same episode and the Cyber Leader from 'The Next Doctor'. Further items transferred from Glasgow to Newcastle included a Host and the costumes of Astrid Peth and Foon and Morvin Van Hoff from 'Voyage of the Damned'. Other exhibits included K-9; a Slitheen; a selection of Autons from 'Rose'; the Moxx of Balhoon from 'The End of the World'; a Weeping Angel; Gadget, the robot from 'The Waters of Mars'; a Tritovore from 'Planet of the Dead'; a Vashta Nerada from 'Silence in the Library'/'Forest of the Dead'; and a Scarecrow from 'Human Nature'/'The Family of Blood'. Finally, the new Davros from 'The Stolen Earth'/'Journey's End' and the previously created Ood mask construction display completed the exhibition in Newcastle.

The End of the Up Close Exhibitions

The exhibitions at Earls Court and in Blackpool ended in 2009. Those in Glasgow, Coventry and Newcastle followed suit in 2010. Finally, in the early part of 2011, the Land's End and Cardiff exhibitions also closed their doors. These closures were indicative of the fact that preparations were being made for a major new attraction, unlike anything that had ever been seen before.

Chapter 9
The *Doctor Who* Experience, London Olympia (2011-2012)

Following Matt Smith's first series as the eleventh Doctor, a brand-new attraction fully immersed visitors into their own adventure with the enigmatic Time Lord. The highlight of the newly-titled *Doctor Who* Experience was a walk-through adventure, preceding a major exhibition packed full of costumes and props, including items from the show's very latest episodes. Rounding things off was the country's only official *Doctor Who* merchandise shop run by BBC Worldwide.

To create the new attraction, BBC Worldwide utilised the skills of Sarner, a company experienced in the design and delivery of leisure entertainment facilities for clients such as Madame Tussauds and the Natural History Museum. Following consultation with *Doctor Who* showrunner Steven Moffat, the plot for the walk-through adventure centred on the Doctor being trapped once again in the Pandorica, as seen in the television story 'The Pandorica Opens'/'The Big Bang'. As visitors made their way along the route, they witnessed spectacular sets combined with atmospheric sounds and special effects, supported by specially-recorded scenes played on monitors, featuring Matt Smith in character as the Doctor.

The *Doctor Who* Experience opened on the second floor of London Olympia on Sunday 20 February 2011, with Matt Smith in attendance, mirroring Jon Pertwee's presence at the opening of the BBC TV Special Effects Exhibition in 1972. Spectacular publicity images of various generations of Daleks on Westminster Bridge and Cybermen outside St Paul's Cathedral were created as part of the associated advertising campaign.

The Walk-through Adventure

After purchasing their tickets, or validating their print-at-home ones, visitors congregated in a queuing area that had *Doctor Who* artefacts on display nearby, such as an Ironsides Dalek from 'Victory of the Daleks' and Rosanna Calvieri's costume from 'Vampires in Venice'. After an introduction from a staff member, they were led into a dark room to watch a specially-edited video montage of the eleventh Doctor in action, featuring clips and music from the 2010 series, before stepping through a 'crack in time' – created by the sliding apart of a pair of double doors with a crack-shaped join down the centre – as their adventure began.

The second room was a specially-constructed set representing the National Museum of *Starship UK*, the vessel on which 'The Beast Below' had been set (although no museum had featured in the episode). Two booths containing Smilers also featured. Within the Museum, lots of items from the show's past were displayed, including a pyramid of Yeti control spheres, similar to that seen in 'The Abominable Snowmen'; the telescope/light chamber prop from 'Tooth and Claw'; and *The Pandorica Opens* painting from the episode of the same title.

The initial dialogue to visitors was delivered by a node as seen in 'Silence in the Library', with a face projected onto the static prop. This was interrupted by alarms, only for the Doctor to appear on a screen, speaking from inside the Pandorica. The Time Lord began by calling out for his companion Amy (Pond) and referring to the assembled visitors as 'shoppers' – a supposed misconception that was continued throughout the adventure and seemed somewhat peculiar given that the venue was not near any retail hotspot (although more cynical critics wondered if it was a nod to the fact that there was a shop at the end of the Experience).

The conclusion to this *Starship UK* Museum section of the adventure came with the arrival of the TARDIS. This impressive illusion was achieved via a clever use of the Pepper's Ghost lighting technique – as previously employed with a model TARDIS at Longleat back in 1987 – coupled with the familiar materialisation sound effect.

Research conducted in advance by BBC Worldwide had shown that one of the things fans most wanted to be able to do at the attraction was to step into and fly the TARDIS, so for the next stage of the walk-through adventure a specially-constructed TARDIS console had been installed, at significant cost, based upon the one seen in Matt Smith's first series as the Doctor. The console room had a floor rigged to make rising and falling movements simulating flight (something that, in the television studio, actors had to convey purely through their performances), and large screens allowing for the Doctor to continue his dialogue and provide instruction. Control boxes on the railings around the console, described by the Doctor as 'remote station controls', allowed visitors to 'fly' the ship. One of the more humorous pieces of dialogue suggested, 'The TARDIS doesn't really like adults, they're boring and drink coffee and go on and on and on.' Visitors eventually exited the console room via a second, 'back' door and made their way into a dark and gloomy corridor.

A familiar heartbeat-like sound effect was then accompanied by the voice-modulated tones of actor Nicholas Briggs, signifying that the adventure's next room represented a Dalek spaceship. Three full-size Dalek props were featured, rigged to move in coordination with the prerecorded soundtrack. The Daleks used were of the 'new paradigm' type seen in 'Victory of the Daleks' – specifically, a white Supreme, a red Drone and a blue Strategist. The Supreme Dalek was placed on its own individual pedestal, drawing the initial attention of visitors, while the Drone and Strategist Daleks then emerged from tunnels on either side of the room. The narrative saw the Daleks identify the visitors as friends of the Doctor – or, as he called them, 'a harmless subspecies known as shoppers'.

The Doctor's video signal having supposedly betrayed the ship's location to a rival group of Daleks of the more traditional bronze design, an exchange of dialogue ensued between the Dalek Supreme and the black Dalek Sec, the latter seen on a screen in close-up footage reused from 'Daleks in Manhattan'. During this exchange – with both Daleks being voiced by Briggs – the background behind the Drone and Scientist Daleks became an impressively large screen showing Dalek spaceships. Visitors could then look on as an epic space battle took place between the two Dalek factions, eventually resulting in the vanquishing of the 'new paradigm' versions (something that Steven Moffat later said he intended to explain in fictional terms why the latter were largely absent from subsequent television episodes).

After exiting the Dalek spaceship, visitors moved into another short corridor, dressed in the same type of bronze panelling as seen in the TARDIS console room, then up a ramp and through a pair of open TARDIS doors. The accompanying Matt Smith-voiced audio warned visitors, 'Whatever you do. Do. Not. Blink.' This served as an introduction to an encounter with the Weeping Angels, on a forest set intended to simulate that seen on the *Byzantium* in 'Flesh and Stone'. Two standard Weeping Angel props were used – one 'weeping', the other 'screaming' – but accompanied by some additional statues like those seen in the episode's 'maze of the dead', initially thought to have been Aplans but revealed to be Weeping Angels in the early stages of regeneration. Also within the forest, a little randomly, were the stone Gorgon and Alan Jackson and Sylvia Gribbins statues from *The Sarah Jane Adventures* story 'Eye of the Gorgon'. Visitors moved along a walkway through the middle of the forest, with one of the Weeping Angels on either side and smoke and strobe effects to accompany the atmospheric soundtrack. Guests were then given a pair of 3D glasses each before being ushered into the final room.

The last stop on the adventure was a room dressed to resemble the Underhenge as seen in 'The Pandorica Opens'/'The Big Bang', although in this case supplemented by a three-tiered platform on which the visitors stood. Opposite the platform, the room was dominated by a stone block representing the Pandorica, to the right of which was positioned the story's 'stone' Dalek, adapted from the orange 'new paradigm' prop seen in 'Victory of the Daleks'. Additional detail was provided by a stone Cyberman leg leaning against the Pandorica, and an excavator's table displaying a stone Cyberman arm.

To the left of the room, a small screen played slides of the archaeological excavations, followed by another clip of Matt Smith's Doctor, in which he was seen to transport from the Pandorica back into his TARDIS console room. The Pandorica seal then slid apart to reveal a large screen and the now-vacated internal seat. This led into a specially-created 3D movie – the reason for the 3D glasses – in which a 'new paradigm' Dalek eyestalk and plunger appeared to move in front of the screen; Cybermen fired their weapons and another reached out in a grabbing motion; a Weeping Angel approached the audience, jumping between positions in the familiar way accompanied by the usual sound effect. In the meantime, on the smaller screen, Matt Smith's Doctor frantically operated his TARDIS controls to try to close the crack in time. Finally, on the larger screen, another Weeping Angel roared toward the audience out of a black background, face screaming and arms reaching out for them, before being sucked back into the closing crack. The Doctor then bid the visitors a farewell – 'Bye-bye, do shopping' – and, after returning their 3D glasses, they exited onto the exhibition floor.

The Exhibition

The exhibition hall provided the biggest collection of *Doctor Who* costumes, props and sets on display for many years, if not ever. Unlike in previous cases such as at Longleat or Blackpool, exhibits were for the most part simply placed onto plinths with a single image background board and information signage instead of being positioned in an environment reflecting their on-screen appearance. However, on the upside, none of the costumes was shielded behind glass, so visitors could inspect every detail and photograph them unrestricted.

After passing the Pandorica cube prop and some oversized *Radio Times* cover replicas on the wall, visitors came to one of exhibition highlights. For the first time ever, costumes representing all of the Doctor's television incarnations were displayed. Replicas were created for the first, second, eighth and ninth Doctors, but all of the others were originals. The third Doctor's costume was the particularly memorable variant from 'Spearhead from Space' and 'The Sea Devils'. Tom Baker's was that seen in stories such as 'The Power of Kroll' and 'City of Death', with flying duck badges on the coat's lapel. The costume for Peter Davison's Doctor featured the trousers he had worn during Season 21, with the simpler striped design.

The first five costumes were mounted on a curved plinth, the next five on another, with a gap in between through which visitors could move into the rest of the exhibition. The oft-ridiculed sixth Doctor costume featured here a red cravat and waistcoat with teddy-bear buttons, as worn in the courtroom sequences and concluding two episodes of 'The Trial of the Time Lord'. The seventh Doctor's costume included his cream jacket as seen in Seasons 24 and 25. The replica ninth Doctor costume included a green jumper as seen in 'Dalek', 'The Long Game' and 'Father's Day'. For the tenth Doctor, a brown pinstripe suit was accompanied by the familiar long overcoat and included a Daniel Hechter tie as worn in stories such as 'New Earth' and 'The End of Time'.

In the centre of the room, opposite the costume plinths, stood a TARDIS police box exterior and a waxwork recreation of Matt Smith's Doctor, dressed in the Donegal tweed jacket and Paul Smith shirt plus red bow tie combination that had debuted in 'The Eleventh Hour'. A sonic screwdriver was placed in the jacket pocket but proved a target for light-fingered visitors. The police box prop was one that had actually been used for the television show; it was in the darker shade of blue seen since the 2010 series and had the St John's Ambulance logo on the right-hand door.

Opposite this display, two green-screen video effects booths provided the exhibition's first merchandise opportunity, as visitors were offered the chance to buy 10x8 photographs showing themselves superimposed onto a choice of two different backgrounds. The first of these backgrounds was the 2010-style TARDIS console room, but unfortunately the proportions were very inaccurate, so that the photographed visitors looked significantly taller than the central console. The second utilised the Pandorica chair, allowing the visitors to pose as if they were trapped inside the Pandorica itself, and in this case the illusion was far more successful. These booths were operated by staff provided by a separate company and not BBC Worldwide employees.

The exhibition became the first to include two original TARDIS console room sets – one classic era and one modern era. The latter was that originally constructed in 2004 for Christopher Eccleston's Doctor and subsequently used by David Tennant, whose regeneration scene was played on a big screen nearby. With the exception of some *Children in Need* studio tours organised in 2008, this was the first opportunity that members of the public had had to see the console up close, complete with quirky elements such as a marine sextant and Gallifreyan post-it notes on the scanner. A few of the coral-esque pillars still remained to complete the set, along with tubing and cables hanging from the ceiling.

The second TARDIS console on display was the version that had debuted in the anniversary story 'The Five Doctors'. Mike Tucker, an individual who had worked on the console over the years, recalled how it had survived due to the foresight of his colleague, visual effects designer Mike Kelt: 'The nice thing about the console was that Mike Kelt, when he designed it for "The Five Doctors", had actually made a very robust storage case for it. That was unusual for anything built for *Doctor Who*, but because Mike knew that this particular prop was going to be lugged in and out of studio on a regular basis, he went to the expense of building this storage case for it. That's one of the reasons I think it has survived so well.

'The advantage the new show has is that the TARDIS is a standing set; it's erected, and it's left there for the duration of the series. When we were making *Doctor Who* [in the classic era], the TARDIS was got in on the morning of recording, set up, and then that evening it was broken down again and taken back to the Visual Effects Department – and that was happening on every story for which it was needed.'

Despite excellent storage, the prop still required some restoration, as it been used regularly from 1983, and even into the 1990s with appearances at various conventions and so on. Tucker again explains: 'It's had a lot of work done to it over the years. I had it refurbished way back when we were doing things like [the *Children in Need* special] "Dimensions in Time". Subsequently it got refurbished an awful lot for the DWAS PanoptiCon conventions, and then finally it was refurbished to go into the exhibition.'

Tucker and his team were involved in this refurbishment but were faced with the challenge of matching switches and buttons originally sourced in the 1980s. 'The switches that were used on it are no longer made, so you're either trying to track down suppliers that have got stocks of these old '80s radio spares switches or you're taking moulds off things and putting new ones in. There have been a few changes over the years, and certainly, as it stands now, there are certain areas of that console where it's probably not as it looked on screen originally; but it's had so many people working on it over the years that it's sort of evolved into a slightly different beast.'

The roundel-patterned walls used for this exhibit were not screen-used. This was because, toward the end of the 1980s, the original walls had suffered badly, as Tucker again remembers: 'By the time we reached "The Greatest Show in the Galaxy", and certainly for "Battlefield", I think there were only one or two walls that had enough roundels left in them for the production team to be able to get the shot they needed. That's why in "Battlefield" the TARDIS interior scene is done in very low lighting: because the walls were in such bad condition.'

Added to the set as a finishing touch was a hat stand positioned in one corner, with the original scarf worn by Tom Baker from 'The Leisure Hive' through to 'Logopolis', despite the fourth Doctor having never actually used that particular console room.

Two more TARDIS exterior props were also present in the exhibition. One was the Melkur-disguised form of the Master's TARDIS as seen in 'The Keeper of Traken'. This had previously been on display in Blackpool, MOMI and Llangollen. The other was the prop that had debuted in 'The Leisure Hive' and been used until the end of the show's original run. This had been restored at the request of the exhibition's artefacts manager Andrew Beech by Mark Barton Hill, following previous work he had done on a replacement lamp and door sign on another TARDIS prop. Hill later recalled: 'I spent three months collecting and playing with suitable blue paints, researching, watching DVDs and developing techniques of distressing and weathering. I then collected the prop from the *Doctor Who* studios in Wales, brought it to Olympia and started to work on it there *in situ* every day for two weeks in January.'[162]

After many years the prop was in a poor state. In addition to a thick layer of dust, the item was missing a base plinth, a door pull sign and a lamp, and featured broken windows and the wrong signage. Hill described the lengthy restoration process: 'I washed it, sanded it, and then painstakingly rebuilt the base plinth and painted it layer by layer, starting with quite a light shade of blue, gradually getting darker with a wipe-on, wipe-off technique using about five different blues and finished with a black wash – just to get that Season 18 feel. I replaced some of the windows with replicas I made myself and made a

---

[162] news.thedoctorwhosite.co.uk/the-restoration-of-a-tardis/comment-page-1/

new lamp and signage, which were all hand-painted.'[163] The impressive final result stood proudly on display in the exhibition – and also revealed that the prop actually had a set of normally-concealed exit doors at the back, used during production as a neat trick to avoid overcrowding in scenes where multiple actors had to be seen to enter the TARDIS all at once.

The Time Lords are of course an important part of *Doctor Who* history, and they were well represented by a trio of costumes. On the left was the one worn by former James Bond actor Timothy Dalton for his appearance as Rassilon in 'The End of Time'. With his powerful gauntlet on the left hand, a practical leather battle tunic was covered by a ceremonial red robe that had undertones of past Time Lord attire. That style of Time Lord costume was represented by a red robe with matching collar, as first seen in 'The Deadly Assassin'. Completing the Time Lord display was the Master's costume, consisting of red waistcoat and white shirt with black trousers, as worn by both Derek Jacobi, initially in the character's human disguise as Professor Yana, and then briefly by John Simm in 'Utopia'.

A display of modern-era companions' costumes was placed between the two TARDIS console room sets. Featured were those of Amy Pond ('The Hungry Earth'/'Cold Blood'), Rory Williams ('The Hungry Earth'/'Cold Blood', with the North Face brand logo carefully coloured out), Donna Noble ('Journey's End'), Martha Jones ('Smith and Jones') and Rose Tyler ('Journey's End'). Young Amelia Pond's costume ('The Eleventh Hour') was possibly also added to tie in with an exclusive product available in the attraction's shop. Opposite these were costumes of River Song (the dress seen in 'The Time of Angels'), Astrid Peth ('Voyage of the Damned'), Captain Jack Harkness ('Journey's End') and Sarah Jane Smith ('School Reunion'). Completing the display was K-9 ('School Reunion'). All of these were original, screen-used items, making up the largest collection of the Doctor's friends' costumes ever to have been put on public display. However, the remainder of the exhibition belonged to the monsters.

Two static Cybus-style Cybermen, one of which was the Cyber Controller seen in 'The Age of Steel', presaged the impending monster encounter. In cabinets nearby, a number of Cyberman helmets were displayed. These included, for the first time ever, a replica of the head design seen in their debut story 'The Tenth Planet'. Others were from 'The Wheel in Space', 'The Invasion', 'Revenge of the Cybermen' (the Leader), 'Attack of the Cybermen' (the Controller) and 'Silver Nemesis'. With the exception of the original design, the remainder had been seen previously in other exhibitions.

This journey through the development of the Cybermen was replicated by one devoted to the Doctor's most famous foes. The Daleks are almost synonymous with *Doctor Who*, and they rightly had a significant presence at the Experience. Their creator, Davros, was on hand, in the form of the original chair and costume from 'The Stolen Earth'/'Journey's End', paired with an

---

[163] news.thedoctorwhosite.co.uk/the-restoration-of-a-tardis/comment-page-1/

exhibition mask based on that worn by Julian Bleach in the story. For the first time, the Daleks themselves were placed in chronological order of appearance, showing that although they had undergone cosmetic changes over the years, the essentials of Raymond Cusick's initial design remained unchanged. The first two in line were replicas, specifically of one of the original Daleks from their 1963 debut story, and of an Emperor's guard from 'The Evil of the Daleks'. These were specially constructed by Dave Brian and Steve Allen and owned by Andrew Beech. Like the exhibition skirt created for Madame Tussauds, they would later graduate to being used in the TV show itself. This first occurred in 'Asylum of the Daleks', necessitating two further replicas being made to ensure that the Dalek display at the Experience still had a full complement of props – and also to keep secret the fact that a new Dalek episode was being recorded in Cardiff. Subsequently, all four replicas appeared on screen in 'The Magician's Apprentice'/'The Witch's Familiar' and can be seen surrounding Peter Capaldi's Doctor in an oft-printed promotional photograph from that story.

The next Dalek in the Experience's chronological line-up was a traditional gun-metal grey-and-black one belonging to Mark Barton Hill. Much of the upper half consisted of parts dating back to 'Planet of the Daleks', but otherwise it was an incredibly accurate replica of a specific prop featured in 'Resurrection of the Daleks', complete with orange ribbons in the weapon. This Dalek had also been on display at Longleat in 2003, positioned behind Davros, and was another that would later go on to appear in 'Asylum of the Daleks'.

As a fitting finale to the classic-era Dalek line-up, the instantly-recognisable Special Weapons Dalek was back for yet another public outing, having been retained by the BBC following the closure of the Blackpool exhibition. When last seen, it had been given a predominantly bronze glaze, but this was rectified for the Experience, with a return to the gritty cream livery seen in 'Remembrance of the Daleks'. This would later become the first original classic-era Dalek prop to appear in the modern series, when it too featured briefly in 'Asylum of the Daleks'.

To the right of the Special Weapons Dalek, the next prop showcased the copper-and-bronze style seen consistently in *Doctor Who* since 'Dalek' in 2005. It is uncertain if this was one of the original screen-used props or one of the previously-constructed exhibition replicas. Finally, the yellow Eternal Dalek, which had made its only on-screen appearance in 'Victory of the Daleks', completed the Evolution of the Daleks display.

Four of these Daleks – specifically those of the 1967, 1984, 2005 and 2010 designs – had been used in the publicity images staged on Westminster Bridge in London prior to the Experience's opening.

Opposite this row of Daleks was presented another: the Dalek Emperor model from 'The Parting of the Ways'. Built by Mike Tucker and the Model Unit, its level of detail was very impressive, and great to be able to see up close.

A trio of exhibits gave a similar chronological demonstration of how the

Sontarans had developed over time while again retaining the basics of their original design. Linx, the original Sontaran from 'The Time Warrior', was represented by a refurbished screen-used costume from the 1970s, paired with a new mask replicating that worn by Kevin Lindsay in the story, with his belt holding a weapon and the original control box. The second Sontaran was another classic-era one, with an original costume from 'The Two Doctors'. This one was taller than the first and positioned holding its helmet in its left hand and the large weapon from the story in its right – the same pose it had held in Longleat in 1991 and then in the Llangollen and Blackpool exhibitions. More recently it had been seen in The Art of *Doctor Who* at the Spaceport on Merseyside, but on that occasion with its arms to the side and not posed as here. The display was completed by a modern Sontaran as first seen in 'The Sontaran Stratagem'/'The Poison Sky'. This was one of the 'crowd scene' Sontarans that had never removed its helmet on screen (avoiding the need for the actor inside to have a prosthetic mask), so the helmet was permanently fixed to the costume – which was probably the same as had been displayed previously at some of the Up Close exhibitions.

One aim decided upon for the Experience was to include more classic-era monsters than had been seen in its Up Close forerunners. This had been reflected in the displays showing the evolution of the Cybermen, the Daleks and Sontarans, but also extended to other items. Artefacts manager Andrew Beech approached Mike Tucker, who had contributed to both classic- and modern-era episodes of the show and was ideally placed to take on the task of renovating older props for display. Tucker recalls: 'Once we knew that this new exhibition was going to be opening up in Olympia, I arranged to meet Andrew down at Newport, where the BBC have a store for all the items previously displayed at Longleat, Llangollen and Blackpool, plus all the things that had survived following the big Bonhams sale. So I went down there with Andrew and we just went through which items still existed and which ones were potentially in a condition to bring back out and put on display again.'

Selection was based on which of those artefacts that the BBC still retained would appeal to visitors and could be realistically restored. Where possible, Tucker and his team at the Model Unit attempted to replicate the construction techniques used originally. 'What was key to me,' notes Tucker, 'and key to the team at BBC Worldwide, was trying to go back and redo these things with the correct techniques that would give them a certain authenticity. The other thing I've got in my favour is that I still have colleagues working with me who were at the Visual Effects Department during the '60s and the '70s; so where possible I actually put people back on the jobs that they were involved with originally, adding another level of authenticity to it.'

This process resulted in the restoration of a trio of artefacts that would feature prominently in the exhibition, and in associated promotional material. These were the K1 Robot from 'Robot', an Ice Warrior from 'The Ice Warriors' and a Zygon from 'Terror of the Zygons'. The K1 Robot took pride of place, having previously appeared in exhibitions at Longleat, Blackpool, MOMI and

Llangollen. Despite having been in storage since the 2009 closure of the Blackpool exhibition, this was a prime candidate for restoration, given its construction of aluminium and timber with very little latex – so often the element that rots and disintegrates over time. A lot of the joints, though, used upholstery foam, and these were in particularly poor condition, as was the head. 'The head was in such a bad state that at first I didn't actually think it was the original head,' says Tucker. 'It looked to me like it might have been a very bad replica. But once we got it back to my workshop and put it on a stand and pulled everything back into shape a little bit, it became apparent that it was pretty much entirely intact and was the original one, it just needed a little bit of care and attention.'

Curiously, at some point during the prop's exhibition life it had been sprayed silver. Removing that paint was therefore one of the first tasks in the restoration process, as Tucker explains: 'Even though the actual prop as seen on screen is just raw aluminium and sheet steel, somebody had sprayed it silver at some point in the intervening years, which had dulled it. So one of our first jobs was literally to strip all the paint off it and take it all back to the metal. Once we'd done that, it already looked a hundred times better than it had previously. Then it was just a question of methodically going through, replacing the pieces of foam that had rotted beyond repair, and a few little bits of detail on the chest. With all these props, anything that has been built 20, 30, 40 years ago, you are trying to track down bits and pieces that the original effects designers and costume designers might have used. Finding some of this stuff proves a bit of a challenge occasionally. So we did a fair bit of taking moulds off things and casting out new pieces. Apart from a couple of bits of detail on the chest, it is largely what was seen on screen, and we didn't have to replace anything.'

Once restored, the Robot looked as good as it had back in 1974, when it was originally created for the show by future Oscar-winning costume designer James Acheson. 'It formed a really nice centrepiece to the new exhibition when that opened in Olympia,' says Tucker, who recalled seeing it previously at MOMI. 'It was almost like a precursor to some of the big robot costumes that Neill Gorton's done for the modern episodes, things that disguise the human shape and add extra height. So it was a bit ahead of its time.'

The second of the major refurbished attractions was an original Ice Warrior costume from the creatures' 1967 debut story. Thought to be the only full original Ice Warrior costume still to survive, this had also been on display before, at MOMI, Blackpool, Llangollen and Longleat, and more recently in Brighton and, prior to its 2008 renovation, the Cardiff Up Close exhibition. The creature's large torso had survived particularly well in the BBC's store because of its fibreglass construction, and contained an indication of the actor who had originally worn it, as Tucker illuminates: 'When we got that back to the workshop, we took the shell apart and that's when we discovered that it still had Bernard Bresslaw's name tag on the inside of it.' Bresslaw had played Varga, the lead Ice Warrior, during the story.

Bob Richardson, an Exhibitions Assistant in the 1980s, remembers, '[At that time] there were a couple of very tatty Ice Warriors, but the rubber parts had gone hard with age, so the claws were very brittle and the rubberised leggings were perished'. It is therefore no surprise to learn that by 2010 these aspects of the surviving Ice Warrior were in even worse condition, as Tucker explains: 'The legs, although they were original, the latex had gone down; it was rotting, basically, and had gone very sticky'. The decision was made to construct a replacement set of legs via the same methods as would have been used originally. First, a repair was made to the rotting latex of one of the originals so that a plaster mould could be taken from it. This mould with then used to create two identical new legs that matched the original.

Further challenges were presented by the costume's head and arms, as Tucker again notes: 'At some point the costume had had a very crude polystyrene replacement head and set of arms made for it.' As a result, Alan Marshall, part of the Model Unit team, had to sculpt from scratch a new set of arms, hands and a head that matched the originals. 'Andrew [Beech] was great,' says Tucker, 'because he provided us with a mass of photographs from the BBC archive showing not only the props on set but also some behind-the-scenes shots of them being put together in the Make-up Department. So we were able to get a lot of very good photo reference to ensure that the head and the arms were accurate to what had been seen on screen.'

The finishing touch was the addition of pieces of brown fur around the costume's various joints. The final result was certainly impressive and authentic-looking, although actually only the torso was screen-used.

Another treat for fans of the classic-era show was the refurbished original Zygon costume – the only one known to have survived from 'Terror of the Zygons'. Again, extensive work was carried out by Mike Tucker's team to bring the costume up to exhibition condition after a long period in storage; a Zygon costume, likely to have been the same one, had not been seen in public since the closure of the original Blackpool exhibition in 1985. In fact, when delivered to Tucker's workshop, the costume was separated out into a number of bin liners, having rotted almost beyond repair.[164] Tucker recalls: 'We basically ended up with a bag of bits, which was all that remained of the arms, the legs and the large peeling fibreglass shape that was the torso. So that was probably the most extensive repair and restoration job we had to do.' The creature's feet did however remain intact, and the inside labels revealed that they had been constructed around a pair of Marks & Spencer's tartan slippers! The fact that these had survived, along with the fibreglass shapes around which the head and torso had been formed, created the potential for restoration, despite the latex having rotted away.

The techniques used to make the original costume had been quite unusual, as Tucker explains: 'The Zygons were made not by sculpting and getting them out of a mould, but by direct build techniques. Once the fibreglass shapes for

---

[164] www.gamesradar.com/making-monsters-for-the-doctor-who-experience/

the three Zygons had been made, all the suckers were handmade and applied, all the textures stippled on with latex; and the arms and the legs were made by cutting upholstery foam into patterns, rolling them into tubular shapes and then again stippling and applying latex and suckers over the top.'

Colin Mapson, who had been visual effects designer on *Doctor Who* stories including 'Image of the Fendahl', 'Nightmare of Eden' and 'Time and the Rani', was assigned the task of restoring the Zygon by replicating those unusual original techniques, as Tucker again describes: 'We took moulds from a few sections of suckers that still survived intact. But the rest of the parts, Colin made up just by making little rolls of foam. We then mixed up a thick latex mix, and the costume was put together in exactly the same way as in the mid-1970s. We had enough bits of the original one to be able to make sure that we matched colours and textures as well as techniques, so that it was as accurate a copy as you could do.'

The final result was spectacular, with the individual suckers and veins on the skin and face-piece sculpted to match those of the costume worn by actor John Woodnutt, who had played the lead Zygon, Broton. 'What we ended up with,' says Tucker, 'was something that looked very authentic and very of the period, although in fact, apart from the central fibreglass core, very little of it actually was the original Zygon. The feet were original, and I think one of the hands we actually managed to salvage, but the rest of it was rebuilt from the ground up.'

While the K1 Robot occupied a central position in the Experience's 'monster zone', the Zygon and the Ice Warrior also provided flashbacks to *Doctor Who* exhibitions of the past. Care was taken, though, to pose all the artefacts more appropriately than had generally been the case in the past, as Tucker explains: 'It was quite nice to have gone full circle, in that we were getting our hands back on these things again, and actually displaying them in what I considered to be a slightly more dynamic way.'

Accompanying the three classic-series costumes were a cavalcade of monsters and aliens from 21st Century *Doctor Who*. These included an Auton ('Rose'); Novice Hame and another Catkind ('New Earth'); and the Face of Boe ('The End of the World', 'New Earth' and 'Gridlock'). A mannequin of Dr Constantine from 'The Empty Child'/'The Doctor Dances' not only wore the character's costume but also had a gas mask attached to the face. It was accompanied by another mannequin representing the Empty Child himself, again with gas mask attached. Other monsters on display included a Scarecrow ('Human Nature'/'The Family of Blood'); a Heavenly Host ('Voyage of the Damned'); and the Hoix ('Love and Monsters'). A pair of Hath ('The Doctor's Daughter') and a Judoon with helmet removed ('Smith and Jones') were joined by an Ood ('The Impossible Planet'/'The Satan Pit' and 'Planet of the Ood'); the Abzorbaloff ('Love and Monsters'); and a Slitheen ('Aliens of London'/'World War Three'). Items on display from 'A Christmas Carol', the last episode to have been broadcast before the exhibition's opening, included Kazran Sardick's chair, the isomorphic control system (looking suspiciously like an organ) and the cryogenic chamber that held Abigail Pettigrew.

Doctor Who's production techniques were also covered. In addition to a display demonstrating the various stages of construction of an Ood mask, as previously seen at the Spaceport on Merseyside and at Earls Court in 2008, there was a newly-created 'Sounds of *Who*' section full of interactive features. A video screen played a short documentary about Delia Derbyshire's work at the legendary Radiophonic Workshop; and visitors had an opportunity to hear their voice recorded and played as a Dalek or a Cyberman, and to add sound effects to a battle scene from 'Victory of the Daleks'. Another feature, on a screen mounted above a small mirror-walled arena, was a video presented by choreographer Ailsa Berk, teaching visitors of all ages how to walk like a Cyberman and a Scarecrow. A mock-up of the *Doctor Who* production office, as had been seen on Merseyside, completed the insight into the show's behind-the-scenes world.

Friday 13 May 2011 saw a new addition to the exhibition in the form of the mysterious Silence, who had debuted in 'The Impossible Astronaut'. This was publicised by way of some posed photographs of the creatures in London, including amusingly on a tube station escalator. In July 2011, there was another addition to the exhibition: a specially-created prop of the Screamer, a monster devised by 12-year-old *Doctor Who Adventures* competition winner Jessica Rickarby, which had featured in the magazine's comic strip.[165] Another competition-winning design, this time for *Blue Peter*, was also exhibited: the junk TARDIS console from 'The Doctor's Wife'. This was added after the episode's broadcast on 14 May 2011. Similarly, at the end of December 2011, following broadcast of 'The Doctor, the Widow and the Wardrobe', that story's Wooden King and Queen arrived.

Fan and WalesOnline journalist David Prince visited the Experience in Olympia once in the summer of 2011 and again the following year, toward the end of its run. 'I went about a fortnight before it closed,' he says. 'You could see then they were really starting to pack stuff up. There was some new stuff – new items and new props – but generally it was the same, just with fewer things there … They'd taken away more than they'd added.' Preparations were clearly being made for the attraction's big move to Cardiff.

Events

During its run at Olympia, the Experience hosted a number of promotional events. On Friday 5 August 2011, *Doctor Who Adventures* magazine held a series of masterclasses giving children an insight into a variety of aspects of magazine publishing.[166] This ranged from designing the cover to picking a free gift to accompany the issue. Two further events were organised and held the

---

[165] www.doctorwhonews.net/2011/07/dwn140711183008-experience-screamer.html
[166] www.doctorwhonews.net/2011/08/dwn100811135012-doctor-who-experience.html

same month. Friday 12 August saw *Doctor Who* choreographer Ailsa Berk running workshops teaching visitors to move like monsters such as the Judoon, a Scarecrow and a Cyberman; and Wednesday 24 August saw a demonstration of the Silurian prosthetics seen in the recently-broadcast 'A Good Man Goes to War', with script editor Gary Russell being transformed into one of the reptiles. A Christmas Grotto celebrated the festive period during part of December 2011, with a £5 charge per child covering a *Doctor Who* gift.

In the final month before the Experience closed in London, a number of small events were organised to coincide with the school half-term holiday. Saturday 11 and Sunday 19 February 2012 saw Ailsa Berk return to run more of her 'Walk Like a Monster' tutorials. Monday 13 and Friday 17 February had Millennium FX demonstrating their work. On Thursday 16 February, members of the show's make-up team transformed visitors into Silurians, Cybermen, Clockwork Droids and Weeping Angels via face painting; and on the same date, as would later become a common occurrence in Cardiff, live action monsters were also present, in the form of actors dressed as a Cyberman and an Ood.

Merchandise

As would doubtless have delighted the tenth Doctor, a 'little shop' was the Experience's final stop. It could also be directly accessed by members of the general public who had not visited the Experience but simply wished to acquire some *Doctor Who* merchandise. The tills were installed in a circular central area reminiscent of the TARDIS console, and two large police box display cabinets were also built for the venue. The shop stocked a wide range of DVDs, action figures and other merchandise, along with some exclusive items, including a souvenir brochure, the photographs in which were some of the same ones used for the exhibition's background boards and so featured actors in costume rather than the displays themselves.

A series of exclusive graphic designs were created for the Experience, featuring a TARDIS exterior, a Dalek, a Cybus-style Cyberman, a Weeping Angel, a Silent, Bessie, the K1 Robot, the eleventh Doctor's sonic screwdriver and the 1983 TARDIS console. These were then printed onto a range of merchandise for sale in the shop: iPhone 4 and 4S covers; badges; mousemats; postcards; and T-shirts, in both adult and child sizes, in navy, orange and light or dark grey colour choices. An Adipose T-shirt was also available for kids.

Another clothing item on offer for younger visitors was a Cyberman hoodie, the zip of which went all the way up over the head so that the wearer's face was fully covered by a Cyberman mask design. However, with incidents of civil unrest occurring in London at the time, an adult version was abandoned for fear it might be used by rioters wishing to conceal their faces.

One other merchandise item exclusive to the Experience in London was an action figure of young Amelia Pond from 'The Eleventh Hour', complete with duffle coat, suitcase and hat. So popular was this figure that customers were restricted to purchasing only one each, and they now achieve quite high amounts on auction website eBay.

The *Doctor Who* Experience at London Olympia finally closed in February 2012, with preparations already under way for its relocation to a purpose-built facility in Cardiff Bay.

Chapter 10
The *Doctor Who* Experience, Cardiff Bay (2012-2017)

As a prelude to the Experience reopening in its new Cardiff venue, BBC Worldwide organised the first official *Doctor Who* convention since Longleat in 1983. Over the weekend of 24 and 25 March 2012, the Wales Millennium Centre in Cardiff Bay hosted multiple guest interview panels, prosthetic and special effects demonstrations and photo and autograph opportunities. Making its first public appearance outside of London Olympia was the impressive display of multiple 21st Century companions' costumes. This was accompanied by an array of monster costume exhibits, including the Hoix ('Love and Monsters'), Varga the Ice Warrior ('The Ice Warriors'); a Slitheen ('Aliens of London'/'World War Three'); and, on an appropriately snow-covered backdrop used as the entrance to the tower seen in the Christmas special 'The Doctor, the Widow and the Wardrobe', the Wooden King and Queen. A number of actors also patrolled the venue in the costumes of monsters such as a helmeted Judoon, a Silurian and a Peg Doll. Leaflets were handed out to promote the Experience, which would be opening in its new venue a short walk away just a few months later.

The Experience's new home was a hangar-like building of some 3,000 square metres, a stone's throw from the BBC's Roath Lock studios, where most of *Doctor Who*'s interior scenes were recorded. Specially constructed to host the attraction, the building had been paid for by Cardiff Council, which then sought to secure sponsorship of approximately £200,000 a year, but without success, leaving a significant hole in its budget.[167]

The Experience's relocation to a venue adjacent to *Doctor Who*'s studio base had the benefits of allowing for closer ties with the show's production team and affording the opportunity for studio and location tours to be organised. Up to 250,000 visitors a year were expected.[168] The building itself operated over two main levels, the immersive adventure and the start of the exhibition being on the ground floor and the remainder of the exhibition being upstairs on the first. Between these two levels, a shop and event room were available, plus staff facilities.

The box office area – which was later clearly seen in the fiftieth-anniversary red-button-transmitted spoof 'The Five(ish) Doctors Reboot' – was decorated with specially-commissioned Anthony Dry artwork, making up the front

---

[167] www.walesonline.co.uk/news/local-news/black-hole-council-budget-after-7819833
[168] www.bbc.co.uk/news/uk-wales-18900040

section of the building. Beyond that solid section, the rest of the building's structure consisted of a framework with a thick tensile membrane stretched over it, forming a dramatic wave shape noticeable across the Cardiff Bay area. In essence it was like a large tent; as a result, it would become very cold during the winter and extremely hot and humid during the summer. This would prove problematic for some of the exhibition's more delicate artefacts. For example, the heat to which it was exposed during the summer of 2012 would result in the original Zygon costume shrinking, accelerating its deterioration and necessitating it being returned to storage until it could undergo further restoration and be put back on display. Another item to suffer deterioration would be the Sontaran mask from 'The Two Doctors'; again, this would have to be removed from the exhibition pending repair. By contrast, staff working in the exhibition during the cold winter had to be issued with hats, gloves and body warmers.

To promote the new attraction in Cardiff, a publicity stunt was arranged. At 8.00 am on 21 June 2012, while BBC Worldwide's Head of Exhibitions Paula Al Lach was conducting an interview outside the venue, a loud explosion was staged. A Cyberman, an Ood, a Silent and a Scarecrow fled the building and, as *The Sun* later phrased it, 'went on a rampage across Cardiff and Newport'. The monsters were photographed at landmarks such as Cardiff Castle and Cardiff Central railway station, tormenting the general public and raising awareness of the Experience's approaching official opening.

On 18 July 2012 the official *Doctor Who* Experience Twitter account teased a new addition to the exhibition. The image tweeted showed an object on the back of a flatbed lorry, covered with a tarpaulin but still revealing a tantalising glimpse of a car number plate, 'WHO 1'. Of course this was Bessie, the Doctor's famous Edwardian roadster that had first appeared in 'Doctor Who and the Silurians'. This original screen-used car was placed in the Experience's box office foyer and provided an early photo opportunity for visitors. Also displayed in cases in the box office foyer were a Cyberman helmet, amusingly claimed to have been dug up during construction of the building, and River Song's shoes, weapon and diaries.

Unlike in the case of some past *Doctor Who* exhibitions, no cast or crew members were present for the Experience's official opening ceremony on 20 July 2012. Instead, a small boy, appropriately dressed in an eleventh Doctor costume complete with fez, cut the red ribbon with the assistance of a young Amy Pond and an even younger child dressed as a Dalek. One of those also in attendance was fan and WalesOnline journalist David Prince. 'I'd been to it twice in London,' he says, 'and loved it. But there it had felt crammed in, so when it moved to Cardiff, I wanted to see this purpose-built building.' Prince's first impressions were positive, although some things, such as the green-screen feature, were not up and running on the opening weekend. 'I went the first day, then went back two or three days later, and even in that short space of time you could see that things had calmed down a bit, they'd managed to get out a bit more, stuff was working.'

Prince visited this Matt Smith-era version of the Experience a total of 30 times between July 2012 and August 2014. His enthusiasm for it became something of a standing joke amongst his friends, with him regularly taking visitors to Cardiff to see the attraction and guiding them around the show's local recording locations. As Prince explains, 'I wanted it to be a success in Cardiff. It was obviously going to be a success. They kept on adding new props and things I hadn't seen before, so that was an initial factor in my visits: going to see these new items.'

The Walk-through Adventure

The Experience's unique walk-through adventure remained, to start with, essentially the same as at London Olympia; but, over time, it gradually evolved. After Amy and Rory departed the show in 'The Angels Take Manhattan', additional Matt Smith dialogue was recorded to explain why the Doctor was calling for these former companions. Similarly, after a new TARDIS console room was revealed in 'The Snowmen', additional dialogue was recorded and played in while visitors moved into the Experience's console room, to explain that it was the old model and that the Doctor considered it 'a bit too orange'. In May 2014, additional Weeping Angels were added to the forest section, having been repaired following storage and use elsewhere, more than doubling the number of actual Weeping Angels in that section. These subtle tweaks aside, though, the walk-through adventure remained essentially unchanged right up until August 2014, making it feel rather dated at times and reducing its impact for repeat visitors.

Lower-Level Exhibition

The new building's design meant that the exhibition space was now spread over two levels, the lower focusing on the Doctor and his TARDIS and the upper being home to the monsters. The first ten Doctors' costumes were now arranged along a single plinth, rather than split between two as at Olympia, with background boards showing photos of the costumes being worn by the respective actors. Christopher Eccleston's costume now included a burgundy sweater, as seen in 'Rose', 'The End of the World' and 'Boom Town', rather than a green one. Once again, a large semi-circular plinth directly in front of this display was the location for the Matt Smith-era TARDIS exterior prop and the costumed eleventh Doctor waxwork. After Smith himself paid the attraction a visit in October 2012, a cast of his handprints was added to the plinth.

Opposite this plinth stood the Melkur statue, positioned with the 1980s TARDIS police box prop as restored by Mark Barton Hill for display at Olympia. Nearby, against black drapes, were display cabinets holding the Doctor's trusty sonic screwdrivers, plus the sonic cane from 'Let's Kill Hitler', and various other artefacts, including the viewing device used to see the

Krafayis in 'Vincent and The Doctor', the tape recorder with which the tenth Doctor trapped the Wire in 'The Idiot's Lantern' and the whisk device from 'Amy's Choice'.

The two TARDIS interior sets featured prominently, as in London, with the 2005-2010 coral-effect version being trimmed in height to fit the available space, and the 1983-1989 one having added to it a TV monitor showing silent clips of TARDIS scenes from 'The Five Doctors', 'Timelash' and 'The Greatest Show in the Galaxy', accompanied by appropriate TARDIS interior sound effects played from an iPod and speaker plugged behind the classic TARDIS roundel walls. A large screen once again projected the tenth-to-eleventh-Doctor regeneration scene by the 2005-2010 interior set. Also displayed, opposite the 2005-2010 console, was the junk TARDIS interior from 'The Doctor's Wife', accompanied by Idris's costume from that episode.

The green-screen area was also found on the ground floor and had been greatly improved since Olympia, with a new 'self-service' system and a choice of four photographic backgrounds. It was overseen by friendly and helpful staff members, this time employed by BBC Worldwide and not an outside company. However, technical problems prevented it from being operational for the opening weekend. The 2010-2012 TARDIS console room once again featured as one of the offered backgrounds, but with the proportions improved so that visitors fitted the environment better and could even pose as if operating the controls. The other three backgrounds placed the TARDIS exterior box respectively in the time vortex, in the American desert during 'The Impossible Astronaut' and on the junkyard planet from 'The Doctor's Wife'. In 2013, a new background was added to celebrate the show's half century, the Totter's Lane set as featured in the *An Adventure in Space and Time* docu-drama replacing the American desert backdrop. Thanks to the enthusiasm of staff in this department visitors could later also pose with replica props, such as a variety of sonic screwdrivers, Tom Baker scarves and fezes, adding to their enjoyment.

Upper-Level Exhibition

Venturing up a metal staircase to the upper floor of the exhibition – a lift was also available – visitors entered a hall of monsters. There were a number of new additions since Olympia, including displays of items from the 2011 series. One of these, and the largest set piece, was the Silent spaceship, which dominated the view. Originally made for 'The Lodger', this had since been reused for 'Day of the Moon'. In addition to the circular set with its four control panels, two Silent costumes were included, one with a normal expression and the other with an open mouth.

The spaceship's circular shape allowed for additional monsters to be displayed surrounding it. Visitors moving around to the left encountered the Face of Boe, as first seen in 'The End of the World'; a Winder from 'The Beast Below', complete with an angry Smiler mask; the original Zygon from 'Terror of the Zygons'; the surviving Ice Warrior from 'The Ice Warriors'; and the K1 Robot from 'Robot'. When it later had to be removed for further restoration work after suffering the effects of the summer heat, the Zygon was replaced by Silurian Restac from 'Cold Blood'. The trio of Sontarans remained as in London Olympia, until 'The Two Doctors' variant became another casualty of the summer heat and had to be removed.

New to the exhibition in Cardiff was the Cyber-conversion unit from 'Closing Time', flanked on either side by a static Cyber Controller and a Cyberman, as both seen in 'The Age of Steel'. A curved wall was created with compartments at varying heights to house the Cyberman heads charting their evolution. At the end of this wall was also a full-size cryogenic chamber prop containing an illuminated Cyberman mask as used during production of 'Closing Time'.

Other artefacts from Matt Smith's second series as the Doctor were to be found the visitor's immediate right after climbing the metal staircase. These included the Doctor's cot as seen in 'A Good Man Goes to War', two Handbots from 'The Girl Who Waited' and two Antibodies from 'Let's Kill Hitler'. Also on display was the spacesuit worn by the Doctor in the latest Christmas special, 'The Doctor, the Widow and the Wardrobe'.

Further along the right-hand side of the exhibition floor, past the Emperor Dalek model from 'The Parting of the Ways' and tucked neatly into a corner, was the same chronologically-arranged display of Dalek designs as had been seen in London Olympia. The 'walk-in' bronze Dalek originally created for the Earls Court exhibition also reappeared; once again, children could venture inside and move the arm and weapon while peering out to gain an appreciation of the viewpoint seen by Dalek operators.

Costumes for the Doctor's companions Rose Tyler, Martha Jones, Captain Jack Harkness, Donna Noble, Sarah Jane Smith, K-9, Amy and Amelia Pond and Rory Williams, which had also been on display at Olympia, likewise reappeared in Cardiff. In 2013 they would be moved to the exhibition's ground floor to accommodate new additions. A notable newcomer to the collection was the Master's costume as worn by Eric Roberts in the 1996 TV movie. This was included in an updated trio of Time Lord costumes that also featured a robe from 'The Deadly Assassin' and Rassilon's attire from 'The End of Time: Part Two'.

Significant space was dedicated to the Wooden King and Queen from 'The Doctor, the Widow and the Wardrobe', sitting proudly on their thrones. On the exhibition's opening in 2012, these were joined by a number of other modern-era monsters that had previously featured in Olympia. These included the Silurian Restac ('Cold Blood'); the Abzorbaloff ('Love and Monsters'); a Hath ('The Doctor's Daughter'); a Scarecrow ('Human Nature'/'The Family of Blood'); a Judoon without helmet ('Smith and Jones'); and an Ood ('The Impossible Planet'/'The Satan Pit'). Finally, a trio of Peg Dolls from 'Night Terrors' were positioned in a corner with a curtained false window, a gigantic D battery prop and the doll's house seen in the episode.

Inside a curved 'U'-shaped structure was the 'Sounds of *Who*' presentation, full of interactive features, that had also been in Olympia. Similarly relocated to Cardiff were the Ood mask demonstrations and the 'Walk Like a Monster' activity. The final exhibits before the exit were a rug and a pair of flags from the Oval Office set from 'The Impossible Astronaut', and a futuristic microwave from 'The Rebel Flesh'/'The Almost People'. The nearby walls were adorned with a montage of production artwork, publicity images and behind-the-scenes photographs, largely from the modern era.

Some of the surviving artefacts were beginning to show signs of wear and tear. In the case of the Slitheen, for example, the heavy arms were starting to become detached from the body, so this costume was not put out on display; instead it was stored within the venue pending repair. The effects of gravity had also caused the left side of the Face of Boe to droop; but in this case, the prop remained on display.

Over time, items were regularly moved around as and when new additions were made; and display plinths were cannibalised and reused, having been transferred from London and not specially constructed for the Cardiff exhibition. The signage for the Ood unfortunately misattributed the writing of 'Planet of the Ood' to Russell T Davies rather than Keith Temple.

On 12 October 2012, a day when the Experience was closed to the public, Matt Smith unveiled a display of artefacts from recently-screened episodes.[169] The specially-made red dress worn by Jenna Coleman as Oswin in 'Asylum of the Daleks' was teamed with the 'Oswin' Dalek and placed in front of the circular doorway seen being boarded up in her opening scene. Her accessory belt included details such as a small whisk. Her red shoes, with socks, which had originally been purchased from high-street retailer River Island, were also on display. As a part of the unveiling, both large robot costumes from 'Dinosaurs on a Spaceship' were occupied by actors and posed for photos with Matt Smith; one of them was retained for display after the event. Also added to the exhibition from the same story were the costumes of Solomon and Nefertiti, plus in the background a set element consisting of a hieroglyph-inscribed Egyptian wall, with a pterodactyl perched above. The final new exhibit was the damaged Weeping Angel and three cherubs as seen in 'The Angels Take Manhattan'.

In December 2012, to celebrate the festive season, a selection of Christmas-special-related items were put on display on the exhibition's upper floor. These included a Robot Santa ('The Runaway Bride'); a Cybershade ('The Next Doctor'); a Sycorax ('The Christmas Invasion'); the cryogenic chamber prop that held Abigail Pettigrew ('A Christmas Carol'); and an Androzani Major harvest ranger costume ('The Doctor, the Widow and the Wardrobe'). The latter was fitted to a mannequin that was larger than the actor who had worn it; this resulted in significant gaps between the armour pieces, revealing the red undersuit.

---

[169] www.youtube.com/watch?v=vQGbcaC6akA

Also included in this Christmas-themed display was David Tennant's original costume of pyjamas, dressing gown and slippers, as worn during 'The Christmas Invasion'. This was retained after the New Year period but moved to the ground floor. The slippers later disappeared; thought to have been stolen by a visitor.

The attraction closed to the public for two days starting on Christmas Eve, and the staff took this opportunity to install a brand-new display of artefacts from the 2012 Christmas special, 'The Snowmen'. Centrepiece of this was a large globe filled with 'snow' – in reality polystyrene balls of the type more commonly used to stuff beanbags. Other features included four tower pillars, one on each corner of the raised set, and a control panel with levers and dials. Four new costumes were also included: Dr Simeon's; Madame Vastra's; Clara Oswald's barmaid attire, inaccurately labelled as her governess costume; and the Doctor's new costume from this story, complete with top hat and scarf, rich purple waistcoat and tailcoat – which would later reappear on screen in Matt Smith's final story, 'The Time of the Doctor'. A Snowman prop was added to the display at a later date, after a period of time spent in the Experience's box office.

'The Bells of Saint John', the episode following 'The Snowmen', saw another costume change for the Doctor; and Matt Smith's waxwork was subsequently redressed in that new regular attire.

Following the broadcast of other 2013 episodes, further new costume additions were made to the exhibition. A particular highlight was the April 2013 installation of the new Ice Warrior, Grand Marshal Skaldak, chained to some torpedo props in a recreation of a scene from 'Cold War'. This version of the costume was the one that allowed the head to fall back and the body to open up, as required at one point by the story's narrative. In early 2014, the other version of the head and body, as worn by actor Spencer Wilding in the episode, was used for appearances in the *Doctor Who* Symphonic Spectacular tour of Australia and New Zealand; however, as only one set of legs and arms had been made for the Ice Warrior, and these were also required for the tour, this meant that there were long periods when the Experience's costume was incomplete and could not be displayed, and the torpedoes consequently stood alone. When the other, complete costume returned from the tour in May 2014, it was placed on a mannequin and added to the exhibition, giving visitors their first opportunity to study this version of the head and body and see the additional detail, particularly of the fleshy chin and teeth.

Another notable addition to the exhibition, in June 2013, was an example of the new style of Cyberman costume first seen in 'Nightmare in Silver'. This was also mounted onto a mannequin, posed with arm extended, providing what proved to be a popular photo opportunity for visitors. Other items exhibited from the same story were Porridge's costume, the chess automaton prop and signage from Webley's World of Wonders.

The only other 2013 series episode represented in the displays was 'The Crimson Horror'. A set element seen as part of the rocket firing system was accompanied by Mrs Gillyflower's costume, as worn on screen by Dame Diana Rigg, and Mr Sweet, the prehistoric red leech. The 'crooked man' creature from the episode 'Hide' was not exhibited immediately. Instead it was held behind the scenes until the 2014 renovation, when it was put out on display.

Costume and make-up areas were added to the upper level of the exhibition. The former boasted a rail of miscellaneous costumes, including those of the Gunslinger ('A Town Called Mercy'); a military Priest ('The Time of Angels'); and Foon Van Hoff ('Voyage of the Damned'). The Cybershade was brought out again and displayed alongside Miss Hartigan's costume from the same story, 'The Next Doctor'. The make-up area featured a stereotypically glamorous mirror with lights around the outside, purchased from a nearby IKEA store; continuity photographs used by the production team; a dummy Vastra prosthetic mask; and a number of actor wigs.

Even though the docu-drama *An Adventure in Space and Time* was yet to be broadcast, the replica original TARDIS console created for the production was installed in the Experience in August 2013, having made its public debut at the previous month's Paris Comic Con. It was placed against an appropriate background of two roundel-patterned walls, one fitted with TARDIS doors. The console had been recreated as accurately as possible, thanks to extensive research, and included the mint green finish the original had been given to avoid the flaring that bright white would have caused on black-and-white television pictures. The installation process was recorded, and a time-lapse video later posted on YouTube.[170] Where the console was originally positioned, visitors exiting the Experience's walk-through adventure were met by the grey and uninteresting back of the set. Consequently it was later moved into the corner previously occupied by the 1983 console, after that in turn was moved to replace the junk TARDIS console from 'The Doctor's Wife', which was then removed from the exhibition.

The show's fiftieth anniversary special 'The Day of the Doctor' generated a host of new artefacts for display, some of which were installed overnight immediately following the broadcast. On the ground floor, the Time Lord table from the epic adventure was given the central position previously occupied by the *An Adventure in Space and Time* console. Next to it were stood the beautiful new Time Lord robe worn by Androgar, and a Gallifreyan soldier costume. Two Gallifreyan weapons were placed on the table itself, along with some oval pieces of paper bearing intricate Gallifreyan script. On closer inspection, the latter seemed to have been kept in a ring binder, as they had holes punched on one side; and they later began to curl up.

On the exhibition's upper floor were displayed even more items from 'The Day of the Doctor'. Given centre stage were the three different TARDIS exterior props featured in the action. These were accompanied by the costumes of their respective Doctors: the tenth, the eleventh and the War Doctor. At a later date, Tom Baker's costume as the mysterious Curator was added to the

---

[170] www.youtube.com/watch?v=cKewl0mwECk

scene. Also displayed were the elaborate dress worn by Joanna Page as Queen Elizabeth I; Billie Piper's costume as the Moment; and the latter's intricately-designed box prop. A Zygon finally returned to the *Doctor Who* Experience, but this time in the form of a costume newly created for 'The Day of the Doctor' rather than a 1975 original. It was accompanied by a Zygon control panel and pod prop seen in the story. A second pod prop was unfortunately damaged in transit – blown over by a gust of wind, causing it to smash – and so was not put on display. Further items from the anniversary special were added to the exhibition in February 2014. These included the two large noticeboards seen on the UNIT Black Archive set – although the Experience's staff had to reattach the accompanying photographs of the Doctor's companions, consulting stills from the episode to ensure they were correctly positioned, as these had all been removed prior to transportation.

Christmas Eve 2013 once again saw the overnight addition of artefacts from the latest Christmas special, ready for the attraction to reopen on Boxing Day after its brief festive-period closure. 'The Time of the Doctor' having seen the eleventh Doctor's departure from the series, the costume initially worn in 'The Snowmen' was put back on display, having suffered a bit more wear and tear and now accompanied by a cane. Another Clara costume also debuted, featuring a tartan skirt and black Yumi bow cardigan that would return in 'Deep Breath'. Another addition to the display was the Punch and Judy box used by the Doctor on Christmas, complete with Monoid puppet. The display was mounted against a backdrop of children's drawings of the Doctor, a large street lamp, a number of wooden toys and other objects from the episode. Two helmets used for Handles, the severed Cyber head, were placed in a glass case, along with the seal of the High Council of Gallifrey, as taken from the Master in the Death Zone in 'The Five Doctors' – probably a screen-used replica rather the 1983 original. Later, Handles was moved from the case and placed on cushions atop a basket within the main display.

Added to the exhibition in February 2014 were two old-age prosthetics worn by Matt Smith during his swansong episode. These were initially located on the central plinth on the exhibition's ground floor, as part of a display celebrating Smith's tenure on the show. Taking pride of place in this display, which remained in place throughout the summer season of 2014, were three costumes worn by Smith's Doctor: the tweed-jacketed Series 5 outfit; the Christmas special costume; and, still placed on the actor's waxwork, the purple-hued Series 7 costume. Additional items were added after costumes that had been displayed at the major, BBC Worldwide-organised *Doctor Who* Celebration convention at ExCel in London in November 2013 (discussed later) were returned to Cardiff for storage. These included Amy Pond's police uniform from 'The Eleventh Hour'; Rory's costume from 'Vampires in Venice'; River Song's attire from the Stonehenge-set scenes of 'The Pandorica Opens'; and Clara's 'Hide' costume and 'The Snowmen' barmaid outfit.

To accommodate the new additions, and because of a need to reuse some of the plinths, K-9 was briefly moved to stand beside the fourth Doctor's costume.

In March 2014, some of the Model Unit's *Doctor Who* work was put on display: specifically two submarine models used for 'Cold War'; a diorama depicting a scene of the TARDIS with a destroyed Dalek, used as part of 'The Day of the Doctor'; and the underside of the Dalek spaceship from 'The Time of the Doctor'. Returned to the exhibition after repair was also the Dalek Emperor miniature from 'The Parting of the Ways', as seen previously at Olympia. Following actress Kate O'Mara's death at the end of the month, the costume she had worn as the Rani in 'Time and the Rani' was added to the 1980s TARDIS console room set as a mark of respect.

May 2014 saw the return to the UK of items from the Symphonic Spectacular tour of Australia and New Zealand. This meant that for the first time the Wooden Cyberman seen in 'The Time of the Doctor' could be added to the exhibition's display of other items from that episode. Also returned was the Skaldak Ice Warrior from 'Cold War', reunited with the torpedo set piece that in its absence had remained empty on the exhibition floor.

At this time, a small display dedicated to 'Asylum of the Daleks' was also installed. This featured the two replica 1960s-era Daleks that had previously been displayed; these were now however covered in cobwebs from their on-screen appearance. Placed alongside them were the other items from the episode that had made their exhibition debut the previous October: the 'Oswin' Dalek and Jenna Coleman's red dress against the boarded-up circular door. This was one of the rare occasions when all four replica Daleks belonging to artefacts manager Andrew Beech were on display in the exhibition at the same time.

During the exhibition's run, display items were regularly adjusted and repositioned. For instance, all of the items from 'The Day of the Doctor' were eventually gathered together on the upper level. These included the large Time Lord table, the Black Archive noticeboards, and a new addition: the chair on which John Hurt's War Doctor sat during the scene where he talks with Clara. Initially, in May 2014, a mannequin bearing the War Doctor's costume was positioned in the chair to replicate the scene, even to the extent of a thermos cup being placed in its hand.

On-site Recording

The Experience became a *Doctor Who* recording location in its own right, not just for the aforementioned 'The Five(ish) Doctors Reboot' spoof but also for 'The Day of the Doctor': David Tennant's scenes in his Doctor's TARDIS console room set were all recorded on the exhibition floor.

The exhibition also proved to be a popular location for recording *Doctor Who*-related documentary material and DVD bonus features. One of these was 'The Ultimate Time Lord', included on *The Complete Eighth Series* DVD and Blu-ray set; presented by Peter Davison. This project gave the actor an opportunity to reunite with the TARDIS console he had used throughout the latter part of his time on the show.

Tours

The Cardiff *Doctor Who* Experience quickly became a popular venue for the show's fans to visit; and this popularity was boosted by the provision of additional exclusive tours, which also created an extra revenue stream for the attraction.

In 2013, a recording locations tour was created. Scripted by author, former *Doctor Who* script editor and former *Doctor Who Magazine* editor Gary Russell, this was conducted by a member of the Experience team, who guided visitors on a walk around approximately a mile and a half of the local Cardiff Bay area, taking in locations such as the American diner seen in 'The Impossible Astronaut'; the Millennium Centre, where scenes from numerous episodes had been recorded; and the so-called Torchwood Tower.

David Prince recalls his first experience of the tour: 'I remember the first one I went on, there was a family from America, and obviously they were doing the whole thing – the walking tour, the Experience, the set tour – and they absolutely loved it. It was everything you could expect or could ever want, apart from the Doctor literally being there. It was fantastic.'

For visitors from outside the local area, the tour provided a rare opportunity to visit places where the show had actually been made, as Prince again notes: 'If you were new to the area, or very rarely came to Cardiff, the walking tours were great. But if you'd been there a couple of times, you could find all the locations on the internet yourself.'

After new episodes had been screened, more locations were added to the tour, such as Mancini's Restaurant exterior from 'Deep Breath'; consequently, the length of the tour was extended from one hour to approximately 75 minutes.

The close proximity of the Experience venue to the BBC Roath Lock studios also allowed for occasional set visit tours to be organised. These gave groups of visitors a rare opportunity to step inside a working BBC studio, the highlight being the opportunity to see in person the standing set of the current TARDIS console room, featured on screen from 'The Snowmen' onwards. For many fans, this afforded a once-in-a-lifetime opportunity to step onto a real BBC set.

The tours naturally had to be suspended during periods when *Doctor Who* was actually being recorded. Concerns that the groups of visitors could disturb other productions under way in Roath Lock also saw admission numbers kept low to start with, although the potential for increased revenue generation seems to have led to a relaxation of this stricture, as David Prince observes: 'The first one I went on, there weren't that many people in the same time-slot. I think there were about ten of us. On later occasions, there were more like twenty.'

This increase in numbers meant that, because of the limited space available, visitors had to be split into smaller groups to be ushered onto the TARDIS set in turn. As a result, people often found that they were spending more time waiting outside the set than actually exploring and taking photographs within it, as Prince again notes: 'The first one I ever went on, it felt like you had so much more time there. Later, they'd obviously seen how much of a money-spinner it was, and they'd said, "Right, how many people can we get on the tour in this amount of time?"'

The set tour nevertheless remained a popular attraction for fans – and the fact that it was available only during limited periods when *Doctor Who* was not in production meant that there was a considerable demand for tickets, as Prince recalls: 'They didn't generally sell out within one day, but within a week of them going on sale, you could pretty well guarantee that they'd all be gone.'

Events

The Cardiff *Doctor Who* Experience hosted a number of events throughout its tenure. An October staple, beginning in 2012, was a Halloween weekend, where several of the monsters would 'come to life' in the exhibition. These were typically a Scarecrow, a Cyberman, a Peg Doll and a Silent. From 2013 on, monsters would also startle visitors in the walk-through adventure; for example, a Smiler breaking out of its booth in the *Starship UK* area.

On three consecutive Saturdays in February 2013, fancy dress competitions were held, with prizes awarded for the best. The theme for 9 February was to dress up as the Doctor; 16 February was dedicated to the monsters; and 23 February was designated for the companions. Even when no such competitions were taking place, Experience visitors would often 'dress for the occasion', as cosplaying became an increasingly popular aspect of fandom.

On Wednesday 3 April 2013, the venue hosted a Monster Day Out event in association with children's magazine *Doctor Who Adventures*. The big draw was an appearance by popular Sontaran character Strax, played as on screen by actor Dan Starkey. A question-and-answer session was held, with Strax answering preapproved questions that allowed Starkey to remain in character throughout. Amusingly, Strax also performed a couple of impressions of other Sontarans, which was not a prearranged idea; these were later included in a YouTube highlights video.[171]

A year later, the Experience presented another Monster Day Out event, with a number of activities taking place on Wednesday 16 April 2014. A Silent, inhabited by monster actor Jamie Hill, posed for photographs on the Silent spaceship set; special effects company Millennium FX held a number of workshops demonstrating how they created some of the monsters seen on the show; writer Cavan Scott held a quiz and signed copies of his *Who-ology* book; and Mike Tucker of the Model Unit held talks and signed copies of his books *Illegal Alien* and *BBC VFX*. Tucker's presentation covered amongst other things the submarine modelwork for 'Cold War'; the Dalek spaceship and other shots for 'The Time of the Doctor'; and the Unit's BAFTA-award-winning work on

---

[171] www.youtube.com/watch?v=_nZxShriR0Y

the fiftieth anniversary story 'The Day of the Doctor'. These talks proved particularly popular and inspirational, as Tucker later explained:

'The talks that I've done down at the Experience are always well attended, and there's always a younger element to the audience who are fascinated by how these things are made. Weirdly, I think they get more fascinated when you reveal some of the slightly more mundane materials used in making some of the props.'

Just as Tucker himself had been inspired by attending the Longleat exhibition and the 1983 Celebration event, he in turn was able to inspire a new generation and encourage them to explore the technical aspects of television production.

Merchandise

The Experience's new Cardiff Bay location incorporated what was described as the only official *Doctor Who* shop, not only in the UK but in the whole world. Located between the attraction's upper floor and ground floor, it was also accessible directly from the ground floor box office whenever the building was open. The cash tills were placed in one corner of the shop, which was decorated with copper and hexagonal light fittings to echo the design of the 2010 version of the TARDIS console. Relocated from the London Olympia shop were also the two large police box display stands, placed in opposite corners by the window.

The shop sold a number of exclusive items, ranging from mugs and postcards to action figures and T-shirts. Remaining stock from the London Olympia shop was also transferred to Cardiff, so to start with visitors could also buy some of those items, such as the K1 Robot, Dalek and TARDIS console T-shirts, and the iPhone cases with sonic screwdriver, Silence, TARDIS console and Cyberman designs.

Another exclusive design was created for the Cardiff Experience. Dubbed the TARDIS explosion, this featured a police box exterior against light blue geometric shapes. It was printed onto navy T-shirts for the shop's opening, and on pens, postcards and magnets later on. A further T-shirt was also produced for the Cardiff shop, with an illustration of the TARDIS leaving a vapour trail as it takes off from Cardiff, illuminating the Welsh shoreline. Both T-shirts were available in adult and child sizes, with the '*Doctor Who* Experience Porth Teigr Cardiff Bay' logo printed on the sleeve (as on staff members' T-shirts).

A merchandise pack was also created to help boost revenue. This included a newly-designed brochure with much stronger visuals than that produced for London Olympia, including photographs of the actual costumes on display. Also included was a T-shirt with another exclusive design, and some postcards. In 2013, a Welsh-language version of the brochure became available. Later that year, however, both the original version and the Welsh translation were replaced by a new brochure design celebrating the show's fiftieth anniversary. In 2014, a new merchandise pack T-shirt replaced the previous one.

As at London Olympia, an exclusive action figure was on offer, this time of Rory Williams with a black gilet and grey shirt. However, the exclusivity was not restricted to the physical shop in Cardiff, as the figure could also be bought online from the official BBC Shop website. As a result, it was much easier to obtain than the previous Amelia Pond figure, and much less scarce later on.

Another item exclusive to the *Doctor Who* Experience shop was a special variant of the eleventh Doctor bust produced by Titan Merchandise. This saw the Time Lord holding a jammie dodger biscuit, as seen in 'Victory of the Daleks', instead of the usual sonic screwdriver. Also exclusive to the Experience were a pair of mugs featuring the Cyberman and Dalek artwork designs by Anthony Dry seen in the new venue's box office area. For the 2012 Christmas period, a limited-edition T-shirt was made available, with a TARDIS star motif; this came in a choice of red or – in ladies' sizes only – purple.

For the first time, all of the classic-era *Doctor Who* DVD range was stocked, enabling fans to fill any gaps in their collections. Also stocked from 2013 onwards was another staple of the collectors' market: the range of original Big Finish *Doctor Who* CD audio dramas. Although the Experience unfortunately failed to capitalise on the potential for actor signings and product launches, attempts were made to promote the DVD range, with each new addition being played on screens in the shop over the weekend preceding its release. In a break from this pattern, 'The Daemons' was screened as a tribute to its director Christopher Barry after his passing in February 2014.

In 2011, the Character company began producing a range of collectable construction figures and playsets, similar to the ever-popular Lego brand. To promote this, a full-size 'new paradigm' Dalek was created out of the construction bricks. It took a team of four people over 328 hours to complete, consisted of 157,460 bricks and weighed 280kg. Positioned in the Experience's box office area, it remained there for several years afterwards.

In 2014, a new phone-case was made available, again in the soft style for iPhone 4 and 4S, with a design featuring the iconic TARDIS police box doors and the *Doctor Who* Experience logo. Other licensed merchandise was brought in too, including a very popular range of TARDIS and Dalek dresses from American manufacturer Her Universe.

The shop was not limited to stocking *Doctor Who* merchandise; for instance, it also sold DVDs of spin-offs *Torchwood* and *The Sarah Jane Adventures*, plus the popular BBC *Sherlock* series and, curiously, the London 2012 Olympics.

The *Doctor Who* Celebration 2013

During the Cardiff Experience's run, *Doctor Who*'s landmark fiftieth anniversary was celebrated with a huge BBC Worldwide-organised convention, held at the ExCeL centre in London over three days from Friday 22 November 2013. Several of the Doctor actors attended, along with various companion actors and production staff from across the fifty years. Autograph and photo sessions were held, and classic episodes were screened, with question-and-answer sessions afterwards. Original props and costumes were displayed, and talks were delivered by various designers and other behind-the-scenes luminaries. Initial tickets were all snapped up within 24 hours of going on sale, although more were made available closer to the time of the event.

Costumes, props and even a set were exhibited right across the venue, including in the official BBC Worldwide shop – staffed by employees from the Cardiff Experience – where a Silent and an original Clara costume from 'Hide' were placed. However, there was also a specific display area for costumes, some of which had not been seen in public for many years, and some not at all.

There were costumes for all of the Doctors – including, for the first and only time in the UK, the outfit worn by Sylvester McCoy during recording in Vancouver for the 1996 TV movie, although the tie was absent. More recent exhibits included David Tennant's blue suit and red shirt as seen in '42' and a Sanctuary Base 6 orange spacesuit from 'The Impossible Planet'/'The Satan Pit'. Also on display was Jon Pertwee's outfit of red smoking jacket, white frilly shirt and purple-lined cape as seen in 'Terror of the Autons', 'The Mind of Evil' and 'Day of the Daleks'. This was displayed next to the Doctor's car Bessie, which had an interesting hanging accessory, the seal of the High Council of Gallifrey from 'The Five Doctors'. Another item from the latter story was Sarah Jane Smith's pink and white-collar costume, which was paired with the Crayford Metro convertible car used by the character in the spin-off *K-9 and Company*.

More recent companion costumes were also on show: Amy Pond's police uniform from 'The Eleventh Hour'; Amy's and Rory's costumes from 'Vampires in Venice'; and the outfit worn by River Song at Stonehenge during 'The Pandorica Opens'. From the tenth Doctor's era were Rose Tyler's lovely 1950s dress and accompanying jacket from 'The Idiot's Lantern'; Martha Jones's red leather jacket and jeans; and Donna Noble's 'The Fires of Pompeii' dress and 'Silence in the Library' outfit. These were accompanied by the costumes of Rose and Jackie Tyler and Mickey Smith from 'The End of Time: Part Two'. Also on display was Adelaide Brooke's outfit from 'The Waters of Mars', last seen in Coventry in 2010.

On the Saturday, Ace's grey dress from 'The Curse of Fenric' and her trademark bomber jacket were also displayed, having been brought out of storage after previous appearances in Longleat, Llangollen and Blackpool. Attending the event that day were Sue Moore and Stephen Mansfield, with a selection of items they had created for the show. These included the Chimeron baby ('Delta and the Bannermen'); Kane's melting face ('Dragonfire'); and heads of the Destroyer ('Battlefield') and three Haemovores, including the Ancient One ('The Curse of Fenric'). Costume designer June Hudson, who amongst other things had created Tom Baker's new look for the 1980 season, was also present the same day, discussing her work and signing autographs.

The show's classic era was well represented, a highlight being an original Yeti costume from 'The Web of Fear', last seen in the second Blackpool exhibition. No *Doctor Who* exhibition would be complete without a Dalek, and a classic gun-metal-grey variant was present. Additional display items included a Tractator and uniforms worn by an Orderly and Plantagenet from 'Frontios'; a Sea Devil from 'Warriors of the Deep'; and a Cyberman from 'Earthshock'. The Cyberman had been renovated by Mark Barton Hill; it was the one with 'destroyed' appearance sold at Bonhams in 2010.[172] Representing the seventh Doctor's era were a Tetrap from 'Time and the Rani' and a Cheetah person from 'Survival'.

A significant proportion of the exhibits naturally came from the post-2005 period. These included the Supreme Dalek from 'The Stolen Earth'/'Journey's End'; an Ood costume without mask; a pink Clockwork Droid dress from 'The Girl in the Fireplace'; Jackson Lake's costume and Miss Hartigan's red dress with umbrella from 'The Next Doctor'; Rosanna Calvieri's dress as seen in 'Vampires in Venice'; and Silurian Eldane's robe from 'Cold Blood'. Merry's costume and various aliens from 'The Rings of Akhaten' were accompanied by the speeder prop on which Clara and the Doctor had been seen to travel through space in that story.

On a table, the redheaded Peg Doll head and Peg Doll arms from 'Night Terrors' were accompanied by a spacesuit helmet from 'The Impossible Astronaut' plus a couple of other helmets. 'The Snowmen' display first seen at the Experience in Cardiff was recreated; accompanying the large snow globe once again were costumes for Matt Smith's Doctor, Dr Simeon and Madame Vastra, and Clara's barmaid outfit.

One particular section of the exhibition was dedicated to the Time Lords. This featured the costumes of the Rani from 'Time and the Rani'; and of Omega, President Borusa and Damon from 'Arc of Infinity', the latter having been worn originally by Runcible in 'The Deadly Assassin'. The Omega and Rani costumes had been in storage since being last seen in public at the Blackpool exhibition in 2009. Unfortunately the mannequin on which the Omega costume was placed would not stand upright, and so was strategically placed against an available wall. Various other Time Lord robes on display included those of the Valeyard and the Keeper of the Matrix from 'Trial of the Time Lord'; and one, last seen at Llangollen, which was of the same design as seen in 'The War Games' but, according to the owner, actually came from 'The Five Doctors'. Iconic robes and collars created for 'The Deadly Assassin' were also present, in red and amber. Also exhibited were the Master's straightjacket from 'The End of Time: Part One' and the costume of the mystic Visionary seen with the High Council on Gallifrey in 'The End of Time: Part Two'.

Spin-off *Torchwood* was afforded a strong display, including costumes of Toshiko Sato and Owen Harper from 'Fragments'; a Ianto Jones suit, a Gwen Cooper costume and one of Rhys Williams' outfits from 'Children of Earth';

---

[172] www.bonhams.com/auctions/18192/lot/134/

and, a particular highlight, Captain Jack Harkness's familiar military coat and navy shirt. The Captain Jack and Gwen costumes were placed on steps in front of a large circular door that had formed part of the Hub set. Also displayed was a costume worn by former *Buffy the Vampire Slayer* actor James Marsters as Captain John Hart.

In one corner, next to the *Torchwood* display, were exhibits from *Doctor Who*'s other contemporary spin-off, *The Sarah Jane Adventures*. The large Mr Smith computer and adjacent window with telescope, which had formed part of the attic set in studio, provided the backdrop for a number of costumes, including examples of those worn by Sarah Jane's young friends Clyde, Rani and Luke, and those of two villains, the Nightmare Man from the episode of the same title and Oddbob from 'Day of the Clown'. A costume worn by Elisabeth Sladen as Sarah Jane herself in 'Prisoner of the Judoon' was placed by the green Nissan Figaro car featured in the show.

These were the first official BBC displays of items from *Torchwood* and *The Sarah Jane Adventures*. *Torchwood* costumes would be added to the Cardiff Experience's exhibition only to mark the spin-off's tenth anniversary in 2016, some four years after the attraction had opened just a short walking distance from where the Torchwood Hub was supposed to be located. From *The Sarah Jane Adventures*, only the Sarah Jane costume from 'Prisoner of the Judoon' would be displayed in Cardiff, and then only briefly.

Wardrobe Workshop

Another feature of the Celebration was a Wardrobe Workshop, in which costume designer Louise Page and two wardrobe assistants discussed their work. Displayed in this area were a few more costumes, including the complete tenth Doctor outfit from 'The Day of the Doctor'; a scorched suit jacket prepared for 'The End of Time: Part One'; a Silurian costume from 'Cold Blood'; and Hila Tacorian's suit from 'Hide'. Visitors could also enter a wardrobe trailer, giving an insight into the Department's work environment when on location. Inside, noticeboards of continuity photographs were accompanied by rails full of miscellaneous costumes, including shirts worn by Matt Smith and ties worn by David Tennant.

Visual Effects and Model Unit

Further exciting displays were to be found at the Visual Effects and Model Unit stand, attended by designers Mat Irvine and Mike Tucker. These included original items used in a variety of *Doctor Who* stories dating back to the 1970s. The oldest were a recording device and a small model version of the police spaceship from 1973's 'Frontier in Space'. Two mechanical 'eight legs' spiders from Jon Pertwee's final story, 'Planet of the Spiders', had also survived the test of time, and were displayed with model city buildings used during the story's production.

The Tom Baker era was well represented too, the earliest item in this case being the medical kit seen in 'The Ark in Space'. From 'The Face of Evil', for which Irvine himself had designed the effects, were Janis thorns, Leela's gun, the large pedestal gun and the model of the cliff with the carving of the Doctor's face, the latter having been first displayed at the Longleat exhibition in 1977.

Irvine had also worked on the fifth Doctor story 'Warriors of the Deep', and from this he was able to display a gun, communicators and a control box; and the Sea Base 4, underwater probe and Silurian vessel models.

Other objects to be seen included the projection device from 'The Stones of Blood'; a TARDIS exterior miniature from 'The Trial of the Time Lord'; a large blaster used by Dibber in 'The Mysterious Planet' segment of the latter story; and Ace's ghetto-blaster from 'Silver Nemesis'. Bringing things into the show's modern era, two K-9 props took pride of place, including the rusted version seen in 'School Reunion', along with a full-size bronze Dalek of the type seen since 2005 and the central section of the Dalek Emperor model used for 'The Parting of the Ways'.

Special Sounds

Another aspect of the show's production to be covered at the Celebration was its sound effects. A replica of part of the legendary BBC Radiophonic Workshop provided a backdrop for a number of its one-time staff, including longest-serving contributor Dick Mills, to discuss their work and sign autographs. This replica environment would later be moved to the *Doctor Who* Experience.

ABC Ultimo Centre, Sydney, Australia

Also celebrating the show's fiftieth anniversary, a small display of *Doctor Who* items was mounted at the ABC Ultimo Centre in Sydney, Australia. This free exhibition, open from 15 August 2013 to 31 January 2014, was organised in conjunction with the *Doctor Who* Experience in Cardiff and featured an enlarged version of its souvenir brochure's centrespread, presenting a timeline of important moments from the show's half-century history.[173]

One item included was Dalek SM2, which now belongs to the Australian arm of BBC Worldwide, having been sent to the country in 1986 following the closure of the Blackpool exhibition. Also from the show's classic era were the prop scanner from 'Paradise Towers'; Sil the Mentor, as first seen in 'Vengeance on Varos'; a replica of the second Doctor's recorder; a third Doctor sonic screwdriver; a fourth Doctor scarf and hat; and the fifth Doctor's celery. Other props and costumes came from the modern era. These included a TARDIS exterior box; a tenth Doctor costume; and an eleventh Doctor costume

---

[173] www.youtube.com/watch?v=KJChniSBAOs

consisting of shirt, bow tie, braces, trousers and boots. Other monsters on show were a Cyberman ('Nightmare in Silver'); a Pig Slave ('Daleks in Manhattan'/'Evolution of the Daleks'); an Ood mask; and a Cybermat ('Closing Time'). Also on display, appropriately for this venue, was the costume worn by Australian star Kylie Minogue as Astrid in 'Voyage of the Damned'.

In January and February 2014, the Symphonic Spectacular Tour (a live presentation of music from *Doctor Who* complete with actors in monster costumes roaming the auditorium and stage) was taken to Melbourne and Brisbane in Australia and Wellington in New Zealand. A selection of props and costumes was included, and this appears to have been the only official *Doctor Who* exhibition staged in New Zealand to date. The Symphonic Specacular also toured the UK in 2015 from Saturday 23 May to Friday 29 May, taking in six cities.

Chapter 11
Doctor Who Experience II, Cardiff Bay (2014-2017)

After the 2014 summer season, the *Doctor Who* Experience was closed to the public from 1 September to 24 October, during which time the entire attraction was renovated – the first significant revamp it had received since being first installed in London back in 2011, when it had been heavily influenced by Matt Smith's debut series broadcast the previous year. A brand-new interactive walk-through adventure was created, with a script by Joseph Lidster, previously a writer for Big Finish and the spin-off shows *Torchwood* and *The Sarah Jane Adventures*. Lidster had visited the Experience's original incarnation with his sister and her children. 'Everyone loved it – especially the kids,' he recalls, 'and I think my sister and I felt like kids again while doing it.' Now, however, the walk-through adventure needed to be updated, not least to reflect the fact that Smith was no longer the Doctor. Lidster explains: 'We wanted the Experience to feel less tied to one era. The previous one was all about Matt Smith's Doctor and ended up with you in the Pandorica. Now there were kids who wouldn't know what the Pandorica was!'

Lidster created a new narrative that saw the TARDIS come under attack from the Crinis, a space jellyfish creature that attached itself to the ship. A deliberate decision was made to try to increase the urgency of the action, as Lidster again explains: 'Elements of the original version such as the Doctor talking to you on monitors when you were in the different rooms were, while fun, slightly outside of the fiction, as was the incidental music. So the one thing I was very keen to see if we could do was to keep everything within the fiction. If we were trapped on Skaro, for example, then we needed to find other ways to establish that, rather than have Peter Capaldi pop up on a monitor and tell us. I wanted to lose that element of it being "safe". The Doctor is gone! We need to find him!

'I suggested that we end up in the junkyard in Totter's Lane that we saw in the very first episode of *Doctor Who* back in 1963 and that the Doctor's been back to a few times over the years. If you're a *Doctor Who* fan, then that's a genuine thrill. If you're not a *Doctor Who* fan, it's still fun, because you're in a spooky old junkyard. If you end up in something more specific or alien such as the Pandorica or the tunnel from "Timelash", then unless you know the reference, it doesn't really mean anything to you.'

Another reason for the reduced focus on the Doctor was that Peter Capaldi's first series in the role was still in production at the time when the new walk-through adventure was being prepared, so Lidster had not yet seen any of his episodes. However, he was still excited by the prospect: 'I'm a huge fan of Peter Capaldi as an actor, and I was given most of the scripts from his first series, so I had a pretty good idea as to what to expect. I do think that the character of the Doctor is often more defined by the actor. They were great scripts but you could imagine pretty much any of the actors – especially the ones from 2005 onwards – saying the lines and putting their own spin on things.'

With the benefit of the scripts made available to him, and other hints from the production team, Lidster set about the task of writing for the character: 'The two main elements I got from them were that he had difficulty initially telling the difference between men and women and that he had a much more realistic – possibly callous – attitude toward death. I particularly wanted to incorporate that. He's quite rude to the visitors and says something like, "I'm pretty certain you won't survive this," which made people laugh and also added to that immersive feeling of real danger about the whole thing.'

Another aim was to deliver a truly immersive celebration of the entirety of the Doctor's adventures, with visitors beginning their journey in the Gallifrey Museum. Lidster again recalls: 'When we were developing the new Experience, we all looked back on previous visits to think about ways to improve it. My one thought was that the walk-through adventure wasn't particularly immersive. It was interactive and exciting and fun but you never particularly felt as if you were in an adventure.'

To further this aim of creating an immersive effect, the Experience's box office area was redressed to resemble the Gallifrey Museum. This meant that the stunning exclusive artwork that had previously adorned the walls was now covered by a drab grey stone effect. Later, the walk-through adventure would be actually extended out into the box office area, and a self-contained pod created for newly-arrived visitors to queue in after entering through the adjacent doors. Here were exhibited some wonderful Time Lord costumes, including that of the Keeper of the Matrix as seen in 'The Trial of the Time Lord' and the Master's from the 1996 TV movie, plus display cases containing other artefacts such as the Time Lord message cubes featured in 'The Doctor's Wife'. In the final year, costumes of Omega ('Arc of Infinity') and the Rani ('Time and the Rani') were also added.

The box office itself became a site for more items to be displayed. These included a Smiler in its booth ('The Beast Below'); an information node ('Silence in the Library'/'Forest of the Dead'; an operational *Doctor Who* pinball machine from the 1990s; and replica props made by the This Planet Earth online merchandisers, including a TARDIS exterior box, three Daleks, a Weeping Angel and an Ice Warrior. During the Christmas 2015 period, a number of artefacts from the show's Christmas specials were added as an extension to the exhibition. These included a Snowman and Clara's and the eleventh Doctor's costumes from 'The Snowmen'; another of Clara's costumes, this one from 'The Time of the Doctor'; the newly-regenerated tenth Doctor's pyjamas and dressing gown combination plus a robot Santa from 'The Christmas Invasion'; the Wooden King and Queen from 'The Doctor, the Widow and the Wardrobe'; and costumes of Jackson Lake and Miss Hartigan from 'The Next Doctor'. Further additions were made following the broadcast of 'The Husbands of River Song', including costumes of River Song and Nardole.

By the time the attraction closed in September 2017, the box office area had effectively become a small exhibition in its own right, with a route extending from the front doors to the entrance to the walk-through adventure. Handprints in concrete of twelfth Doctor actor Peter Capaldi and Clara Oswald actress Jenna Coleman were accompanied by the costumes they had worn in 'Deep Breath'. Also displayed were Tom Baker's costume as the Curator ('The Day of the Doctor'); the Matt Smith waxwork with the eleventh Doctor's purple-hued Series 7 costume; a Spoonhead ('The Bells of Saint John') clutching the venue's wi-fi password; the Library node from 'Silence in the Library'/'Forest of the Dead'; and *The Pandorica Opens* painting that had featured in the original walk-through adventure. A portrait of Nicholas Courtney as the Brigadier, based on a photograph taken during recording of 'Battlefield' and seen during 'Death in Heaven', was mounted on the wall by the cloakroom, accompanied by a modern UNIT uniform as first featured in 'The Sontaran Stratagem'.

Inside the first darkened room of the Museum were displayed further Gallifreyan artefacts, including the Time Lord table and the Moment prop from 'The Day of the Doctor'; *The History of the Time War* book from 'Journey to the Centre of the TARDIS'; and even the Key to Time prop from the classic-era show's Season 16, although this latter item was pushed to one side and not given the attention and direct lighting it really deserved.

Visitors arriving in this room were greeted by a Museum Guide – an in-costume Experience staff member – who issued each of them with a lanyard with a 'time crystal' attached. An introductory video was then played, with voiceover provided by actress Lalla Ward in character as one-time fourth Doctor companion and now Time Lord President Romana – a casting coup about which Joe Lidster recalls being 'hugely excited'. The video introduced Gallifrey and the Time Lords, with appropriate clips from modern-era episodes and a montage of the Doctor's various incarnations. 'I was really pleased with that whole opening segment,' says Lidster, 'as it covered everything from *Doctor Who* and reminded you that the whole 50-odd years was all about one man, his friends and the monsters he'd fought.'

As the video – or, as the Museum Guide referred to it, the Time-Space Visualiser image – came to a close, viewers saw a sequence of the TARDIS in flight and being attacked by the Crinis space squids. The Museum Guide would aid in the drama as suddenly the video screen broke open down the centre to lead onto the next room. As seasoned visitors would have realised, this was a reuse of the 'crack in time' effect from the original walk-through adventure – one of a number of limitations within which Lidster had to work when writing the new version. Other such limitations were that the general layout of the rooms had to remain fixed, and that the Matt Smith-era TARDIS console room and Dalek spaceship sets had to be retained, owing to the large amount of money invested in their construction.

These restrictions did not, however, hamper Lidster's creativity, as he explains: 'I think most writers like limitations, and I know I do. Having that structure was really useful, and it meant we could focus on developing – and hopefully improving on – what was in that part of the Experience.' Even where rooms could not be substantially altered, Lidster was able to suggest lighting changes to create a different feel. The adventure's second room, however, was one that could be completely redressed.

What once was *Starship UK* now became the TARDIS's architectural reconfiguration system, dominated by an impressive tree-like artefact bearing illuminated ovoid pods, as seen in 'Journey to the Centre of the TARDIS'. While not an aspect of the show that would have been immediately recognisable to more casual viewers – particularly as time went by – this made a lot of sense within the context of the walk-through adventure's story, as the space squids' attack on the system provided an explanation for the reappearance of the old, Matt Smith-era console room set. Video clips, played on a monitor, showed Peter Capaldi's Doctor reacting to this surprising turn of events, and also finding himself in several other, even earlier TARDIS console rooms. Although amusing, this sequence naturally had Capaldi playing the part in his grumpy Series 8 mode, rather than in the more mellow style he would come to adopt in subsequent series, and this unfortunately dated the adventure – something its creators had attempted to avoid.

Capaldi's material for the adventure was directed by Paul Wilmshurst, who also handled the television episodes 'Kill the Moon', 'Mummy on the Orient Express' and 'Last Christmas'. Shot on 4 August 2014, it had Capaldi performing on the Experience's own 1963-, 1983-, 2005- and 2010-style TARDIS console room sets, plus the current standing set at the Roath Lock studios.

A major remnant of the original adventure followed, as visitors moved through the police box doors and into the replica Matt Smith-era console room. 'We knew the TARDIS console room couldn't physically change,' notes Lidster. 'It had to stay as the initial Matt Smith console room. My suggestion, therefore, was to change the lighting. If we could make it less orange then it would feel more like a generic console room and less tied to one era.' For younger fans, the thrill of flying the TARDIS could still be enjoyed, and for those who had visited the Experience before, interactions with the on-screen Peter Capaldi Doctor offered something new.

The 'time crystals' attached to the visitors' lanyards would change colour and vibrate throughout the adventure, courtesy of wireless technology, further enhancing the interactive element. Lidster' narrative for the adventure also involved locating three further crystals to help the Doctor; and the first of these was to be found in the next room, which once again featured the Daleks. 'The room with the Daleks had to stay as a room with the Daleks,' says Lidster, 'but

I suggested changing it to their home planet, Skaro, rather than keeping it as a Dalek spaceship. I wanted the guests to feel like they were stepping out onto their first alien planet, so I suggested how we could use the TARDIS view screen and lighting in the corridor leading into the room etc to really make it feel like they'd landed somewhere.'

As the 'new paradigm'-style Daleks had now effectively disappeared from the television show, this had to be reflected in the new walk-through adventure, as Mike Tucker explains: 'When [Sarner] did that revamp they were very keen to try to do this ruined Skaro environment, and given that the large, multi-coloured "new paradigm" Daleks had been sort of phased out of the show, they wanted to bring back more of the bronze ones. We had the parts from probably about half-a-dozen of them delivered to my workshop, and out of those parts I needed to make two or three good ones and another couple of just wrecked pieces to go in the background. So we put together all the bronze Daleks that were in their sort of battered state for that walk-through piece.'

The ruined Skaro landscape, littered with battered and destroyed Daleks, was hugely impressive, and the Model Unit deserved high praise for helping to create this completely redressed set. The creepiness of the scene was enhanced by atmospheric lighting effects, again at Lidster's prompting, as he recalls: 'I suggested that the room be dark initially and then slowly light up. The previous Dalek room had been very loud and exciting. You walked in and there were Daleks and music and explosions and so on. I suggested that more mystery might be nice. When we went through it on the launch day, it was great to see kids – and adults! – being genuinely unnerved by that. They walked into the room not knowing what to expect and then, slowly, Daleks started to come alive around them.'

The trigger for waking up the Daleks was the removal of the first crystal needed to help the Doctor, with a younger member of the group of visitors being invited to pluck it from the side of what had been the Supreme Dalek. In order to escape from Skaro, the group needed to stand on a 'pressure pad' bearing a Dalek design, jumping up and down to activate it. They then moved swiftly on to the next section of the adventure, which again featured the same monsters as before, but was vastly improved.

'It had to stay as the Weeping Angels' room,' explains Lidster, 'but I made suggestions as to how lighting etc could make it scarier.' What had previously been simply a path through a creepy forest, extended earlier in 2014 with the addition of further Weeping Angel statues, was now converted into a graveyard, utilising gravestone props for Clara Oswin Oswald and Rory Williams and his wife Amelia plus pieces of the old Underhenge set. The path through the room was made twistier and longer to traverse, and this added to the increased tension. Curiously, the incongruous stone Gorgon prop from *The Sarah Jane Adventures* continued to be used, brightly lit and prominently positioned in the middle of the pathway. The second missing 'time crystal' was also located in this Weeping Angels graveyard.

The final room had previously been the Underhenge set, concluding the

Pandorica storyline of the adventure's original version. Now, though, the finale instead saw visitors stepping inside the Totter's Lane junkyard, created using the set built for the *An Adventure in Space and Time* docu-drama of 2013. The third and final missing 'time crystal' was obtained in this room and inserted into a device that activated the revamped attraction's new 3D movie. This version of the movie featured the Crinis, Daleks and Weeping Angels, tying together the adventure's narrative.

Not all of Joe Lidster's ideas for the adventure came to fruition, as he reflects: 'The one element we couldn't get, sadly, was to use clips from "An Unearthly Child" – the first ever TV episode. I wanted a clip of Ian and Barbara entering the junkyard to be used in the opening montage, and then for us to return to it at the end. So, as visitors, you would have collected all of the crystals, saved the day, and the Doctor would have congratulated you before telling you to shut up. We'd then have heard Ian and Barbara entering the junkyard, and the Doctor would have told everyone to get out quickly before they messed up his timeline. Sadly, because of rights issues, that couldn't happen.'

This new adventure was unveiled to the public on Friday 24 October 2014. Also in attendance for the opening was an actor in costume as the Teller from that year's story 'Time Heist', posing for photographs while under the supervision of its keepers. Members of the press were given a preview of the walk-through adventure first thing that morning, before the doors opened to the public. Reaction was positive. David Prince later wrote about the new version for WalesOnline and approved of all the changes: 'The new Gallifrey Museum, I like that storyline. For me, even though I've been there six times now, it still feels fresh … I think it runs more smoothly now than it ever did with Matt Smith, it runs more cohesively.' However, there was no escaping the fact that the revamp had been achieved on a limited budget, as Prince summarised: 'The narrative with Capaldi, that felt great, that was a much-needed step. But then, when you're walking through, you notice that not that much has actually changed. But credit where credit is due, they had to change it and keep down the costs.' Budgetary constraints might also perhaps have accounted for the fact that the crystals on the visitors' lanyards did not always vibrate and change colour as intended; Prince noted that his had worked properly on only two of his six visits.

After handing back those lanyards, and the 3D glasses with which they had been issued, visitors then emerged from the walk-through adventure onto the TARDIS control room set created for *An Adventure of Space and Time*, and from there onto the rest of the exhibition.

Lower Exhibition

The exhibition floors were also redeveloped as part of the revamp. New items were added, and although most of these had been seen in public before, generally at the Up Close exhibitions or the *Doctor Who* Celebration event, some from Peter Capaldi's first season did make their exhibition debuts.

The *An Adventure in Space and Time* TARDIS control room set was presented in such a way as to give visitors the impression of having just walked into a 1960s BBC studio. Following a display of replica Daleks, created both for the exhibition itself and for *An Adventure in Space and Time*, a number of behind-the-scenes photographs were presented. Also on show from the docu-drama were a Menoptra costume and a table of props, including period newspapers. Later, costumes worn in the production by David Bradley as William Hartnell and Claudia Grant as Carole Ann Ford were positioned beside the TARDIS console, as if the first Doctor and his grand-daughter Susan were stood at the controls. These were accompanied by costumes worn by Jessica Raine as producer Verity Lambert and Brian Cox as *Doctor Who*'s principal creator Sydney Newman.

The next display attempted to replicate the environment of the BBC Radiophonic Workshop, as had been seen at the *Doctor Who* Celebration, complete with a set of exposed piano strings as used to make the familiar sound effect of the TARDIS engines. Adjacent to this was placed a recreation of a scene from 'The Dalek Invasion of Earth', with a TARDIS police box stood in front of a brick wall with a poster reading, 'IT IS FORBIDDEN TO DUMP BODIES INTO THE RIVER'. This approach of positioning behind-the-scenes displays alongside immersive recreations of events from the Doctor's adventures on screen arguably made for some rather jarring juxtapositions.

As in the previous version of the exhibition, the main focus of the ground floor displays was the TARDIS. The three different interior sets remained but were now joined by no fewer than five exterior props, plus an additional one with a green-screen effects background inside. The 1980s police box prop was used in another newly-conceived scene recreation, being placed with a screen-used K-9 prop on a pebbled surface intended to represent Brighton beach, as seen in the opening sequence of 'The Leisure Hive'. The TARDIS console used by the fifth to seventh Doctors was another item to be repositioned, now placed next to the 1960s-style control room set.

In the initial revamp, the existing recreation of the barn scene from 'The Day of the Doctor', with the three TARDIS exterior props accompanied by the Moment, was relocated from the exhibition's upper floor to the ground floor. Later, however, it was moved back to the upper floor and replaced by a new green-screen area, offering a total of eight background choices for photographs that visitors could purchase.

Another repositioned exhibit was the Doctor's car Bessie, which was now tucked neatly beneath the stairs leading to the upper floor. By the end of Matt Smith's era, however, the lower floor had become so crammed full of large items and sets that it really offered only limited scope for being refreshed in the revamp, as David Prince notes: 'When it first opened back in 2012, it felt like they'd got a lot of space to grow into, whereas later it started to get kind of cramped, especially downstairs.' The upper floor, though, offered greater potential for the introduction of new features to engage the interest of even the most seasoned of visitors.

Upper Exhibition

The upper floor became more freely flowing in the revamp, with no preferred route around the exhibits. In addition, the items on display would be shifted around and changed over time – the Silent spaceship and Skaldak the Ice Warrior, for instance, were amongst the items included on reopening, but were later removed to make way for new exhibits.

The fiftieth anniversary episode 'The Day of the Doctor' was well represented, in the form of the costumes worn by the tenth Doctor and Elizabeth I, plus a Zygon and associated equipment, all of which had been on display previously. Items from 'The Time of the Doctor' also remained on display as before.

Some of the items previously seen at the *Doctor Who* Celebration at the ExCeL centre were given a further public airing. Sarah Jane Smith's costume from 'The Five Doctors', Ace's costume from 'The Curse of Fenric', a Yeti from 'The Web of Fear' and the 'Earthshock' Cyberman boosted the number of classic-era artefacts on display. Additions from the 21st Century episodes included Rose Tyler's costume from 'The Idiot's Lantern' and the Supreme Dalek from 'The Stolen Earth'. All of these items had been in storage since the 2013 Celebration event.

One of the most substantial displays focused on the Cybermen. The helmets displayed since 2011 were now all presented in a single case, accompanied by a line of full Cyberman costumes and related items. Included were a refurbished 'Earthshock' costume; the Cyber Controller from 'The Age of Steel'; a Cybershade from 'The Next Doctor' (incorrectly stated on the signage to have been transmitted in 2009 rather than 2008); the conversion unit from 'Closing Time'; a standard Cybus-style Cyberman from 'Rise of the Cybermen'/'The Age of Steel'; a 'Nightmare in Silver' Cyberman; the wooden Cyberman from 'The Time of the Doctor'; and a cryogenic unit with Cyberman helmet inside from 'Closing Time'.

The refurbished 'Earthshock' costume was provided by Mark Barton Hill and had been previously displayed at the 2013 Celebration event. It was comprised of parts from two different original costumes, sold as Lots 134 and 135 at Bonhams in 2010. One had previously been a destroyed Cyberman, dating back to 'Earthshock' itself; the other provided the immersion suit plus other pieces.[174,175] As detailed in previous chapters, the destroyed Cyberman had been a regular display item at Longleat after 'Attack of the Cybermen' and had later appeared at the second Blackpool exhibition. Hill had purchased it at Bonhams specifically with a view to restoring it, as he explains: 'Having seen it way back at Longleat year after year, lying on the floor, I realised that it was actually older and of greater value than the ones standing beside it in better condition – and would be well worth saving and cleaning up one day … Little

---

[174] www.bonhams.com/auctions/18192/lot/134/
[175] www.bonhams.com/auctions/18192/lot/135/

did I know that, years later, I would be there breaking the bank to get hold of it and do just that.' The helmet had required relatively little restoration work – the fitting of replacement handles and mouthpiece for instance – but the suit had been a more difficult proposition. It having become quite rigid over the years, its placement on a mannequin was initially accompanied by the distressing sound of cracking latex rubber. The end result, however, proved well worth the effort.

Next to the Cyberman display was positioned the Walk Like a Monster attraction, now mounted in a curved and mirrored pod. Nearby, an assortment of monsters from the show's post-2005 era were also on show, most of them having previously appeared at the various regional Up Close exhibitions. These included the Face of Boe; Novice Hame; a female Clockwork Droid in pink dress; the Abzorbaloff; a Scarecrow; a Hath (with mask showing signs of deterioration); a Winder costume with Smiler mask; and a helmeted Sontaran from 'The Sontaran Stratagem'. Rosanna Calvieri's costume from 'Vampires in Venice' was reunited with her throne, previously positioned in the *Starship UK* room of the original walk-through adventure. Completing the monster menagerie were the Restac Silurian costume; two Antibodies from 'Let's Kill Hitler'; and a Silent. Additional Silents were later hung upside-down from the lighting framework above.

Also displayed initially were a Sycorax ('The Christmas Invasion'); an Ood ('The Impossible Planet'/'The Satan Pit'); and a chained Weeping Angel accompanied by two cherubs ('The Angels Take Manhattan'). Later, though, these items were removed to make way for others.

A selection of exhibits from the show's classic era were grouped together. These included the Rani's costume from 'Time and the Rani'; the refurbished Linx Sontaran from 'The Time Warrior'; the Melkur statue ('The Keeper of Traken'); and the K1 Robot ('Robot').

Also added to this area was a Yeti from 'The Web of Fear', accompanied by signage erroneously picturing the earlier design as seen in 'The Abominable Snowmen'. This costume had received no significant restoration since its appearance at the 2013 Celebration event. Areas of the fur fabric and face all needed work, but more significantly it was now missing both of its feet and its right claw, and even its left claw was not an original. The costume was the same one as seen at Longleat in 1988 and later at MOMI, Llangollen and the second Blackpool exhibition; and in fact it still held the same pose, with left arm across the torso, adopted for the latter two venues.

As part of the exhibition's revamp, the Daleks were removed from their previous plinth and placed instead on the exhibition floor. Initially they were arranged in a circle, and the established chronological line-up was bolstered by the addition of the Emperor Dalek miniature from 'The Parting of the Ways', a second gun-metal-grey and black Dalek (a refurbished original from 'Planet of the Daleks') and the Supreme Dalek from 'The Stolen Earth'/'Journey's End', these two Daleks having also appeared at the 2013 Celebration event. The ever-popular Special Weapons Dalek from 'Remembrance of the Daleks' also chalked up another exhibition appearance. The walk-in 'operate a Dalek' prop was also once again present on the exhibition floor.

Moved upstairs from the ground floor, along with the display case of sonic screwdrivers, was the line-up of all the earlier Doctors' costumes, ending with Matt Smith's outfit from his debut series. Added to the line-up now was also the War Doctor's costume, positioned between the eighth and ninth Doctors'. Elsewhere on the upper floor, the eighth Doctor's more recent costume from 'The Night of the Doctor' was paired with Ohila's robes from that minisode. Peter Capaldi's main costume, which had debuted in 'Deep Breath', was also exhibited, with hands tucked into the trouser pockets in a pose that revealed the jacket's red lining.

Numerous companion costumes were also on display, some of which had been seen at the Experience before, while others – including Ace's grey dress from 'The Curse of Fenric' – had been retrieved from storage, having previously been on show at the 2013 Celebration event. Sarah Jane Smith was particularly well-represented, with costumes from 'The Five Doctors', 'School Reunion' and *The Sarah Jane Adventures* story 'Prisoner of the Judoon'. Rose Tyler's pink dress and jacket from 'The Idiot's Lantern' was also added, joining her outfit from 'The Stolen Earth'/'Journey's End'. Completing the array of companion costumes were examples of those worn by Captain Jack Harkness ('The Stolen Earth'/'Journey's End'), Martha Jones ('Smith and Jones'), Donna Noble ('The Stolen Earth'/'Journey's End'), Rory Williams ('Vampires in Venice' and 'The Hungry Earth'/'Cold Blood'), Amy Pond ('The Eleventh Hour' and 'The Hungry Earth'/'Cold Blood') and young Amelia Pond ('The Eleventh Hour'). These were all placed in front of the noticeboards from the UNIT Black Archive as seen in 'The Day of the Doctor'.

Significant new additions were made to the exhibition following the broadcast of Peter Capaldi's first series. Items from his debut story 'Deep Breath' included the Half-Faced Man prop, complete with exposed clockwork mechanism; a miniature of the hot air balloon; a Mancini's Restaurant sign; the Doctor's initial grubby costume; and Clara's emerald dress. Also displayed were the costumes worn by the Paternoster trio, Vastra, Jenny and Strax, each clutching one of the special tools conceived for the story by *Blue Peter* competition winners.

The rest of the 2014 series was well represented too, via brand-new displays and exhibits, some of which featured episode-specific poster designs specially created for a range of new merchandise items available exclusively from the Experience's shop. From 'Into the Dalek' came Rusty the Dalek, while 'Robot of Sherwood' was the source of several exhibits, including one of the robot knights, costumes of the Sherriff of Nottingham, Robin Hood, Clara and Marian, and a target with three arrows shot through the centre.

A creepy scene from 'Listen' was recreated, with the unidentified shape beneath the bed sheet and the pyjamas of the young Rupert/Danny Pink. From 'Time Heist', items included costumes of Clara, Psi, Saibra and Madame Karabraxos/Ms Delphox. The Teller and its minders were added after being used for promotional duties during the revamped Experience's opening.

Another notable villain to be displayed was the Skovox Blitzer from 'The Caretaker'. Other exhibits from that episode included two costumes worn by Danny Pink, specifically a suit and his Coal Hill Cadet Squad uniform; Clara's outfit; Courtney Woods' school uniform; the Doctor's backpack; and in the background a Coal Hill Secondary School sign.

Next, from 'Kill the Moon' came a Spider germ – a larger prop than visitors might have anticipated – and the spacesuits worn by Lundvik and Clara. The following episode, 'Mummy on the Orient Express', received a bit more attention, with props and set elements from the episode supporting a display of outfits worn by Clara, Maisie and the singer Foxes. The central monster, the Foretold, was also displayed when not being worn by original actor Jamie Hill, who worked at the Experience. It was complemented by the mysterious sarcophagus that had housed it on screen.

From 'In the Forest of the Night' came a lion statue prop, which looked as if it had come straight from Trafalgar Square in London, plus costumes for Danny Pink and Clara.

The series finale, 'Dark Water'/'Death in Heaven', provided a number of popular exhibits, including Missy's costume, the replica 'The Invasion'-style Cyberman helmet prop, and the modern-day Cyberman helmet with open front plate that had revealed Danny Pink inside. Items from 'Last Christmas' were added later, including Santa Claus, Ian and Wolf costumes, plus a selection of props and an area of set dusted with a light amount of fake snow. On a hospital bed, a crew member with an attached dream crab was also displayed.

The redevelopment certainly proved a hit, as in March 2015 the Experience won the Best in Leisure & Tourism prize at the Cardiff Life awards, beating other nominees including the prestigious Celtic Manor resort.[176] It also generated a new wave of exclusive merchandise, with the Gallifrey Museum appearing on stationary and mugs, and a design featuring the Crinis appearing on postcards and T-shirts. Another updated version of the souvenir brochure was also created.

Certain high-profile classic-era artefacts had been retained by the BBC following the closure of the Blackpool exhibition in 2009. Of these, the K1 Robot, the Zygon and the Ice Warrior had already been retrieved from storage and restored for the Experience's 2011 opening. A few more had been brought out for display at the 2013 Celebration event in London. Now, the services of Mike Tucker and his team at the Model Unit were enlisted to explore the possibility of restoring further items to add to the Experience's exhibition.

Davros, creator of the Daleks, had always been a popular display item, having first featured at the Longleat exhibition mere months after the character's 1975 television debut in 'Genesis of the Daleks'.[177] Now, the Model

---

[176] www.doctorwhonews.net/2015/03/doctor-who-wins-cardiff-life-awards.html
[177] *World of Horror* No.8.

Unit set about recreating his 'Resurrection of the Daleks' appearance. The black jacket revealed the signs of having been altered for multiple actors, beginning with the original, Michael Wisher, whose handwritten name could still be identified inside, as Mike Tucker illuminates: 'The jacket still had Wisher's name written in the back of it. And it had a little vent of a different material cut into the back of it, and extensions put onto the sleeves. When Terry Molloy came down to the workshop one day, he said, "Oh yeah, that's because I was actually slightly bulkier than Michael Wisher was!" So they had had to expand the costume slightly to fit him.'

The likelihood is that the BBC Costume Department had actually produced more than one jacket for Wisher, as Tucker again explains: 'The BBC Costume Department usually made duplicates of everything, so it's very possible that there was more than one jacket. That's difficult to prove one way or the other. What we can prove is that one of the original "Genesis" jackets definitely got reused for all the subsequent Terry Molloy stories.'

Davros's chair also turned out to originate from 'Genesis of the Daleks'. 'Fundamentally,' says Tucker, 'the plywood base of that is the same chair built for Michael Wisher back in "Genesis". So that's got an amazing history there ... Tony Harding, who was responsible for it in the first place, came along to the workshop when we doing the refurbishment, and he confirmed that it is the chair he built back in 1975.' During production of 'Genesis of the Daleks', Harding had been a BBC visual effects assistant; later he had graduated to visual effects designer on stories including 'The Invisible Enemy', 'The Power of Kroll' and 'The Awakening'.

The original Michael Wisher mask, also worn by David Gooderson in 'Destiny of the Daleks', had rotted into a bag of brown goo by this time. However, Tucker's team were able to reuse the original plaster mould created by BBC visual effects sculptor Stan Mitchell for the later mask worn by Terry Molloy back in 1983. 'I was very lucky with that,' Tucker confirms, 'in that I was able to track down and successfully reuse the original mould that Stan Mitchell had made.' Despite the mould being over 30 years old, it was successfully used to create a latex-and-expanding-foam head for the Davros exhibit. This was painted and an eye fitted so as replicate the original look as closely as possible. 'That's an example of a replica prop being almost as close to screen-used as you can get,' says Tucker, 'because we were using the original mould to recreate it.'

Davros's hand was also recreated by Model Unit team member Alan Marshall. The head and hand were then fitted to an altered fibreglass mannequin, with additional foam parts fitted to fill the jacket. Mike Tucker was keen to ensure that the figure held a recognisable pose, with Davros's right hand hovering ominously over the controls on his chair. 'I felt it was very important to the look of that prop,' he affirms, 'and we couldn't find a mannequin that had that exact pose. So we took a basic mannequin and chopped it around until we got something that looked right.'

Using Plastazote foam, a blue rear head-brace was constructed to replace the original, which had been lost over time. The original control panel, having suffered damage, was also replaced with a new one, but with as many of the original pieces reused as possible – including the hatch from beneath which Davros retrieved his triangular mind-control device in 'Resurrection of the Daleks'.

Mike Tucker is proud of the final results of his team's work: 'I was very pleased with the way Davros particularly came out. Again it was just that key thing that I'm determined to do: that we go back and we try to do everything as accurately as possible to what was done originally.'

The stunning final result was unveiled at the Cardiff Experience on 24 October 2015, accompanied by the original Emperor Dalek/Davros from 'Remembrance of the Daleks'. The Emperor had also required some restoration work, having been on show previously at Space Adventure, MOMI, Longleat and the second Blackpool exhibition before going into storage. Damaged hemispheres on the skirt section were removed and replaced, and badly flaking paintwork was completely stripped and repainted. The top section was refitted to the skirt, with a new collar and replacement white discs, which covered the joining bolts. A second Davros head was cast from the original mould and fitted inside the dome, accompanied by wires and cables, completing the screen-accurate restoration.

Further items would be added to the exhibition after appearing in *Doctor Who*'s 2015 series – a development of which subscribers to the Experience's e-mail newsletter received advance notice. First, however, a number of those new items were given a debut public airing at two *Doctor Who* Festival events staged in November 2015.

Doctor Who Festival – ExCeL Centre

Two years after the fiftieth anniversary Celebration event, BBC Worldwide hosted another major *Doctor Who* convention, again at the ExCeL Centre in London. Titled the *Doctor Who* Festival, this marked Peter Capaldi's first official convention appearance. Once again, this three-day event allowed fans to meet the stars for autographs and photos, but also to see costumes and props from the latest series, which was still being broadcast at the time. Unlike with the Celebration, tickets for the Festival were available for months before the event, which was even advertised with leaflets around the country. Many fans were unhappy with the hike in ticket prices. In 2013, the standard adult ticket for the Celebration had cost £45.00 per day. In 2015 it cost £65.00, equating to a 45% increase. Similarly, the special TARDIS tickets, allowing a degree of preferential access, were increased in price from £95.50 to £110.00 for an adult and from £218.00 to a staggering £285.00 for a family.

The event took place over the weekend of 13 to 15 November 2015, and as usual featured several guest panels, which were largely repeated on each of the three days. Scriptwriter Mark Gatiss and Millennium FX's Kate Walshe discussed creations such as Mr Sweet and the new Ice Warrior, with monster actor Jon Davey at one point appearing on stage in full Mire outfit from 'The Girl Who Died'. Making an appearance on the Sunday was also a Sandman, as seen in 'Sleep No More', broadcast the day before. The second panel, titled Meet the Writers, was hosted by Matthew Sweet and saw Sarah Dollard, Peter Harness and Steven Moffat discussing their work. Finally, Toby Hadoke hosted a similar Meet the Cast panel, starring Peter Capaldi, Michelle Gomez and Ingrid Oliver, again accompanied by Steven Moffat. Jenna Coleman joined this panel on the Saturday and Sunday, taking a break from working on the ITV drama *Victoria*.

With the event focusing on the adventures of the twelfth Doctor, the costumes and props on display all came from his tenure, including the series still being broadcast. While props were placed on a standard props table as found in a *Doctor Who* studio, many of the costumes were presented on mannequins, with costume rails, coat hangers and plastic wrapping behind, creating a feel of the Costume Department. Costumes were also accompanied by plastic pockets of notes and continuity photos, again as used during production.

The latest series-opener, 'The Magician's Apprentice'/'The Witch's Familiar', was well represented, Missy's new purple ensemble appearing alongside costumes of Ohila of the Sisterhood of Karn; Clara; the Shadow Architect; young Davros; and Colony Sarff. Also on display were the open Dalek prop that had housed Clara and, last but not least, the Doctor's own costume, accompanied by his electric guitar and amp.

Exhibits from 'Under the Lake'/'Before the Flood' included costumes worn by Clara and Cass plus a Vector Petroleum wetsuit.

From 'The Girl Who Died' came Clara's orange spacesuit, complete with helmet and boots; Clara's and Ashildr's Viking costumes, together with the 'Ye Swan with two necks' pub sign; Odin's costume; and all manner of props, including a large horn and some ornate-looking wood carvings. These items were all positioned in a Viking Hall recreation dubbed the Production Village, where the show's assistant director team conducted presentations, including one by production designer Michael Pickwood. One of the more glamorous outfits on display was Me's red dress from 'The Woman Who Lived', which was accompanied by her highwayman outfit, a Tyburn distance-marker prop, plus Leandro and Clara costumes.

The two-parter 'The Zygon Invasion'/'The Zygon Inversion' had concluded on BBC One the weekend prior to the event, and so a number of exhibits were provided for visitors to see. These included costumes of Clara, Bonnie and Kate Stewart; a UNIT soldier uniform; two Osgood outfits, one of them the duffle coat and scarf seen in her final scene; the two decision boxes; a rocket-launcher in its case, as featured in the cliff-hanger; and a Zygon pod.

Perhaps surprisingly, Peter Capaldi's maroon velvet jacket costume was displayed before actually debuting on screen in the following week's episode, 'Face the Raven'. It had however already been photographed during recording on the streets of Cardiff and for a *Radio Times* photoshoot.

A TARDIS police box made of Lego bricks was on show in the arena, promoting the Lego Dimensions video game. Millennium FX also had a display of their work, including a Mire costume; an Ood mask; a Madame Vastra head; Slitheen skins; Sycorax, Clockwork Droid and Sontaran heads; a Colony Sarff facepiece; the Foretold mask; Dalek duplicate skulls; and prosthetic pieces.

One of the more substantial exhibits was the complete studio set used for Davros's sick room in the series-opener, including the adjoining corridor and the 'only chair on Skaro'. Another set reassembled at the ExCeL Centre was Clara's flat, where visitors could have their photograph taken by a professional photographer.

Doctor Who Festival – Moore Park

Another *Doctor Who* Festival event, albeit on a smaller scale, was held at Moore Park in Sydney, Australia over the following weekend, 21-22 November 2015. Once again Peter Capaldi, Mark Gatiss and Steven Moffat were in attendance, with panels, photo and autograph opportunities on offer. Seventh doctor Sylvester McCoy also appeared for a panel. Although advertised, Billie Piper had to pull out mere days before the event, but was replaced by Ingrid Oliver.[178] Various costumes and props were also flown 'down under' for display, including a Sandman, an Ood and a Zygon. Once this event concluded, these items were prepared for relocation to Cardiff for display in 2016.

Doctor Who Experience – Series 9

As foreshadowed in the e-mail newsletter announcement, exhibits from the 2015 series finally went on display at the *Doctor Who* Experience in Cardiff from 2 March 2016. This necessitated significant rearranging and updating of the upper exhibition space. Notably, the number of items from the 2014 series was significantly reduced, the only ones retained being the Half-Face Man and the hot air balloon model ('Deep Breath'); Rusty the Dalek ('Into the Dalek'); Madame Karabraxos's costume and the Teller ('Time Heist'); the Skovox Blitzer ('The Caretaker'); and the Foretold with sarcophagus ('Mummy on the Orient Express').

Most of the new additions had been seen previously at the 2015 ExCeL centre event. The most substantial of them was Davros's sick room set, which took the place of the Silent spaceship set that had been present since 2012. Either side of the corridor leading into the sick room were positioned the Dalek props, guarding the entrance, with their creator lurking inside. The 'new paradigm' Eternal Dalek, having not appeared in 'The Magician's

---

[178] www.smh.com.au/entertainment/tv-and-radio/billie-piper-pulls-out-of-doctor-who-festival-four-days-before-its-sydney-launch-20151117-gl1d8l.html

Apprentice'/'The Witch's Familiar', was subsequently removed from the exhibition but would later return before the attraction closed. Near to the sick room set were also placed the costumes of the young Davros and Colony Sarff. The latter even had a small toy snake added, appearing to slither out from underneath the robe. Inside the sick room set, complete with a selection of props and Davros himself, were positioned Missy's purple outfit and Clara's costume, plus the open Dalek prop. The Doctor's costume from the story was also displayed, beside 'the only chair on Skaro'.

The display for 'Under the Lake'/'Before the Flood' featured Clara's and Cass's costumes and the Vector Petroleum wetsuit as seen at the Festival event, accompanied now by the towering presence of the Fisher King. Opposite this were placed items from 'The Girl Who Died', specifically Clara's Viking attire and costumes of Odin and the Mire. Next to these came Me's red dress and highwayman outfit and the Leandro and Clara costumes from 'The Woman Who Lived'. In all of these displays, the costumes worn by Jenna Coleman as Clara took centre stage, a reminder that the actress had departed the show at the series' conclusion.

Beside the Fisher King were placed a number of costumes and props from 'The Zygon Invasion'/'The Zygon Inversion'. As at the Festival, these included costumes of Clara, Bonnie, Kate Stewart and a UNIT soldier; two outfits worn by Osgood; and the two decision boxes, with the rocket-launcher in its case. These were positioned in front of one of the UNIT Black Archive noticeboards from 'The Day of the Doctor'.

All but two of the rest of the 2015 series exhibits were exclusive to the Experience. One of the exceptions was the Sandman from 'Sleep No More', which had previously appeared at the Festival event on the Sunday only. New exhibits from 'Sleep No More' included outfits worn by Clara and Rasmussen; one of the military uniforms; a dress worn by a hologram singer; and the Morpheus Pod prop.

'Face the Raven' was represented by a section of the screen-used Trap Street set that had formed the backdrop for the ultimate demise of Clara, whose costume from the episode was displayed here, along with those of Rigsy, Ashildr and Anahson. Also present was the cage that had held the titular raven.

Behind all these exhibits, in the centre of a wider area prior to the exit toward the shop, were displayed the teleport and the weathered eleventh Doctor costume seen during 'Heaven Sent'. Opposite these was the scary Veil creature, accompanied by prop skulls, the Clara painting and the spade used by the Doctor during the same episode. Providing the exhibition's finale, in a corner opposite the shop entrance, were a number of impressive costumes from the series finale, 'Hell Bent'. Immaculately displayed on mannequins were the General's uniform, the President's robes, Ohila's costume and a Cloister Wraith or Slider Time Lord costume. On the final plinth were the twelfth Doctor's outfit worn in the diner scenes, Clara's diner waitress outfit and Ashildr's costume.

Also added to the exhibition was Peter Capaldi's maroon velvet jacket costume – the other item from the series' later episodes to have been seen previously at the Festival event. This was initially positioned beside a TARDIS police box, along with his main costume and his grubby initial outfit from 'Deep Breath'. Adjacent to these was set up a significant display of costumes worn by Jenna Coleman, again marking her departure from the show. Included in this were outfits worn in 'Asylum of the Daleks', 'Deep Breath', 'Robot of Sherwood', 'Time Heist', 'Hide', 'The Time of the Doctor', 'Listen', 'The Caretaker' and 'Mummy on the Orient Express'. Later, the TARDIS exterior prop adorned with the Clara memorial painting from 'Face the Raven' was also added to the display, having previously been retained in studio to be seen by visitors taking the official set tour. It replaced the other TARDIS exterior prop that had stood in this position previously, and remained there even after recording of the next series began at the end of June 2016. At the same time, the two twelfth Doctor suits from 'Deep Breath' were relocated to join the other incarnations' costumes, allowing the focus of the display to be solely on Clara.

Another, smaller display was dedicated to River Song. This included costumes from 'The Name of the Doctor' and 'The Time of Angels', positioned alongside the Doctor's cot provided for the infant Melody Pond in 'A Good Man Goes to War'. Three costumes from the Christmas special 'The Husbands of River Song', which had been previously shown in the box office area, were also added to this display in the main exhibition, bumping off River's costume from 'The Pandorica Opens'.

Doctor Who Experience – Series 10 and further restorations

For a limited time, from 14 May 2016 and into the following month, the *Doctor Who* Experience was able to display the denim jacket and Prince T-shirt that had formed part of the costume worn by new companion Pearl Mackie in the special scene that introduced her character Bill Potts. These were positioned with the maroon velvet jacket costume worn by the twelfth Doctor during the same scene, and the scene itself was played on a small monitor at the end of the upper floor exhibition before visitors made their way into the official shop.

2016 saw further additions being made to the Cardiff exhibition, and further restorations of monsters from the show's classic era. Vital to the success of these restorations was the work of Mike Tucker and the Model Unit. On 16 July 2016, Tucker returned to the exhibition and was able to unveil a fresh restoration of the original Zygon, which had been removed from display following the summer of 2012. In what was considered 'phase two' of the restoration project, the Zygon was joined by costumes of Omega from 'Arc of Infinity' and a Tetrap from 'Time and the Rani', both of which had required work after spending several years in storage, save for a brief appearance at the Celebration event in 2013.

Where the Omega costume was concerned, the work required was relatively minor. The helmet piece, although elaborate in design, was constructed of fibreglass, and so had withstood the test of time intact. The costume itself, once it was placed on a mannequin it fitted better than the one used previously, just needed to be cleaned up, with the accumulated dust and grime carefully removed from the fabric. During his presentations at the Experience, Tucker explained: 'All it really takes is buying a modern mannequin and redressing the costume in a slightly better pose ... An item that's been bundled up in a box or quite badly displayed becomes an easy item for us to pull from the archives and re-present.' The results provided a rare representation of Peter Davison's second year as the fifth Doctor and *Doctor Who's* twentieth anniversary season.

Back in 1987, the Tetrap had been a collaborative effort between the Visual Effects Department, who had constructed the head and arms, and the Costume Department, who had provided the body suit. Mike Tucker had himself worked on 'Time and Rani' as an effects assistant; he had been responsible for the remote control work on Urak, the lead Tetrap, and also for helping actor Richard Gauntlett in and out of the costume. Significant sections of the surviving head had been cast in foam latex, which by 2016 had suffered significant deterioration – not helped by the fact that the actor inside had sweated profusely during the story's recording, before the costume had first gone into storage. In particular, the latex around the cheeks and jaw had begun to rot.

The restoration in this instance was assisted by Colin Mapson – who, as Mike Tucker explains, 'was the designer who actually came up with the Tetraps in the first place.' Like the Omega costume, the Tetrap had in the past been mounted on a mannequin that was less than ideal, so the Model Unit's first task was to fit it to a more suitable one and in a more sympathetic pose. Given the Tetrap's similarity to a bat, when last displayed in Blackpool from 2004 to 2009 its arms had been outstretched laterally to demonstrate its wingspan. A similar pose was again favoured, but with the arms angled forwards. Once the costume was on the new mannequin, repairs could be undertaken to the damaged areas.

Some of the paint had worn off the creature's exposed belly, requiring touching up. The wings were in reasonable condition, although the supporting struts needed repairing, and again the paintwork required refreshing. Fortunately Tucker discovered an original Tetrap jaw in his attic, and this was fitted to the mask to replace the rotted section. Overall, the final result featured approximately 95% original material.

At the unveiling of these exhibits, the Experience promoted an online poll in which fans could vote to select which pairing of classic monsters would be next to undergo the restoration process. The options listed – confirming that, due in part to the efforts of artefacts manager Andrew Beech, they all still survived in storage – were the Morbius monster ('The Brain of Morbius'), a Mandrel ('Nightmare of Eden'), a Sea Devil ('Warriors of the Deep'), a Tractator ('Frontios'), the L3 Drathro robot ('The Trial of the Time Lord': 'The Mysterious Planet'), a Vervoid ('The Trial of the Time Lord': 'Terror of the Vervoids'), a Haemovore ('The Curse of Fenric') and a Cheetah Person ('Survival').

Victorious in the public vote was the fourth-Doctor-era pairing of the Morbius monster and the Mandrel. Both artefacts were then delivered to the Model Unit's workshop and the restoration process began.

The Morbius monster was in particularly poor condition. It had been constructed using yellow upholstery foam, which had hardened over time and was now disintegrating. In contrast, the Mandrel had a more traditional construction of leather and faux fur pieces, although it had a latex head that needed attention.

Those items unsuccessful in the public vote, namely the Sea Devil, the Tractator, Drathro, the Vervoid, the Haemovore and the Cheetah Person, plus other former exhibits such as an Axon last seen in Blackpool, were for the time being retained in storage by BBC Worldwide.

On 1 August 2016, the Experience was also able to put on display a replica of the 1977-1981 TARDIS console room, painstakingly recreated by Mark Barton Hill. The original console had been last on display at the 1983 Longleat Celebration, having been replaced for the production of 'The Five Doctors'. This new replica included some original control pieces, and within the recreated walls an original roundel. Positioned on the hat-stand within the set were Tegan's handbag and stewardess hat, generously donated by costume designer June Hudson.[179] The console had previously made a brief cameo appearance during a special trailer that had formed part of the fiftieth anniversary celebrations in 2013, and so was displayed on the upper exhibition floor in a section celebrating that special year. This section had been created after the barn set and trio of TARDIS exterior props from 'The Day of the Doctor' had been moved upstairs from the ground floor. They were accompanied by the costume worn by Billie Piper as the Moment; a Time Lord soldier costume; and Paul McGann's eighth Doctor outfit and Ohila's costume from 'The Night of the Doctor'.

Also in August 2016, a black Dalek Sec was added to the exhibition; and later a Sil costume first seen in 'Vengeance on Varos' was briefly placed in the classic monster area. To celebrate a decade of *Torchwood*, on 22 October 2016 – exactly ten years after the debut episode, 'Everything Changes', was transmitted – a selection of costumes and props from the spin-off went on display. *The Sarah Jane Adventures* continued to be overlooked.

Departing from the usual practice of items being exhibited only after being seen on screen, to promote the upcoming Christmas special 'The Return of Doctor Mysterio' the costumes of Nardole, the twelfth Doctor, the Ghost and Lucy Fletcher were placed in the box office area, in front of the large Harmony Shoal map from the episode. Also added to the foyer for visitors to see were handprints of Matt Smith, David Tennant, Billie Piper and John Barrowman. These had been on display previously during 2013 before being removed in the following year's redevelopment.

---

[179] news.thedoctorwhosite.co.uk/4th-5th-doctor-console-now-on-display-at-the-dwe/

Tours and Events

The Experience continued to run the walking location and TARDIS set tours when possible. A small number of other events were also advertised. First, as school half-term fun for younger visitors, Tuesday 17 and Thursday 19 February 2015 saw puzzle activities and a caricature artist in the exhibition.[180] On 30 March 2015, to celebrate ten years since *Doctor Who* returned to TV, Peter Capaldi made a surprise appearance at the Experience in character as the Doctor; a YouTube video was later posted, showing highlights of his appearance and some words from Steven Moffat.[181] Capaldi was interviewed and replied to prepared questions read out by schoolchildren, and also posed for photos as he explored the exhibition.

In the only advertised appearance at the Experience by a former Doctor, Colin Baker attended the venue on Saturday 10 October 2015. Visitors participated in a question-and-answer session, and Baker signed items for fans.

As previously mentioned, the Model Unit's Mike Tucker guested on three occasions to unveil newly-restored classic-era items: on 24 October 2015, a special Dalek Day event marked the arrival of the complete Davros from 'Resurrection of the Daleks' and the Emperor Dalek/Davros from 'Remembrance of the Daleks'; on 16 July 2016, the Zygon, Omega and Tetrap costumes returned to public display; and over the bank holiday weekend of 27 and 28 August 2016, it was the turn of the Morbius monster and the Mandrel to be unveiled to the public.

The Halloween weekend tradition of featuring live-action monsters was continued in 2015. The following year, this became referred to as 'Wholloween', with the Foretold, a Whisperman, a Cyberman, a Peg Doll, the Vigil and the Mire all coming to life in the exhibition as the costumes were donned by actors.

A new wave of advertising for autumn 2016 encouraged visitors to celebrate 50 years of the Cybermen. An official announcement read: 'Later in the Autumn the *Doctor Who* Experience will be celebrating 50 years of the Doctor's most challenging adversary, the Cybermen, with a special 50th event – more details coming soon!'[182] As things transpired, however, this event never materialised. Instead, news broke that the Experience's days were numbered …

The End of the *Doctor Who* Experience

On 7 November 2016, WalesOnline reported that the *Doctor Who* Experience was to close at the end of summer 2017.[183] This was based on a short quote provided by BBC Worldwide, which simply stated: 'The *Doctor Who*

---

[180] www.doctorwho.tv/whats-new/article/half-term-fun-at-the-doctor-who-experience/
[181] www.youtube.com/watch?v=nMi8c8uglmI
[182] www.doctorwho.tv/whats-new/article/autumn-at-the-doctor-who-experience
[183] www.walesonline.co.uk/whats-on/whats-on-news/cardiffs-doctor-who-experience-close-12138399

Experience has enjoyed a fantastic five-year run in Cardiff Bay but, sadly, our five-year sub-lease from the City of Cardiff Council will come to an end in Summer 2017.' Further elucidation was provided in a statement by a Council spokesman: 'The land currently occupied by the *Doctor Who* Experience is owned by the Welsh Government and their development partner, Igloo Regeneration. It was leased to the City Council for five years to enable [the Experience's] relocation from Olympia to Cardiff on a temporary basis. It has always been the intention for the site to be developed as part of the ongoing Porth Teigr regeneration project. The agreement was always intended to be for five years only, reflecting the nature of the attraction. The decision to close the Experience at the end of the lease next summer has been mutually agreed by all parties involved, including the operators BBC Worldwide.'[184]

Another, unstated, reason for the decision not to continue or relocate the attraction could perhaps have been the fact that *Doctor Who* had been absent from television throughout 2016, resulting in a downturn in visitor numbers. As David Prince noted at the time, 'When the show's not on air, it is quiet. Or quieter, I should say. As soon as the show's back on, generally that's when it picks up, and especially when they announce that there are new props going in. It's bad enough that [in 2016] there hasn't been any new *Doctor Who*. If they're going to close the Experience, that's going to be another nail in the coffin. Not that the show itself is going to decline, but it's not going to help it.'

Despite the shadow hanging over the attraction, on Saturday 22 April 2017 the Experience hosted an event launching a new range of *Doctor Who*-themed Mr Men books. The range's writer and illustrator Adam Hargreaves, son of Mr Men and Little Miss creator the late Roger Hargreaves, visited the attraction, drew characters in the recognisable Hargreaves style and signed copies of the first four books, *Dr First*, *Dr Fourth*, *Dr Eleventh* and *Dr Twelfth*, copies of which were available for purchase. Hargreaves was also interviewed by Luke Spillane of the *Doctor Who Fan Show* (a tie-in on the official BBC YouTube channel) and took audience questions during three sessions throughout the day.

The event also boasted two world exclusives. First was the premiere screening of an animated version of *Dr Twelfth*, narrated by Michelle Gomez. Second was the reveal of the next four books in the range, to be published later in the year: *Dr Second*, *Dr Seventh*, *Dr Eighth* and *Dr Ninth*.

Also added to the exhibition at this time were the remnants of eight original classic-era monster costumes. This was to promote a final public costume restoration vote, the winner of which would be restored for the summer 2017 season. The monsters that had lost out in the previous public vote were given another chance. These were a Sea Devil ('Warriors of the Deep'), a Tractator ('Frontios'), the L3 Drathro robot ('The Trial of a Time Lord': 'The Mysterious Planet'), a Vervoid ('The Trial of a Time Lord': 'Terror of the Vervoids'), a Haemovore ('The Curse of Fenric') and a Cheetah Person

---

[184] www.blogtorwho.com/doctor-who-experience-to-close-in-summer-2017/

('Survival'). The last two costumes added to the new vote were the Yeti from 'The Web of Fear' and a Silurian from 'Warriors of the Deep'.

All eight costumes were in very poor condition. The Tractator for instance had a noticeable split across the neck, and the Silurian's feet had completely rotted away, exposing the framework structure that had held it upright during previous exhibition appearances in Longleat, Llangollen and Blackpool. Drathro was just a collection of pieces, and the Vervoid suit was crumpled up into a transparent box. Online voting closed at 5pm on Friday 5 May; in-person voting at the Experience itself closed at the end of the following day. The victor turned out to be the Yeti, even though it had already featured in the exhibition since 2014. Perhaps surprisingly, the seven costumes that had been unsuccessful in the poll were left on display for the remainder of the summer season, despite their poor and deteriorating condition.

On 14 June 2017, BBC Worldwide announced that the Experience would close its doors for good on 9 September. *Doctor Who* finally returned to the nation's screens from 15 April to 1 July for Peter Capaldi's swansong series, and items from its episodes were unveiled at the exhibition on 8 July – the last update of the displays.

The series' opening episode, 'The Pilot', was represented by a small recreation of the Doctor's study set, including desk, chalkboard and other pieces of set-dressing. Within the set were placed two of Bill's outfits; the Doctor's costume, featuring a red hoodie under a black coat; and Nardole's costume, including his red duffle-coat. Two of Heather's costumes from the episode were also displayed, as was the Movellan costume, recreated to match that of their first appearance in 'Destiny of the Daleks'.

Opposite 'The Pilot' display were positioned items from the series' second episode, 'Smile', including another of Bill's outfits and two Emojibots, plus additional pieces of set-dressing. Adjacent to these were located three costumes from the next story, 'Thin Ice': the Doctor's, Bill's, and a diving suit donned by one of the guest characters.

The fourth episode, 'Knock Knock', was also represented by its respective Doctor and Bill costumes, displayed alongside the wooden Eliza. A photo opportunity was provided in the form of the wooden wall that trapped the character Pavel during the story. Visitors could place their own faces through the hole in the wall and pose as if trapped within the house's infrastructure.

The only exhibits from the series' fifth episode, 'Oxygen', were one of the spacesuits seen during the story and a couple of equipment props. Adjacent to these, however, stood the large vault doors seen in several episodes, which opened outwards to reveal Michelle Gomez's Missy outfit. From the flashback sequences of 'Extremis', the Doctor's costume, the executioner robes, the execution lever and a banner were also displayed.

An exhibit covering the Monk trilogy of stories, 'Extremis', 'The Pyramid at the End of the World' and 'The Lie of the Land', was afforded the space occupying the right-hand wall prior to the exhibition's exit door. Two of Bill's costumes, one of Nardole's and a red soldier uniform were positioned in front of a Monk painting. To the left, a cage housed two Monks, the Doctor's costume with velvet coat, and other pieces of ephemera from the episodes. On the other side of the cage was the controlling Monk, credited as the Giant Monk.

Opposite, on the left-hand wall, were placed exhibits representing 'Empress of Mars'. These included the spacesuits worn by the Doctor and Bill; Iraxxa's tomb and full costume; an Ice Warrior; the peculiar Victorian spacesuit; a Union flag; and two of the props used to depict Victorian soldiers scrunched up into cubes by the Martian weaponry.

'The Eaters of Light' received a more modest display, consisting of Kar's costume; a Roman uniform; the outfits of Bill and Nardole; two of the prop stones, one with a crow sat upon it; plus some tools and other props.

Concluding the exhibition were items covering 'World Enough and Time' and the series finale, 'The Doctor Falls'. Pride of place here went to two of the Cybermen recreated in the style of those originally seen in 'The Tenth Planet'. Oddly, the headpieces on which their masks were displayed did not fully fill them, so the effect was not as dramatic as it could have been. Accompanying the two Mondasian Cybermen, and placed in front of the green prop doors seen during 'World Enough and Time', were two patients, one in a wheelchair, along with Mr Razor's costume, both of Bill's outfits, and the Master's costume as worn by John Simm. To the right of this display was the exit to the gift shop.

8 July 2017 saw the return of the location walking tours; and on the same date, Mike Tucker unveiled the restored Yeti from 'The Web of Fear'. In the lengthy restoration process, the costume had been taken off its old mannequin, placed on a new one in a more fearsome pose, and stripped back to reveal required repairs on a combination of perishing upholstery foam and latex. Incidentally uncovered was a name written inside the suit, revealing that it was the one worn originally by actor Gordon Stothard as Yeti number three during production of 'The Web of Fear'. As the feet and claws were missing, they needed to be sculpted from scratch. The eyes were also illuminated once again; the original bulbs were long gone, but new LED lights were inserted in their place – the only significant deviation from the policy of relying on the same techniques as would have been used back in the 1960s. Special guest for the event was Terry Molloy, who took the opportunity to view the restored Davros and Emperor Davros on display. To the delight of those in attendance, Peter Capaldi also made an unannounced appearance, posing for photos and signing autographs.

Although the previous year's planned event to celebrate their fiftieth anniversary had not come to fruition, the Cybermen did provide the theme for the Experience's final Monster Event, which took place on 22 July 2017. The day included workshops and Q&A sessions with Kate Walshe of Millennium FX, presented by Luke Spillane from the *Doctor Who Fan Show*. Visitors could also be converted into Cybermen, and actors dressed in Mondasian Cybermen costumes roamed around the displays. The day was completed with a screening of 'World Enough and Time' and 'The Doctor Falls' in the exhibition area.

The last event held at the attraction took place on 5 August 2017, with fans invited to attend in cosplay as some of their favourite characters.

The Experience's final day of opening, Saturday 9 September 2017, saw fans flock there in pilgrimage. Tickets for the day sold out in advance – one of very few times during the five-year run that this had occurred. Christel Dee and Luke Spillane, employed by BBC Worldwide and largely known for the *Doctor Who Fan Show*, presented three Facebook Live videos streamed from the venue across the day. Officially-organised monsters united with costumed fans around the exhibition. In view of the impending closure, the shop had very low stock levels, and some of the fittings had already been removed. However, limited numbers of postcards, posters, brochures, T-shirts and other miscellaneous items could still be purchased. The extra space available also meant that MilleniumFX could set up a stand in the shop, offering visitors – including Christel Dee in one of the Facebook Live videos – a chance to have prosthetic pieces affixed to their faces.

At the end of the day, a special video was broadcast on the large screen on the upper exhibition floor. This used specially-recorded footage from inside the Gallifrey Museum, accompanied by the Cloister Bell sound effect, along with Nicholas Briggs-voiced audio from the Matt Smith-era walk-through adventure, warning that the time and space rift in Cardiff was open. Jamie Hill donned the Giant Monk costume from the Series 10 episode 'The Lie of the Land' in a makeshift recreation of that story's conclusion. This triggered an explosion effect, provided by Danny Hargreaves of RealSFX, and a specially-edited montage video celebrating the attraction's five year run. The latter was subsequently uploaded to YouTube.[185] Peter Capaldi had also recorded a farewell message, which was broadcast to the crowds. Lastly, Brad Kelly, General Manager of the *Doctor Who* Experience for its five-year run in Cardiff, thanked visitors for coming and led a final hip-hip-hooray.

A few months later, Peter Capaldi departed the role of the twelfth Doctor, passing the torch on to Jodie Whittaker. Two years after the *Doctor Who* Experience closed, the building in which it had been housed was dismantled, leaving little trace that it had ever been there. Despite the increased attention *Doctor Who* has received with the arrival of the thirteenth Doctor, no new official exhibition has since been opened. The Experience's closure has also thrown into doubt the future of the exhibited items. Many of them no longer remain in the BBC's hands; instead they have been sold off and are now in the possession of committed fans and collectors.

---

[185] www.youtube.com/watch?v=U59ru5LlCrU

Chapter 12
Other Exhibitions

On several occasions over the years, *Doctor Who* items have been displayed at other museums and exhibitions across the UK. These have been organised largely by fans and collectors rather than by the BBC, and have often featured well-made replicas instead of, or as well as, original props and costumes.

Spaceblasters, Warrington Museum

To tie in with *Doctor Who*'s thirtieth anniversary, a number of items were displayed as part of Warrington Museum's Spaceblasters exhibition. Open from 20 November 1993 to 8 January 1994, this featured replicas of two Time Lord costumes, Daleks, Cybermen, a Silurian, K-9, the TARDIS police box, and Sea Devil, Jagaroth and Davros masks. These all formed part of a Galactic Encounter section that also included a Gremlin, and a Stormtrooper helmet from *Star Wars*.[186]

Derby Industrial Museum

In 2002 the Derby Industrial Museum displayed a number of *Doctor Who* items, including replicas of a Dalek, a TARDIS police box and K-9, plus costume design sketches for the Foamasi and other memorabilia. Also on display, carefully positioned as if entering the TARDIS, was a mannequin wearing a replica of Sylvester McCoy's costume.

Scotland

Prop and model maker Raymond MacFadyen organised a number of exhibitions featuring *Doctor Who* items in Scotland. His first was in Kilmarnock in 1998, drawing an estimated 12,000 visitors. Others followed in Nairn and Forfar the next year. During the summer of 2002, Pittencrieff House Museum in Dunfermline was the venue, this time drawing in excess of 13,000 visitors.[187] Next came an installation at the Smith Art Gallery and Museum in Stirling. Displayed at all these exhibitions were some impressive examples of MacFadyen's work, including models of the Jagaroth spaceship and the Emperor Dalek's throne room and full-size replica Daleks, Davros and a TARDIS console. The Stirling exhibition also included items of merchandise

---

[186] www.richardwho.co.uk/exhibitions/Spaceblasters1993-1994/index.asp
[187] www.richardwho.co.uk/collectors/raymondmacfdyen/index.asp

from the collection of Colin Young. MacFadyen and Young joined forces once again in 2004 for another excellent display, this time at the Motherwell Heritage Centre.[188]

Dorking Museum, Surrey

Collectors Matt and Sarah Parish provided a selection of items from their collection for a display at Dorking Museum in Surrey, opening on Saturday 20 October 2007.[189] Included were masks such as those of the Bus Conductor robot from 'The Greatest Show in the Galaxy', a Silurian from 'Warriors of the Deep' and Omega from 'Arc of Infinity'. A Haemovore was accompanied by a prop bomb from 'The Curse of Fenric', with a Dalek and an Ice Warrior also on display, along with examples of *Doctor Who* merchandise from over the years.

Merchandise Museum

On the subject of merchandise, 2016 saw writer, historian and collector David J Howe run a campaign to raise money to help him achieve a lifelong ambition to create a *Doctor Who* Merchandise Museum. As an expert in this field, Howe has amassed a large collection of artefacts, which also encompasses some original costumes and props. A suitable building having been purchased in Lincolnshire, work has since been under way to establish the Museum, although at the time of writing, due in part to extensive flooding in the area at the end of 2019, and the CoronaVirus Pandemic of 2020, this has yet to be completed and opened to the public.

Made in Wales Exhibition

The Made in Wales Exhibition, which currently has no permanent home but provides items for display at conventions and other events, aims to celebrate television shows made in South Wales and currently consists of a collection of original, screen-used costumes from *Doctor Who*, *Torchwood* and *The Sarah Jane Adventures*, many of them having been purchased in past Bonhams auctions. Part of the motivation for this is to preserve the legacy of the two spin-off shows in particular, given that they are no longer in production. The collection includes costumes worn by John Barrowman, Eve Myles and Elisabeth Sladen, plus Freema Agyeman's maid outfit from 'Human Nature'/'The Family of Blood' and her costume from the 2007 series finale 'Last of the Time Lords'.

---

[188] www.richardwho.co.uk/exhibitions/MotherwellHeritageCentre/index.asp
[189] www.richardwho.co.uk/exhibitions/DorkingMuseum20071020/index.asp

Chapter 13
Where Are They Now?

Just as some of the early episodes of *Doctor Who* no longer reside in the BBC archive, many of the props, costumes and other items created for the production over its decades-long history no longer exist. Some were given a distinct lack of care and attention before being simply discarded once damaged or considered no longer useful. Others simply decayed over the years and became lost in the mists of time and space – perhaps unsurprisingly, given that it was never envisaged they would need to last beyond the immediate shooting schedule. Even some items that could potentially have been saved for display at *Doctor Who* exhibitions were not always kept, as storage space was at a premium.

'We couldn't keep everything,' confirms former Exhibitions Assistant Bob Richardson, 'and each new season of *Doctor Who* created a whole new batch of props and costumes that we had to store.' This problem was exacerbated by the fact that the Exhibitions Unit had to share its storage space, Unit 4 in North Acton, with BBC Records, who kept their stock there. As a result, a yearly clear-out was required, with a few skips hired to dispose of items. Richardson explains the process:

'We had to dispose of items constantly, as the cost of hired storage space was very high. At the time when I worked for BBC Exhibitions, we never had a sale of items to the public and would simply throw things into the skips for disposal. It sounds terrible, but I was also asked to shred or smash anything that was thrown away. Some fans knew where our store was and would go "skip diving" in the evening and at weekends. Anything we threw out was "trashed" to prevent possible resale.'

While it is heartbreaking for dedicated fans to hear of *Doctor Who* items being deliberately destroyed, it must be remembered that in many cases the items in question were already deteriorating. With only a limited budget available to the Exhibitions Unit for repairs and restoration, it was inevitable that some pieces would be deemed beyond repair and disposed of. Richardson shares a story about one of the original Yeti costumes from 'The Web of Fear':

'Sadly, he'd had a good soaking from a leak in the roof, and the dampness had reacted with the formaldehyde foam padding, which made it stink quite badly – it smelled very strongly of stale urine! We dismembered him and sent the "claws" to Blackpool for display. They never arrived – or if they did, they were stolen by someone before they ever reached the display cabinet.'

Fortunately, surviving items have more recently come to be seen as valuable collectors' pieces, and the BBC has periodically auctioned selections off instead of disposing of them, while retaining others in storage for their own possible future use. The 1983 Longleat Celebration, for example, featured auctions of props and costumes; and Bonhams auction house in Knightsbridge, London held the first of their *Doctor Who* sales on Saturday 11 May 1991. Auctions also took place at Longleat during August events in 1996, 1997, 1999, 2000 and 2001. As a result, fans have been able to acquire many items, and some of these have since been displayed in smaller exhibitions across the UK and even in America.

The 2010 Bonhams Sale

A particularly large Bonhams sale was held in February 2010 and included many items from the recently-closed Blackpool exhibition that were now considered damaged beyond repair or otherwise surplus to requirements. The revenue from this would no doubt have contributed to the up-front costs of creating the *Doctor Who* Experience.

Bonhams had been the BBC's auctioneer of choice since the 1990s. One of those to attend their sales was Kevan Looseley, who recalls: 'We went to the first of the Bonhams auctions, and they hadn't at the time got someone to sort out what they were actually selling. So it was, "Lot 1: Ten *Doctor Who* costumes." We would go along to a viewing in advance and notice that a certain lot had a really nice piece in it, and the rest were all rubbish; but for the one costume we wanted, we were going to bid for that lot. One of the things we got was Romana's outfit from "Destiny of the Daleks" – the pink two-piece – and for a while we owned that. But a lot of the stuff was actually bits from *Blake's 7* and god knows what.'

Bonhams included *Doctor Who*-related items in their general media auctions quite regularly, a number of lots in 2009 coming not from the BBC but from the collection of Angels the costumiers; these included the jacket worn by Jon Pertwee in 'The Time Warrior'. However, the 2010 sale was the first since 1991 to be devoted entirely to *Doctor Who*. The auction catalogue listed not only items from the now-closed Blackpool exhibition but also other costumes from the show's post-2005 era and vehicles used in *Torchwood* and *The Sarah Jane Adventures*. Media coverage featured a photograph of one of the Cyberman costumes included in the sale; this appeared on the front page of *The Times* on the auction day, 24 February 2010. The following day, other newspapers, including *The Sun*, the *Daily Mail* and the *Western Mail*, ran articles about the results of the sale.

One person who couldn't attend was Christopher Daniels, who had worked at the Blackpool exhibition up until 2009. He recalls his emotions at the time: 'I picked up the *Metro* when I was on the bus going to work on the morning of the sale. I opened it up and there was a picture of all these costumes that I'd explained to so many people, lined up to be sold off. It was quite a kick in the teeth.'

Some of those items included the Pirate Captain from 'The Pirate Planet', which had made the first of its several exhibition appearances at Blackpool in 1979, and the Cyberscope prop from 'Silver Nemesis', which had also been displayed at a number of venues over the years. The motorised Kroll miniature, another item first displayed at Blackpool in 1979, and later seen at Longleat, Llangollen and the second Blackpool exhibition, fetched £780 including buyer's premium. Also sold were the costumes of Sil, Kiv and the Alien Delegate from 'The Trial of the Time Lord': 'Mindwarp', which had been seen together at the Longleat, MOMI, Isle of Wight, Llangollen and Blackpool exhibitions.

The stars of the auction were, predictably, the Daleks, with two screen-used props up for grabs. Dalek N1 had been part of the USA tour in the late 1980s and the MOMI and Llangollen exhibitions during the 1990s before concluding its journey at the second Blackpool exhibition in 2009. It sold for over £20,000 and is now in a private collection, back in the USA once again. Dalek I2-I4 achieved over £15,000, and is likewise now in the USA, displayed at the EMP Museum in Seattle, Washington, along with a 1980s Cyberman costume.

In later years, Bonhams continued to sell off items from *Doctor Who*, *Torchwood* and *The Sarah Jane Adventures*, mainly in their biannual Entertainment Memorabilia auctions. In December 2011, for example, a Clockwork Droid from 'The Girl in the Fireplace', without mask but with the dark navy costume as seen at many of the Up Close exhibitions, was sold for a whopping £5,000.[190]

Fortunately, some of the artefacts sold at the various auctions over the years have not simply disappeared into private collections but have since been made available by their new owners for public display – in some cases for the first time.

The Who Shop Museum, London

Husband-and-wife team Kevan Looseley and Alexandra Looseley-Saul run a *Doctor Who* Museum at their Who Shop in East London, just around the corner from what had been West Ham United's football ground Upton Park. The shop itself has roots that can be traced back to the Longleat Celebration of 1983, as Kevan explains: 'The shop was basically born out of that convention. I went to that, and so did Alex's brother, but we didn't know each other at the time, and the shop all came about because of that.'

Alexandra illuminates further: 'My brother went to the event, brought [merchandise] back, and I said, "Why have you dragged it all the way back from Wiltshire? This is London." He said, "Yeah, but there's nowhere [in London where you can get it]." I was, at that stage, already doing a business project, and I thought, "Well, okay, let's see if we can amalgamate it." And I did. I amalgamated the shop into the project, and then it was the shop that worked, over and above the project, so it carried on going from that point.'

---

[190] www.bonhams.com/auctions/19037/lot/162/

The new venture, dubbed the Who Shop, operated initially, from 1 December 1984, from a warehouse in Wapping. Later however it moved to premises near East Ham tube station, where it remained for many years. At the same time, Alexandra and Kevan built up a substantial collection of original *Doctor Who* costumes and props. Even back in the Wapping warehouse days, the possibility of exhibiting these was being discussed, as Alexandra explains: 'At one stage we were going to do an exhibition there, but the chap that approached me about it, it just didn't work out with him.' It would take a few more years, but around 1994 an exhibition was eventually mounted at Albert Dock in Liverpool. As Kevan explains, 'It was only supposed to run for a couple of weeks. It was going to be a temporary thing. In the end it remained open for a few months instead.'

Alexandra also recalls that original Who Shop exhibition in Liverpool: 'While we had our own screen-used props, other people who were into the show had bought items too, and they loaned us some of their bits and pieces as well. It was in a warehouse, ground floor. Beautiful big cold stone. One of the film companies loaned us some dry ice machines, so we used to have permanently floating monsters, with dry ice around them! It was brilliant and great fun. But in the end, the actual site itself was too expensive for what we needed it to do.'

The cost of the Albert Dock site, coupled with the ongoing pressures of running the shop in London, proved prohibitive, so a move to a combined venue was sought. As Alexandra again explains, 'We came back to London and we just kept on looking for other places to be able to do something. And then, lo and behold, we got a premises where we could put our museum with all our bits and pieces in.'

Prior to the move, in November 2009, items from the collection were simply placed on walls around the shop. However this new venue on Barking Road afforded enough space for the collection to be displayed properly. Hence the Who Shop Museum was born. Although it displays *Doctor Who* costumes and props, it is quite deliberately referred to as a museum rather than an exhibition, as Alexandra confirms: 'Ours is a museum. Ours is an appreciation of the products, of the costumes. We are not an exhibition. To me, it's a different thing. I like museums. I don't necessarily like exhibitions, because they tend to have a different feel to them.'

While exhibitions can offer immersive experiences within the fictional world of the show, the Who Shop Museum enthusiastically acknowledges the practical aspects of television programme-making – or, as Kevan phrases it, 'This shows how they made costumes in those days.' Giving an insight into the practical craft of costume design and construction is also aimed at encouraging the next generation, as Alexandra believes: 'It's more inspiring, when it's the museum side of things as opposed to the exhibition.'

Inside the shop a TARDIS exterior prop, very similar to that used in the Peter Cushing Dalek movies, stands proudly. It actually originates from Elstree Studios and appeared in 'Tin God', a 1965 episode of ITV crime series *Gideon's*

Way.[191] It was later used by the *Doctor Who* Appreciation Society, for instance appearing onstage at PanoptiCon conventions. In 1981, having been refurbished, it appeared alongside fifth Doctor Peter Davison on a float as a part of the Lord Mayor's Show in London. During the same period, it also featured in an advert for the Honda C50-C moped.[192] This TARDIS exterior now provides a mere hint of the treasures held within the Museum itself.

The entrance to the Museum is located in the back left-hand corner of the shop, through the doors of a second TARDIS police box, which was itself utilised by the BBC in recording of material for their *Doctor Who* Night broadcast on BBC Two in November 1999.

Having entered the Museum, the first item visitors encounter, on the left-hand side, is a wonderful relic from a *Doctor Who* exhibition long since closed, as Kevan Looseley explains: 'One of the things we do own from Longleat is the diamond logo that used to be on the side of the TARDIS; we've got that now. It was out in all weathers, this thing, but when we got hold of it, I didn't try to repaint it, I just painted a couple of coats of clear varnish to seal in the flaking paint so it's not going to get any worse. I didn't want to touch it up in case it took away the authenticity of the thing. But it's not in that bad a condition, to be honest.'

One of the oldest items in the exhibition was used in a Hartnell-era story that no longer exists in the BBC's archive. 'One of the things we've got is Marco Polo's tunic,' says Kevin. 'The exact one [actor] Mark Eden wore. It's the same one that appears in all the publicity photos.' This tunic from the seven-part historical 'Marco Polo' was sold at Bonhams in June 2009. Another item bought for the Museum in the same auction was a chain-mail costume seen on a statue that briefly traps the Doctor's companion Ian Chesterton in the third episode of the following story, 'The Keys of Marinus'.[193] As Kevan explains, this was not actually made for *Doctor Who*: 'They just grabbed it out of stock. It's a chain-mail jacket that they only needed for ten seconds on screen, so they didn't make anything fancy. We bought the thing, and the helmet is metal rather than fibreglass or plastic. Inside, it had newspaper stuffed in the top, which some wardrobe guy had put in as a bit of padding for the poor devil that had to wear it. The newspaper was a copy of the *Daily Sketch* dated 1950-something. It's still in there now ... So it's pre-*Doctor Who*. It just got used in *Doctor Who*.' A label inside the costume suggests that it was sourced by the BBC from Bermans and Nathans costumiers.

Another reused costume piece that now resides in the Museum is the villain Tegana's belt from 'Marco Polo', which was also worn by Ian Chesterton in 'The Crusade'. A Crusader robe, sourced by the BBC from another costumiers, Angels, is another Museum item from the latter story. Also from a Hartnell-era story, 'Galaxy 4', is a Drahvin gun, which was reused later

---

[191] www.youtube.com/watch?v=PnQ7jYMSJsM
[192] www.youtube.com/watch?v=YfP6cFwy0Pg
[193] firstdoctorcostume.blogspot.co.uk/2015/06/bonhams-costume-sale-16th-june-2009.html

in 'Genesis of the Daleks'.

Items displayed in a cabinet include a helmet worn by Sil's bodyguard in 'Vengeance on Varos', and other helmets seen in 'Revelation of the Daleks' and 'Dragonfire'. Also displayed is Sutekh's mask from 'Pyramids of Mars', although this is not the genuine article but a replica made from the original mould – possibly one of those featured in exhibitions during the 1970s and 1980s.

Some of the other props seen in the Museum include the dove pan magic trick used in 'The Talons of Weng-Chiang', Unstoffe's water bottle from 'The Ribos Operation', the book of Kroll from 'The Power of the Kroll', the communicator plate from 'The Creature from the Pit', and backpacks used in 'Enlightenment'.

A 1980s-era Cyberman costume, part replica but part original, also stands in the Museum, and has been seen on television – but not in *Doctor Who*. Kevan donned the costume to appear opposite Jon Culshaw as the fourth Doctor for one of a number of sketches in the *Dead Ringers* comedy show. The costume that Culshaw wore on that occasion is also in the Museum and was originally created not for Tom Baker to wear but to be placed on his Madame Tussauds waxwork – although, as Culshaw proved, it was nevertheless wearable.

Further original costumes in the Museum from the fourth Doctor's era include items from 'The Androids of Tara' and 'State of Decay', plus a set of Time Lord robes from 'The Deadly Assassin', although it is possible that the skullcap of the latter is one of the reproductions made for 'Arc of Infinity'.

The costume worn by Stratford Johns as Monarch the Urbankan in the fifth Doctor story 'Four to Doomsday' had its first public airing at the Blackpool exhibition in 1982 but now is back on public display in the Who Shop Museum. Additional costumes from the 1980s include Shockeye, complete with blunted wooden knives, from 'The Two Doctors'; those of Queen Katryca and Balazar from 'The Trial of the Time Lord': 'The Mysterious Planet'; a *Hyperion III* crew member's uniform from 'The Trial of the Time Lord': 'Terror of the Vervoids'; the Chief Caretaker's attire from 'Paradise Towers'; and the Android from 'Timelash', complete with weapon. Kevan describes this latter weapon as 'this weird ray-gun contraption that goes completely over your arm; bits of that are made of Airfix model Eagle Transporters from *Space 1999*'.

One of the larger items in the Museum is the TARDIS console used in the stage show *The Ultimate Adventure*. This famously had lines of dialogue written on it by Jon Pertwee to aid his memory during performances. It failed to sell when listed in a November 2005 Bonhams auction, but has since found a home at the Who Shop.

Museum items from *Doctor Who*'s 21st Century episodes include Matt Smith's Soothsayer costume from 'The Wedding of River Song' and Rory's Roman Centurion uniform from 'The Pandorica Opens'/'The Big Bang'. From *The Sarah Jane Adventures* come two costumes worn by Elisabeth Sladen in the lead role, including her wedding dress from the story 'The Wedding of Sarah Jane Smith', along with the wedding suit worn by Nigel Havers in the same story, plus an outfit worn by Daniel Anthony as Clyde Langer.

One of Alexandra's favourite items comes from a classic modern-era episode, 'Vincent and the Doctor', as she explains: 'We've got a Vincent Van Gogh costume from that beautiful, beautiful episode, so I absolutely adore that.'

A highlight of the Who Shop Museum for many visitors is its three Daleks, including a Special Weapons Dalek. The latter is a replica, nicknamed 'Rambo', built by Kevan Looseley himself. A silver and blue Dalek is also a replica, nicknamed 'Chunky' due to its larger size, and was originally made by Julian Vince for Virgin Publishing; this too featured in the BBC's *Doctor Who* Night recordings in 1999, and then on a *Radio Times* cover celebrating the show's fortieth anniversary in 2003. However, the other Museum Dalek, in a traditional gun-metal-grey and black colour scheme, is thought to be an original, as Kevan explains:

'We've got an original 1970s Dalek from "Planet of the Daleks". It's been restored. Originally it was quite clapped out. It was thought to have been one of the "goon" ones, but looking at it, I don't think that's right. It's workable, whereas the "goons" for the most part were just background ones that didn't do anything. Our one's got a seat and the whole pivot mechanism for the head. It's definitely an original prop, but I think someone actually sat in it and operated it, rather than it being just one of the background ones.' Due to its poor condition when first acquired for the Museum, and the extensive refurbishment it has since undergone, it is difficult to confirm for which television story this Dalek was originally built. However, as Kevan notes, '75% of the thing is the original prop.' A fourth Dalek – another replica – stands not in the Museum itself but in the shop area outside.

One of the smaller Museum items, displayed in a cabinet, is another of Alexandra's personal favourites. 'Jon Pertwee always used to try to take it away with him every single time he came to the shop, bless him; the Metebelis crystal.' Alexandra recalls how fond Pertwee was of this item, which would always come up in conversation during his visits to the Who Shop: 'Whenever Jon used to come along, he'd always say, "Ooh, can I just have a look at my crystal, please? I just want to hold it in my hand again," and he'd have his photograph taken with it. Then I'd look again and think, "Hang on a second, it's not where I left it." It was in his pocket! Only one was made and it wasn't even blue. It was a clear resin painted blue afterwards, which became noticeable as some of that paint began to wear away with too much handling. It would've been back-lit to give it the glowing appearance on screen. As a result, flash photography of that item is not allowed.'

A machine gun prop on display in the Museum was used by Kevan Looseley when he played the role of a UNIT soldier in additional material recorded for the special edition DVD release of 'Day of the Daleks'. Previously, however, this weapon had actually been seen held by a Stormtrooper in *Star Wars*, as Kevan explains: 'The Stormtrooper guns shown in close-ups were British Army Sterling sub-machine guns with bits stuck on. The background ones though were replicas of the actual guns, resin cast on a wooden frame. I managed to get hold of one of these props. Then, when I got to do "Day of the Daleks", I had to retro-convert it back into a Sterling. I took off all the bits and pieces; rebuilt the magazine; took off the telescopic sight, which the real machine gun wouldn't have had; put a camera strap on it for the harness.'

Further items on display in the Museum include one of the prop hands from 'The Hand of Fear'; Lady Cranleigh's dress from 'Black Orchid'; Captain Jack's safe door from the Hub set in *Torchwood*; an Auton bride from 'Rose'; and the Steward costume from 'The End of the World'. The latter two had previously featured in a number of the Up Close exhibitions. Other interesting relics the Museum holds from past *Doctor Who* exhibitions include a prop of Morbius's brain in a jar, likely to be the same one seen at Longleat during the 1970s, and a 1979-dated plan of the Longleat exhibition.

The Museum also features a few items from shows other than *Doctor Who*, including *Red Dwarf*, and is well worth a visit.

The Time Machine, Bromyard

In the small Herefordshire town of Bromyard is a hidden treat for science fiction fans. Owner Andy Glizzard has acquired a vast collection of props and costumes over the years, and once even appeared on the BBC's *Celebrity Antiques Road Trip* giving Colin Baker a tour of his exhibition.[194] A cellar beneath a former bakery and Victorian tea room provides a home for a wide variety of science fiction items. In addition to *Doctor Who*, these come from *Star Wars*, *Red Dwarf*, *Life on Mars* and the Gerry Anderson shows *Thunderbirds*, *Captain Scarlet* and *Stingray*. Unfortunately the period nature of the original building means that it is accessible only to those able or indeed brave enough to venture down into the cellar. Exhibits are accompanied by notes explaining what they are, and where possible by photographs of their appearances on screen or in publicity photographs. The exhibition is also adorned by posters, largely taken from the *Doctor Who Adventures* magazine.

Exhibition tradition of entry through a TARDIS police box continues, and the steep staircase down into the cellar is reminiscent of the descent into the original Blackpool exhibition. Many of the *Doctor Who* exhibits have been acquired from auctions over the years. For example, a number of costumes worn by Billie Piper during her time as Rose Tyler are on display, having been purchased from Bonhams in 2010 and not previously exhibited elsewhere. These include her outfits from 'The Empty Child'/'The Doctor Dances', 'Bad Wolf'/'The Parting of the Ways', 'Tooth and Claw' and 'Rise of the Cybermen'/'The Age of Steel', plus her nightwear from 'Doomsday'. Additional items include Martha Jones's recognisable main costume seen in 'Smith and Jones' and other episodes; the leather jacket she wore in the TARDIS departure scene in 'Human Nature'/'The Family of Blood'; John

---

[194] www.youtube.com/watch?v=e01dgj608j8

Smith's suit and the Daughter of Mine costume from the latter story; Matt Smith's wedding suit outfit from 'The Big Bang'; a Graske mask; and costumes of a number of peculiar aliens seen during the scene set in a bar in the second instalment of 'The End of Time'.

The exhibition's focus is not solely on the show's modern incarnation; it also includes a number of items from the classic era. One of the most interesting pieces is an old Silurian mask, claimed to be from the creatures' debut story, 'Doctor Who and the Silurians'; any doubt as to its authenticity is due largely to the fact that it remains in quite reasonable condition, despite its supposed age – although this could be seen as a testament to the good care that Andy Glizzard has taken of it. Other original classic-era items include Kalid's kimono from 'Time-Flight'; a soldier costume from 'The Androids of Tara'; a Dalek trooper boiler suit and helmet from 'Resurrection of the Daleks'; the L1 tracker robot from 'The Trial of a Time Lord': 'The Mysterious Planet'; a jacket worn by a member of 'The Happiness Patrol'; plus helmets from 'The Invasion' and 'The Mutants'. Also present is a TARDIS exterior prop allegedly used by Jon Pertwee's Doctor, probably not in *Doctor Who* itself but more likely in an unofficial production.

A total of five Daleks are also present, all thought to be replicas. One of them was previously positioned by the entrance door of the Llangollen exhibition and featured on one of its advertising leaflets; another is a silver-and-blue one used during recording of the *30 Years in the TARDIS* anniversary documentary; and another was constructed for the *An Adventure in Space and Time* docu-drama.

Other items in the exhibition include examples of the replicas marketed commercially by Millennium FX – Ood, Cyber Leader, Sycorax and Davros heads and a tenth Doctor sonic screwdriver – along with replicas of classic and modern Cybermen, K-9, a Zygon and a Hath. A replica Mechanoid, possibly that seen in the second Blackpool exhibition, is also to be found in the collection.

The Museum of Classic Sci-Fi

Another fan and collector, Neil Cole, has mounted his own exhibition of items from science fiction productions, again in a cellar in an English village – in this case Allendale, Northumberland. Cole has spent years preparing the basement and cellar of Osborne House for this purpose. Included are a number of original *Doctor Who* artefacts, many of which have featured in earlier exhibitions over the years and have benefited from substantial restoration by Cole himself.

One of the items in most need of repair when Cole acquired it was a Terileptil from 'The Visitation', consisting of the red-hued body coupled with the scarred animatronic head. Purchased as Lot 137 in the 2010 Bonhams *Doctor Who* sale, it had last appeared in public in Blackpool, prior to that exhibition's closure in 2009, and before that in Llangollen, where the two components had first been paired together; previously the components had formed parts of separate Terileptil costumes seen in the Longleat and original Blackpool exhibitions. The years since the creature's only television appearance in 1982 had taken their toll – in fact at Llangollen and Blackpool it had been placed on the floor in display cases to conceal its significant deterioration. Although the torso and back of the red-hued Terileptil remained, the legs were missing; and so too were the feet, having been repurposed for the alien delegate creature seen in 'The Trial of the Time Lord': 'Mindwarp'.

Neil Cole's first task was to fix the Terileptil to a suitable mannequin, reuniting the front chest piece with the scaly back. Much of the shoulder and neck detailing had deteriorated. The rubber components that did remain, however, were coated by Cole in a resin, to give them a gloss finish and crucially to preserve them. Expandable foam was then used to support the costume and provide a base for new features to fill the gaps. For example, two new arms were sculpted, based on screen shots of the originals. Although predominantly green on screen, the scarred animatronic Terileptil mask had discoloured over time to a more orange colour, which fortunately matched nicely with the red body. The lower lip and neck section however needed significant fixing, with a fibreglass under-structure and clay to add texture on top.

Another of Neil Cole's items, surviving from multiple previous *Doctor Who* exhibitions, is the Garm from 'Terminus'. In the course of its most recent former appearance, in the 21st Century Blackpool exhibition, the creature's right arm had fallen off; subsequently it had been angled away from visitors to hide this fact – a tactic amusingly also used by Bonhams in the photograph taken for their auction catalogue. Although the arm was no longer attached, it did still survive, albeit not in great condition. Another concern was the fact that when previously exhibited the costume had been placed on an oversized mechanical frame that stretched and tore the material. However, the Garm's head, constructed of a rubber composite, was in reasonable condition, as was the vinyl body armour, so these areas required only subtle restoration.

A new base was created, using the holes already created in the boots for its original display. A more suitably-shaped frame for the torso was then built so that the fabric of the tunic was no longer being stretched and damaged. When combined with the other costume pieces, the final result was an impressive display once again. The Garm's significant height has also been restored, and the creature now looks far more like it did originally in 1983.

By the time Cole purchased the Garm from the original Bonhams buyer through eBay, the left arm had also deteriorated. At the time of writing, both arms are currently undergoing restoration. 'I suspect carving new arms would be best,' says Cole, 'using the surviving pieces as accurate reference.' However, the currently armless Garm remains proudly on display in the Museum, where it has been visited by none other than Stephen Gallagher, writer of 'Terminus'.

Another item still requiring restoration to the arm pieces is one from Colin

Baker's debut story, 'The Twin Dilemma'. Mestor the Gastropod was first displayed at Blackpool in 1984. It then appeared on the USA tour, at the MOMI exhibition, at Longleat in 1990 and then at Llangollen before finally concluding its journey in Blackpool once more. Now in Neil Cole's collection, this costume has also required gentle restoration. Unfortunately it too needed a bespoke under-frame to support it properly and to provide a better shape; the face also required minor renovation. After subtle repairs and general preservation work, Mestor was ready to be seen in public once again. As with the Garm, work is ongoing to restore the arm pieces fully.

Already reconstructed for display at the exhibition is a Haemovore from 'The Curse of Fenric'. Referred to as the 'Arctic Explorer Haemovore', this consists of a screen-used costume, mask and lower arm. Completing the impressive exhibit is a wig that originally appeared on another Haemovore: the one dressed like a 1920s flapper.

One exhibit that needed only limited restoration was that of Kane's melted hands and face from 'Dragonfire' – replicas originally created for the Longleat exhibition and first put on display in 1988. To keep them in immaculate condition, a preservative has simply been added.

Other *Doctor Who* items in Cole's collection include original Silurian and Sea Devil pieces from the Jon Pertwee era; a Galsec rifle from 'The Sontaran Experiment'; the black Cyber scout and a Cryon from 'Attack of the Cybermen'; the Chimeron baby from 'Delta and the Bannermen'; and the original Haemovore concept bust. Artwork from renowned *Doctor Who* artist Andrew Skilleter is also displayed, alongside a variety of other science fiction-related exhibits.

Preparations for the opening of the Museum of Classic Sci-Fi were featured in the third episode of the Netflix show *Amazing Interiors*.[195] This showed Neil Cole, his father-in-law and the rest of the family attempting to get the Museum up and running, revealing the huge amount of effort required to renovate the cellar, let alone to install a science fiction museum inside. Focus was given to the restoration of the Terileptil and the construction of an intricate fibreglass panel. For the show, Cole was set the task of completing the Museum's opening section and unveiling it to a small number of visitors. After recording for the programme concluded, work continued on completing the remainder of the exhibition.

The Museum officially opened to the public on Saturday 20 October 2018. To mark the event, long-time *Doctor Who* alumnus John Levene was in attendance.[196] Visitors received an exclusive signed art print complete with a personal dedication from the former Sergeant Benton. Additionally, a special evening dinner event took place at the Golden Lion in Allendale, Levene sharing memories and stories with those in attendance.

With the Museum now officially open, work continues on acquiring,

---

[195] www.blogtorwho.com/sci-fi-museum-featured-on-netflix-show-amazing-interiors/
[196] www.blogtorwho.com/sci-fi-museum-grand-opening-today/

restoring and preserving further exhibits from previous *Doctor Who* exhibitions; a testament to the enthusiasm and dedication of Neil Cole.

Items held by private collectors

Many other fans have, over the years, gratefully purchased *Doctor Who* artefacts and, while not able to display them publicly, continue to look after them as prized possessions.

The DVD release of 'The Awakening' includes a special feature in which designer Tony Harding and craftsman Richard Gregory discuss their creation of the large Malus prop for 'The Awakening'. Both express surprise that the prop still exists, as Harding admits, 'So much of the stuff from the BBC went to the skip.'[197] Fortunately, because the prop was retained by BBC Enterprises for use at the exhibitions, it avoided this fate. It first appeared at Longleat in 1984 and later at the Isle of Wight, Llangollen and second Blackpool exhibitions. Paul Burrows, described as 'custodian of the Malus', purchased it at Bonhams in 2010; he explains in the feature how he then mounted it on his living-room wall.

Perhaps the single item seen by the most people over the years is the replica TARDIS console that was originally created for the Longleat exhibition and later relocated to the second Blackpool exhibition. After a staggering 45 years on display over the two exhibitions, it was finally sold by Bonhams in June 2010. The purchaser was Peter Trott from Kent, who recalls his reaction on seeing the item in the auction catalogue: 'When I found out that the console was going to be at Bonhams, I kind of thought, "Right, that's mine." I went up there with a tape measure to check whether I could get it in the house or not. In fact, when I bought it, that was still questionable.'

Unfortunately the console was missing one of its six panels and required extensive restoration to return it to its former glory, as Trott again explains: 'I'm not much of a restorer – I don't build Daleks or other things as such – but I just started from scratch and thought, "How can I replace that panel?" I managed to source photographs – which wasn't easy, because it was the panel that was furthest away [from visitors at the exhibitions] … The other panels all seemed to get photographed to death, but there was one that was up against a mirror. It was on the far side, so was always the least photographed.'

Using the photographs that he did manage to source, Trott spent a lot of time and effort trying to replicate the missing panel, locating the same materials originally used: 'Luckily, the electronics were still there – the things that made all the lights flash – so all I had to do was to make sure that I got the same bulbs and put them in the right places. I also looked at video footage on YouTube that shows them lighting up. So, as best as possible, I matched it all up. I think if you compared my panel to the original one, you'd find very little difference.'

---

[197] *Making the Malus, Doctor Who*: 'The Awakening' DVD (2011).

Having completed this painstaking restoration, in August 2016 Trott sold the console on to fellow collector Thomas Seymour. Incredibly, Seymour later managed to track down the original panel that had gone missing prior to the 2010 auction and reunite it with the rest of the console.

Still owned by Peter Trott is Dalek L1, which was originally built for Longleat and later appeared at the second Blackpool exhibition. This was not purchased at the same Bonhams auction as the TARDIS console but came into Trott's possession a few years later. On collecting it, he discovered that the internal mechanisms installed to give it movement when on display were still largely operational. The motor that had allowed the dome to rotate had been removed, but the left-and-right movement of the telescopic arm with plunger attachment, the up-and-down movement of the eyestalk, and the in-and-out movement of the small flipper inside the weapon were all still functional. Some restoration was required to the body, however, as a number of the shoulder slats were missing. 'I looked at how the old ones were made,' says Trott, 'and just basically followed the pattern.' Close paint matching was needed, too, to touch up the various dings and scratches the casing had incurred since the prop was removed from exhibition. Remnants of the original gold colour were still visible at the rear toward the base. Trott also removed the screen-used 'Remembrance of the Daleks' plunger and telescopic arm, replacing it with a more traditional sucker. Dalek L1 now takes pride of place in his collection and has even appeared on ITV's *This Morning*. 'You photograph these things,' he reflects, 'but you don't think they're going to end up in your living room!'

The five other Daleks built for the exhibitions have had a mixed afterlife. After appearing at MOMI during the late 1990s, Dalek L2 was sold to a prop hire company. In 2002 it was displayed at Planet Hollywood in London. Six years later it reappeared in Peterborough. Most recently, however, it has been seen at the London Film Museum on London's South Bank, where curiously it was repainted black and gold, given a claw attachment in place of the traditional sucker and incorrectly described as a 'screen-used movie Dalek'.

Dalek SM2 was sent to Australia in 1986 following the closure of the Blackpool exhibition and remains in the care of the Australian arm of BBC Studios; it was last seen in Sydney during 2013.

The three other exhibition Daleks fared less well. In 1986, Dalek B1 sacrificed its neck cageing and eyestalk for Dalek 6-ex before the latter was auctioned for charity (discussed shortly). Dalek SM1 donated neck pieces to Dalek N5. Likewise, Dalek B2 became a source of spare parts to repair other existing props for the production of 'Remembrance of the Daleks'. What bits remained of these Daleks are likely to have been junked.

After the closure of the second Blackpool exhibition, the walk-in Dalek, Dalek 1-7, was initially retained by the BBC and then sold at Bonhams in June 2010. Amazingly, the two panels that had been removed from it nearly twenty years earlier to create the walk-in feature had been kept by former producer John Nathan-Turner. They were sold at a Longleat auction in 2000, and finally reunited with the rest of the casing and restored by Mike Tucker of the Model Unit. This Dalek has since come into the possession of long-time collector Chris Balcombe.

Dalek 2-8, also known as the 'Wilkie' Dalek, had been displayed at a number of exhibitions over the years before being placed into storage. It was then sold at Bonhams on 23 June 2010. Purchased by the Prop Gallery, it now resides in the collection of Hollywood director and *Doctor Who* fan Peter Jackson.

Also in Jackson's collection is Dalek 6-ex – a prop with a very long and complicated history. Originally created for display at Madame Tussauds, it later appeared at the 1983 Longleat Celebration; featured with disc jockey Ed Stewart in some photographs for *Radio Times*; and graced the back cover of the latter publication's special magazine marking *Doctor Who*'s twentieth anniversary. Having been kept in good condition, it was then repainted in a more traditional gun-metal-grey and black colour scheme for on-screen use in 'Resurrection of the Daleks', also featuring in promotional photographs taken in the shadow of Tower Bridge. Later during the story's production, it was repainted again, in black with white hemispheres, to take on the role of the Supreme Dalek. After a *Blue Peter* appearance promoting the twentieth anniversary, it was returned once again to the grey-and-black colour scheme for use in 'Revelation of the Daleks'. That however was Dalek 6-ex's final on-screen appearance. It was then positioned outside the Blackpool exhibition, suffering the attentions of the public and the British weather throughout 1985. Following the exhibition's closure, it was restored – as mentioned previously, using parts taken from exhibition Dalek B1 – and given a fresh light-grey-and-black livery before being donated by the BBC for a charity auction at Christie's in London, adding a respectable £4,600 toward the Red Cross's efforts to raise money for Sudan with the support of the BBC *Woman's Hour* Appeal. After further restoration and a return to the Tussauds' light blue, black and silver colour scheme, the prop was sold again in 2005, this time fetching a staggering £36,000 for the Great Ormond Street Hospital Children's charity. It was auctioned once more in 2009; sold on to the Prop Gallery in 2011; and then finally concluded its journey by becoming part of Peter Jackson's collection.

Ben Croucher, a collector living in London, now owns the costumes of Sil the Mentor, a Vervoid and a Sea Devil, all purchased in Bonhams auctions. 'I used to visit that [Longleat] exhibition with my family every summer (as well as getting lost in the maze there!),' says Croucher. 'The Vervoids were one of the few *Doctor Who* monsters that really scared me as a child, so I could never linger too long outside their display! I never imagined that one day I'd have one of them in my own house. Back then, I didn't even realise that owning props/costumes from the show was actually possible. These days, it's my own children that seem to be just as frightened of them as I was back then.'

Other items sold at Bonhams in 2010 include Nyssa's mask and a Haemovore in medieval clothes, both of which now reside in the collection of Jenny Martin; and the Giant Brain prop from 'Time and Rani', which fetched

£180 at Bonhams but was resold on eBay in June 2014 for £565.55.

The miniature TARDIS exterior model that had been placed on space backgrounds at MOMI and Llangollen was sold at Bonhams on 29 June 2011 for £900 including buyer's premium and now resides in a private collection. The Taran Wood Beast from 'The Androids of Tara', first displayed at Blackpool in 1979, was sold at Bonhams in December 2013 for £1,250 and is also held by a private collector.

Bonhams is not the only source from which collectors have acquired *Doctor Who* items, however. In fact, one particular item was acquired directly from BBC Enterprises' Exhibitions Unit. One-time Exhibitions Assistant Bob Richardson recalls: 'When I was there in 1979, one of the things we still had was the Servo Robot from "The Wheel in Space". It was still relatively "new" – the story had been transmitted only a decade earlier – but despite that, its rubber legs had perished and been thrown away.' The absence of the legs explains why this item was never included in an official exhibition – although it was briefly displayed at the *Doctor Who* Appreciation Society's PanoptiCon convention in 1978. Later, as Richardson again explains, 'that prop was given to a fan as a gift to thank him for his assistance in identifying props and monsters held in storage.' The Servo Robot now resides in the collection of Colin Young.

The items detailed above are by no means the only *Doctor Who* props and costumes currently in private hands – on the contrary, there are many others. Nevertheless, a significant number are still retained by the BBC for possible future use, some of them having been restored and preserved during the *Doctor Who* Experience's run, and it can only be hoped that one day it will be possible for them to be returned once more to public display.

Afterword
The Legacy of *Doctor Who* Exhibitions

Doctor Who is a phenomenon that reaches far beyond the confines of the television screen. It has always been a trailblazing show, at the forefront of many production innovations since its launch in November 1963. In 2005, it returned to television after a long break and reinvigorated communal family viewing. Of particular relevance to this book, its successful branching out into public exhibitions of props and costumes, starting in the 1970s, has since led on to similar ventures from other franchises such as *Game of Thrones* and *Harry Potter*. The touring event Friendsfest, based on the popular American sitcom *Friends*, parallels *Doctor Who*'s USA tour of the 1980s. A touring *Star Trek* exhibition has also popped up in Blackpool, former home of two *Doctor Who* exhibitions, to celebrate that show's fiftieth anniversary. The thrill of seeing costumes, props and sets from films and television shows is indisputable.

Times have changed, and there is now a general acknowledgement of the value of such items being preserved for possible exhibition purposes. No longer are things discarded as easily as they once were. However, with the closure of the *Doctor Who* Experience in Cardiff, the outlook for further official *Doctor Who* exhibitions is decidedly uncertain. A few items from Jodie Whittaker's first series, broadcast in 2018, have appeared at the Madam Tussauds attraction in Blackpool, and also at MCM London Comic Con from Friday 25 to Sunday 27 October 2019, but there has been nothing more substantial in this regard since she took on the role of the thirteenth Doctor.

There have been occasional rumours of BBC Studios planning a major theme park attraction, with *Doctor Who* as a significant element of it, but whether or not that will ever come to fruition is uncertain. For the time being, there is no real prospect of any new, BBC-endorsed *Doctor Who* exhibition being created. In the meantime, perhaps the future lies with independent exhibitions run by fans and collectors.

As writer Joseph Lidster so eloquently phrases it, 'Seeing *Doctor Who* exhibits is genuinely thrilling and exciting. I think kids love it, and it makes adults feel like kids again. *Doctor Who* is an amazing adventure that takes us all away from the mundane reality of life – and to see elements from it up close is just magical.' Anyone who enjoyed one of the many *Doctor Who* exhibitions described in this book will certainly agree with that sentiment.

DOCTOR WHO EXHIBITIONS

Welcome to Blackpool Tom Baker.

'Hello! Goodbye! It's good isn't it? Hmm? If you want to, you can tell your friends about the exhibition ... I don't mind. In fact I'd like it.' The Doctor

BEDWYR GULLIDGE

Gallery

There are many hundreds of photographs from all the exhibitions mentioned in this book online. Just use Google! But here we have gathered some of the advertising posters and press photographs and coverage from the events.

Press coverage of the *Daily Mail* exhibition (1964/5).

BB OPERATE THE DALEKS AT BOYS' AND GIRLS' EXHIBITION

BB EXHIBITION STAND ATTRACTS THOUSANDS

RIGHT up to date in a youngsters "with it" way were the members of the 1st Friern Barnet, 1st Barnet, 73rd and 174th London Companies who operated two original "Daleks" at the Boys' and Girls' Exhibition in London.

The *Daily Mail* had sent a last minute request to the BB and the Army Cadets to supply operators for these Dr. Who favourites.

During the exhibition the BB Boys gradually took over the duties of the Army Cadets who were rather rebellious in their operating.

Thousands of Boys and girls queued to get a peep at the Daleks.

The London District Field Officer enticed one of the machines to take a wander down to the BB stand (front cover picture). The machine couldn't refuse — if it had, there would have been a withdrawal of operators!

At the BB stand there was a competition in the form of a jig-saw puzzle. A continuous stream of Boys (and girls) tried their hand at completing the puzzle in a record time.

Thousands of copies of Stedfast Mag. and Life Boy Link were distributed and many potential recruits left their names and addresses.

216

DOCTOR WHO EXHIBITIONS

From the *Daily Mail* Boys' and Girls' Exhibition (1964/5).

Top: *Daily Mail* Boys' and Girls' exhibition (1966/7). Bottom: Science Museum (1972/3).

DOCTOR WHO EXHIBITIONS

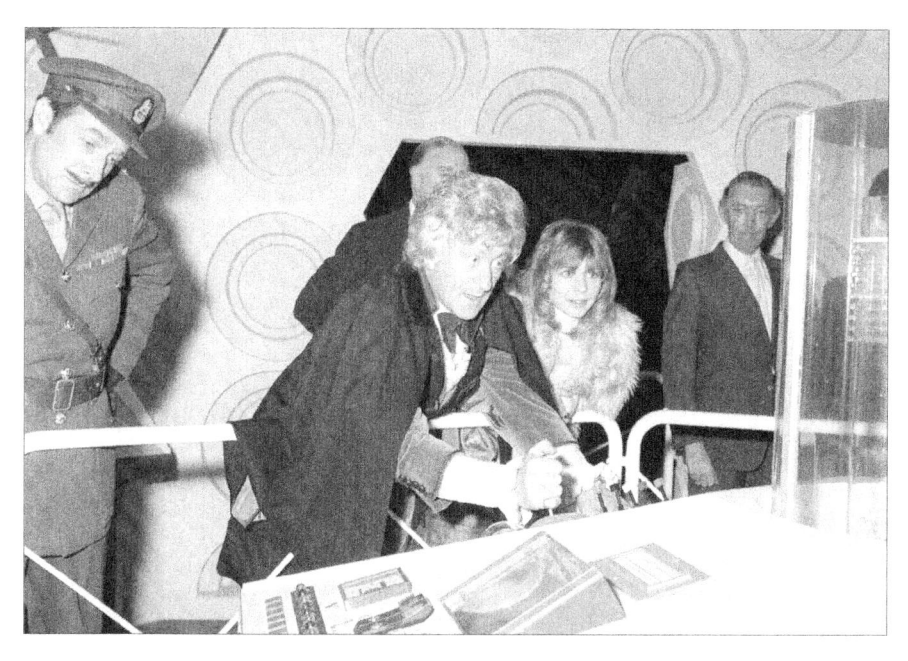

Top: Science Museum (1972/3); Bottom: Blackpool exhibition opening (April 1974).

Cover for promotional flier promoting the exhibitions in 1974.

DOCTOR WHO EXHIBITIONS

Reverse of promotional flier promoting the exhibitions in 1974.

Poster advertising the Blackpool exhibition in 1975.

Poster advertising the Blackpool exhibition in 1976.

Poster advertising the Blackpool exhibition in 1980.

DOCTOR WHO EXHIBITIONS

Commemorative Programme for the big Longleat event in April 1983.

Poster advertising the Blackpool exhibition in 1985.

DOCTOR WHO EXHIBITIONS

Tom Baker as "Dr Who"

Poster sold at the Madame Tussauds *Doctor Who* exhibition in 1980/1.

Tour logo and interior view of the travelling *Doctor Who* exhibition (1987/8).

DOCTOR WHO EXHIBITIONS

The Celebration Bus Tour. Bottom: Colin Baker, Janet Fielding and Nicola Bryant, along with a Cyberman and a Cryon at the initial press call for the Tour (1987/8).

Front of the Souvenir Brochure for the Llangollen *Doctor Who* Experience (1995/2003).

DOCTOR WHO EXHIBITIONS

Advert for the Brighton Pier exhibition (2005).

Front of the Exhibition Guide for the exhibition at Earls Court (2008/9).

Front of the Exhibition Guide for the *Doctor Who Up Close* exhibition at the Coventry Transport Museum (2009/10).

Poster for the London *Doctor Who* Experience (2011/12)

DOCTOR WHO EXHIBITIONS

Doctor Who Experience outside view and promotional posters (2012/17).

Poster and Show Planner front and back for the *Doctor Who* Celebration at London Excel in November 2013, celebrating *Doctor Who*'s 50th anniversary.

DOCTOR WHO EXHIBITIONS

A small selection of *Doctor Who* merchandise from various exhibitions over the years. Pictured are mugs, clocks, coaster, badges, eraser, key fob, notepads, bookmarks, cheque book cover, calculator, car sticker, pens, pencils, screwdriver set, magnets, rulers and CD case. Plus entry tickets for the Longleat and Blackpool exhibitions. (Courtesy David J Howe)

Appendix
Chronology of Referenced *Doctor Who* Stories

The following is a chronological list of *Doctor Who* stories referenced in the main text of this book.

Marco Polo (1964)
The Keys of Marinus (1964)
The Dalek Invasion of Earth (1964)
The Rescue (1965)
The Crusade (1965)
The Chase (1965)
Galaxy 4 (1965)
The Daleks' Master Plan (1965/66)
The Tenth Planet (1966)
The Moonbase (1967)
The Abominable Snowmen (1967)
The Ice Warriors (1967)
The Tomb of the Cybermen (1967)
The Web of Fear (1968)
The Wheel in Space (1968)
The Dominators (1968)
The Invasion (1968)
The Krotons (1968/69)
The Space Pirates (1969)
Doctor Who and the Silurians (1970)
Terror of the Autons (1971)
The Claws of Axos (1971)
Day of the Daleks (1972)
The Curse of Peladon (1972)
The Sea Devils (1972)
The Mutants (1972)
Carnival of Monsters (1973)
Frontier in Space (1973)
The Green Death (1973)
Invasion of the Dinosaurs (1974)
Death to the Daleks (1974)
The Monster of Peladon (1974)
Planet of the Spiders (1974)
Robot (1974/75)
The Ark in Space (1975)
The Sontaran Experiment (1975)

Genesis of the Daleks (1975)
Revenge of the Cybermen (1975)
Terror of the Zygons (1975)
Pyramids of Mars (1975
The Android Invasion (1975)
The Brain of Morbius (1976)
The Seeds of Doom (1976)
The Masque of Mandragora (1976)
The Hand of Fear (1976)
The Deadly Assassin (1976)
The Face of Evil (1977)
The Robots of Death (1977)
The Talons of Weng-Chiang (1977)
The Invisible Enemy (1977)
Image of the Fendahl (1977)
Underworld (1978)
The Invasion of Time (1978)
The Ribos Operation (1978)
The Pirate Planet (1978)
The Androids of Tara (1978)
The Power of Kroll (1978/79)
The Armageddon Factor (1979)
Destiny of the Daleks (1979)
City of Death (1979)
The Creature from the Pit (1979)
Nightmare of Eden (1979)
The Horns of Nimon (1979/80)
The Leisure Hive (1980)
Meglos (1980)
Full Circle (1980)
Warriors' Gate (1981)
The Keeper of Traken (1981)
Logopolis (1981)
Castrovalva (1982)
Four to Doomsday (1982)
Kinda (1982)

DOCTOR WHO EXHIBITIONS

The Visitation (1982)
Black Orchid (1982)
Earthshock (1982)
Time Flight (1982)
Arc of Infinity (1983)
Snakedance (1983)
Mawdryn Undead (1983)
Terminus (1983)
Enlightenment (1983)
The King's Demons (1983)
The Five Doctors (1983)
Warriors of the Deep (1984)
The Awakening (1984)
Frontios (1984)
Resurrection of the Daleks (1984)
Planet of Fire (1984)
The Caves of Androzani (1984)
The Twin Dilemma (1984)
Attack of the Cybermen (1984)
Vengeance on Varos (1985)
The Mark of the Rani (1985)
The Two Doctors (1985)
Timelash (1985)
Revelation of the Daleks (1985)
The Trial of a Time Lord: The Mysterious Planet (1986)
The Trial of a Time Lord: Mindwarp (1986)
The Trial of a Time Lord: Terror of the Vervoids (1986)
Time and the Rani (1987)
Paradise Towers (1987)
Dragonfire (1987)
Remembrance of the Daleks (1988)
The Happiness Patrol (1988)
Silver Nemesis (1988)
The Greatest Show in the Galaxy (1988)
Battlefield (1989)
Ghost Light (1989)
The Curse of Fenric (1989)
Survival (1989)
Doctor Who (1996)
Rose (2005)
The End of the World (2005)
The Unquiet Dead (2005)
Aliens of London (2005)
World War Three (2005)
Dalek (2005)
The Long Game (2005)
Father's Day (2005)
The Empty Child (2005)
The Doctor Dances (2005)
Boom Town (2005)
Bad Wolf (2005)
The Parting of the Ways (2005)

The Christmas Invasion (2005)
New Earth (2006)
Tooth and Claw (2006)
School Reunion (2006)
The Girl in the Fireplace (2006)
Rise of the Cybermen (2006)
The Age of Steel (2006)
The Idiot's Lantern (2006)
The Impossible Planet (2006)
The Satan Pit (2006)
Love and Monsters (2006)
Fear Her (2006)
Army of Ghosts (2006)
Doomsday (2006)
The Runaway Bride (2006)
Smith and Jones (2007)
The Shakespeare Code (2007)
Daleks in Manhattan (2007)
Evolution of the Daleks (2007)
The Lazarus Experiment (2007)
Human Nature (2007)
The Family of Blood (2007)
Blink (2007)
Utopia (2007)
Voyage of the Damned (2007)
Partners in Crime (2008)
The Fires of Pompeii (2008)
Planet of the Ood (2008)
The Sontaran Stratagem (2008)
The Poison Sky (2008)
The Doctor's Daughter (2008)
Silence in the Library (2008)
Forest of the Dead (2008)
Turn Left (2008)
The Stolen Earth (2008)
Journey's End (2008)
The Next Doctor (2008)
Planet of the Dead (2009)
The Waters of Mars (2009)
The End of Time (2009/10)
The Eleventh Hour (2010)
The Beast Below (2010)
Victory of the Daleks (2010)
The Time of Angels (2010)
Vampires of Venice (2010)
Amy's Choice (2010)
The Hungry Earth (2010)
Cold Blood (2010)
Vincent and the Doctor (2010)
The Lodger (2010)
The Pandorica Opens (2010)
The Big Bang (2010)
A Christmas Carol (2010)
The Impossible Astronaut (2011)

Day of the Moon (2011)
The Doctor's Wife (2011)
A Good Man Goes to War (2011)
Let's Kill Hitler (2011)
Night Terrors (2011)
The Girl Who Waited (2011)
Closing Time (2011)
The Wedding of River Song (2011)
The Doctor, the Widow and the Wardrobe (2011)
Asylum of the Daleks (2012)
Dinosaurs on a Spaceship (2012)
A Town Called Mercy (2012)
The Angels Take Manhattan (2012)
The Snowmen (2012)
The Bells of Saint John (2013)
The Rings of Akhaten (2013)
Cold War (2013)
Hide (2013)
Journey to the Centre of the TARDIS (2013)
The Crimson Horror (2013)
Nightmare in Silver (2013)
The Night of the Doctor (2013)
The Day of the Doctor (2013)
The Time of the Doctor (2013)
Deep Breath (2014)
Into the Dalek (2014)
Robot of Sherwood (2014)
Listen (2014)
Time Heist (2014)
The Caretaker (2014)
Kill the Moon (2014)
Mummy on the Orient Express (2014)
In the Forest of the Night (2014)
Dark Water (2014)
Death in Heaven (2014)
Last Christmas (2014)
The Magician's Apprentice (2015)
The Witch's Familiar (2015)
Under the Lake (2015)
Before the Flood (2015)
The Girl Who Died (2015)
The Woman Who Lived (2015)
The Zygon Invasion (2015)
The Zygon Inversion (2015)
Sleep No More (2015)
Face the Raven (2015)
Heaven Sent (2015)
Hell Bent (2015)
The Husbands of River Song (2015)
The Return of Doctor Mysterio (2016)
The Pilot (2017)
Smile (2017)
Thin Ice (2017)
Knock Knock (2017)
Oxygen (2017)
Extremis (2017)
The Pyramid at the End of the World (2017)
The Lie of the Land (2017)
Empress of Mars (2017)
The Eaters of Light (2017)
World Enough and Time (2017)
The Doctor Falls (2017)

References

Auction Catalogues

Bonhams. (2009). *Entertainment Memorabilia including items from the Angels Collection of Television and Film Costumes*. Auction 16808.
Bonhams. (2010). *Doctor Who: The Auction. Costumes and Props from the BBC Archive*. Auction 18192.
Bonhams. (2011). *Entertainment Memorabilia*. Auction 19036.
Bonhams. (2011). *Entertainment Memorabilia*. Auction 19037.

Books

Berry, S. (Ed). (2013). *Behind the Sofa: Celebrity Memories of Doctor Who*. Gollancz.
Hearn, M. (2013). *Doctor Who: The Vault*. BBC Books.
Howe, D J & Blumberg, A T (2000). *Howe's Transcendental Toybox*. Telos Publishing.
Howe, D J, Stammers, M, Walker, S J. (1992). *Doctor Who: The Sixties*. Doctor Who Books, Virgin Publishing.
Howe, D J, Stammers, M, Walker, S J. (1994). *Doctor Who: The Seventies*. Doctor Who Books, Virgin Publishing.
Howe, D J, Stammers, M, Walker, S J. (1996). *Doctor Who: The Eighties*. Doctor Who Books, Virgin Publishing.
Marson, R. (2013). *JN-T: The Life and Scandalous Times of John Nathan-Turner*. MIWK Publishing.
Marson, R. (2016). *Totally Tasteless: The Life of John Nathan-Turner*. MIWK Publishing.
Sladen, E. (2012). *Elisabeth Sladen: The Autobiography*. Aurum Press Ltd.

DVDs

Doctor Who: 'Attack of the Cybermen'. (2009).
Doctor Who: Earth Story: 'The Gunfighters'/'The Awakening'. (2011).
Doctor Who: 'Robot'. (2007).
Doctor Who: 'The Ark in Space': *Special Edition*. (2013).
Doctor Who: The Complete Fourth Series. (2008).
Doctor Who: The Complete Eighth Series. (2014).
Doctor Who: 'Day of the Daleks'. (2011).
Doctor Who: 'The Five Doctors': *25th Anniversary Edition*. (2008).
Doctor Who: The Legacy Collection: 'Shada'/More Than 30 Years in the TARDIS. (2013).
Doctor Who: 'The Leisure Hive'. (2004).
Doctor Who: 'The Mutants'. (2011).
Doctor Who: 'The Tomb of the Cybermen': *Special Edition*. (2012).
Doctor Who: 'The Trial of a Time Lord'. (2008).
Doctor Who: 'The Underwater Menace'. (2015).
Longleat '83 – The Greatest Show in the Galaxy? (2014).
The Doctors – 30 Years of Time Travel And Beyond. (2004).

Guides and Brochures

Doctor Who Celebration. (1983). Longleat House.
Doctor Who Experience. (1996). Llangollen.
Doctor Who Up Close. (2005). Brighton Pier.
Doctor Who Up Close. (2009). Coventry Transport Museum.
Doctor Who Experience. (2010). Olympia, London.

Doctor Who Experience. (2012). Cardiff.
Doctor Who Celebration. (2013). Excel Centre, London.
Doctor Who Experience. (2014). Cardiff.
Doctor Who Festival. (2015). London.

Interviews

Peter Trott, 27 September 2015.
David Boyle, 3 November 2015.
Joseph Lidster, 10 December 2015.
Mike Tucker, 8 January 2016.
Kevan Looseley and Alexandra Looseley-Saul, 20 May 2016.
Christopher Daniels, 29 May 2016.
Bob Richardson, 16 September 2016.
Andrew Smith, 9 October 2016.
David Prince, 21 October 2016.
Gordon Roxburgh, 11 April 2020.

Magazines and Fanzines

DWB: Number 56.
Doctor Who Weekly/Monthly/Magazine: Issues 48, 53, 73, 79, 92, 113, 115, 127, 140, 145, 150, 163, 175, 189, 209, 236, 237, 245, 336, 341, 361.
Doctor Who: The Complete History. (2015). Volume 26.
Gallifrey fanzine. Number 4.
Crystal of Kronos fanzine. Issue 2.
Nothing at the End of the Lane. (2015). Issue 4.
TARDIS fanzine. Volume 1, Number 5.
TARDIS fanzine. Blackpool Extra.
TARDIS fanzine. Volume 2, Number 6.
TARDIS fanzine. Volume 4, Number 5.
The Essential Doctor Who: *The Time Lords* (2016).
The New Scientist. Volume 56, Number 823.
TV Zone. (1993). Issue 6.
World of Horror. No. 8.

Newspapers

Evening Gazette. 14 June 1973.
Evening Gazette. 5 July 1973.

Press Release

BBC Enterprises. BBC TV Special Effects Press Information.

Websites

NB The links given below are all 'live' at the time of writing but – like all internet links – cannot be guaranteed to remain so indefinitely.

www.bbc.co.uk/liverpool/capital_culture/2004/04/garden_festival/index.shtml#
www.bbc.co.uk/news/uk-wales-18900040 (*Doctor Who* exhibit opens to fans in Cardiff)
www.blackpoolgazetteandherald.newsprints.co.uk/search/scu/p/u/185607/1/doctor%20who%20pictures

DOCTOR WHO EXHIBITIONS

www.blogtorwho.com/doctor-who-experience-to-close-in-summer-2017/
www.blogtorwho.com/sci-fi-museum-featured-on-netflix-show-amazing-interiors/
www.blogtorwho.com/sci-fi-museum-grand-opening-today/
www.bonhams.com/auctions/18192
www.coventrytelegraph.net/news/coventry-news/new-props-costumes-doctor-who-3071264
www.dalek-mania.co.uk/EX.htm
www.dalek6388.co.uk/daleks-in-exhibitions/
www.dalek6388.co.uk/where-are-they-now/
www.drwhoexhibitions.co.uk/
www.drwholongleat.com/index.html
www.drwholongleat.com/id4.html
www.doctorwhonews.net/2005/10/brighton-exhibition-moves-to-leicester_9924.html
www.doctorwhonews.net/2010/12/dwn171210112508-lands-end-exhibition.html
www.doctorwhonews.net/2011/07/dwn140711183008-experience-screamer.html
www.doctorwhonews.net/2011/08/dwn100811135012-doctor-who-experience.html
www.doctorwhonews.net/2015/03/doctor-who-wins-cardiff-life-awards.html
www.doctorwho.tv/whats-new/article/half-term-fun-at-the-doctor-who-experience/
www.doctorwho.tv/whats-new/article/autumn-at-the-doctor-who-experience
www.campaignlive.co.uk/article/dr-exhibition-host-special-halloween-weekend/855846
www.firstdoctorcostume.blogspot.co.uk/2015/06/bonhams-costume-sale-16th-june-2009.html
www.gamesradar.com/making-monsters-for-the-doctor-who-experience/
www.liverpoolecho.co.uk/news/liverpool-news/heads-roll-spaceport-doctor-who-3458606
www.longleat.co.uk/main-square/the-bat-cave
www.museumofclassicsci-fi.com/
news.bbc.co.uk/cbbcnews/hi/newsid_4540000/newsid_4541800/4541857.stm
news.thedoctorwhosite.co.uk/the-restoration-of-a-tardis/comment-page-1/
news.thedoctorwhosite.co.uk/4th-5th-doctor-console-now-on-display-at-the-dwe/
www.richardwho.co.uk/auctions/index.asp
www.richardwho.co.uk/exhibitions/index.asp
www.sevenzero.net/steve_cambden_blackpool.html
www.sixthdoctorcostume.blogspot.co.uk/2010/11/bonhams-costume-sales-previous-auctions.html
www.smh.com.au/entertainment/tv-and-radio/billie-piper-pulls-out-of-doctor-who-festival-four-days-before-its-sydney-launch-20151117-gl1d8l.html
www.thedilleys.net/dwepa.htm
www.thepropgallery.com/kane-edward-peel-bbc-exhibition-melting-head-dragonfire
www.thepropgallery.com/soliton-gas-machine-the-visitation
www.thewhoshop.com/museum
www.timemachineuk.com/index.html
www.walesonline.co.uk/news/wales-news/time-up-doctor-who-exhibition-1847875
www.walesonline.co.uk/news/local-news/black-hole-council-budget-after-7819833
www.walesonline.co.uk/whats-on/whats-on-news/cardiffs-doctor-who-experience-close-12138399
web.archive.org/web/20110815194718/www.doctorwhoexhibitions.com/09/previous.html
www.youtube.com/watch?v=drIjQ88mXPM (Dalek Five's skirt is converted to become Davros' chair)
www.youtube.com/watch?v=ZdZBX7CL0pk (*Lion Country*)
www.youtube.com/watch?v=XD7hTYaTOp4 (Tooley St *Doctor Who* Exhibition 1988)
www.youtube.com/watch?v=nMi8c8uglmI (The Doctor Surprises Fans at the *Doctor Who* Experience – *Doctor Who*)
www.youtube.com/watch?v=KJChniSBAOs (Sydney *Doctor Who* Exhibition – ABC Ultimo 2013)

www.youtube.com/watch?v=_nZxShriR0Y (Kids ask Strax – Commander Strax's Q&A – *Doctor Who*)

www.youtube.com/watch?v=cKewl0mwECk (Time-lapse – First Doctor's TARDIS Console – *Doctor Who*)

www.youtube.com/watch?v=vQGbcaC6akA (Matt Smith visits the *Doctor Who* Experience in Cardiff – BBC)

www.youtube.com/watch?v=e01dgj608j8 (Doctor Who Colin Baker visits the Time Machine museum)

About The Author

Bedwyr Gullidge worked at the *Doctor Who* Experience in Cardiff Bay for the entirety of the Matt Smith era of the attraction. During that time, he operated a Dalek, appeared in 'The Five(ish) Doctors Reboot' and put a wooden Cyberman back together, amongst other tasks. An uncredited Runner/Assistant Director on the *Doctor Who* episodes 'Dark Water'/'Death in Heaven', 'Last Christmas', 'The Return of Doctor Mysterio' and 'Thin Ice', he wrote for *Gallifrey Times* and *Doctor Who* Online before becoming Assistant Editor for BlogtorWho.com. He also established the 'Made in Wales' Exhibition to display items from his significant costume collection at events and conventions. *Doctor Who Exhibitions: The Unofficial and Unauthorised History* is his first book.

Based in South Wales, he works as a Cardiac Physiologist at the University Hospital of Wales, Cardiff.

Other Cult TV Titles From Telos Publishing

Back to the Vortex: *Doctor Who* 2005
J Shaun Lyon

Third Dimension: *Doctor Who* 2007
Stephen James Walker

Monsters Within: *Doctor Who* 2008
Stephen James Walker

End of Ten: *Doctor Who* 2009
Stephen James Walker

Cracks in Time: *Doctor Who* 2010
Stephen James Walker

River's Run: *Doctor Who* 2011
Stephen James Walker

Time of the Doctor: *Doctor Who* 2012 and 2013
Stephen James Walker

The Television Companion (*Doctor Who***) Vols 1 and 2**
David J Howe, Stephen James Walker

The Handbook (*Doctor Who***) Vols 1 and 2**
David J Howe, Stephen James Walker, Mark Stammers

The Target Book (*Doctor Who* **Novelisations)**
David J Howe

A Day in the Life (Guide to Season 1 of *24***)**
Keith Topping

Inside the Hub (Guide to *Torchwood* **Season 1)**
Something in the Darkness (Guide to *Torchwood* **Season 2)**
Stephen James Walker

Liberation (Guide to *Blake's 7***)**
Alan Stevens and Fiona Moore

Fall Out (Guide to *The Prisoner*)
Alan Stevens and Fiona Moore

A Family at War (Guide to *Till Death Us Do Part*)
Mark Ward

Destination Moonbase Alpha (Guide to *Space 1999*)
Robert E Wood

Assigned (Guide to *Sapphire and Steel*)
Richard Callaghan

Hear the Roar (Guide to *Thundercats*)
David Crichton

Hunted (Guide to *Supernatural* Seasons 1-3)
Sam Ford and Antony Fogg

Triquetra (Guide to *Charmed*)
Keith Topping

Bowler Hats and Kinky Boots (Guide to *The Avengers*)
Michael Richardson

By Your Command (Guide to *Battlestar Galactica*, 2 Vols)
Alan Stevens and Fiona Moore

Transform and Roll Out (Guide to The Transformers Franchise)
Ryan Frost

The Complete Slayer (Guide to *Buffy the Vampire Slayer*)
Keith Topping

Songs for Europe (Guide to the UK in the Eurovision Song Contest: 3 Volumes)
Gordon Roxburgh

Prophets of Doom (Guide to *Doomwatch*)
Michael Seely and Phil Ware

All available online from
www.telos.co.uk

ADVERTISEMENT

WE BUY & SELL
DOCTOR WHO PROPS

Matthew Doe of TBT Props is one of the world's leading specialists in Doctor Who props and costumes.

TBT Props buy and sell Doctor Who props, costumes, production paperwork and artefacts from individual collectors and exhibitions all over the world and we are always keen to see what you have to sell.

Our previous pieces have included the Cyber Controller costume from Tomb of the Cybermen, an original screen-used Ice Warrior head and screen-used Daleks.

So if you have an original prop that you would consider parting with, or if you are just looking to add to your collection, please get in touch!

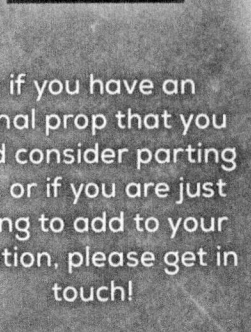

tbt Props

www.tbtprops.com
www.movie-reliquary.com
contactus@movie-reliquary.com
+44 (0) 1209 242526

ADVERTISEMENT

A chronological history of classic 'Doctor Who'
illustrated by an extensive collection of original surviving production material including monsters, props, costumes and published artwork

The internationally famous Museum of Classic Sci-Fi

A tribute to the nostalgia of the classic Exhibitions
Inspired by the original Blackpool & Longleat 'Dr. Who' Exhibitions of the 1970's

A visual archive of classic Science-Fiction
Celebrating the pioneers of the genre in both literature and film
Illustrated by a unique collection of original movie props, costumes and artwork

- Osborne House - Allendale - Northumberland - NE47 9BJ -
www.facebook.com/neilcoleadventuresinscifimuseum
www.museumofclassicsci-fi.com
YouTube: neil cole

NETFLIX
As seen on NETFLIX 'Amazing Interiors'

Printed in Great Britain
by Amazon